THE EMERGING AMERICAN CHURCH

DAN SCOTT

BRISTOL
BOOKS

THE EMERGING AMERICAN CHURCH
Copyright © 1993 by Dan Scott
Published by Bristol Books

First Edition, January 1994

Unless otherwise indicated, all Scripture quotations are from the *Holy Bible, New International Version* © 1973, 1978 by the International Bible Society. Used by permission.

Cover design by: Rocky Zornes/Dan Wright

ISBN 0-917851-75-7

BRISTOL BOOKS
An imprint of Bristol House, Ltd.
3131 E. 67th Street • Anderson, IN 46013
Phone: (317) 664-0856
Fax: (317) 622-1045
To order, call our toll-free line: 1-800-READ

This book is tenderly dedicated
to the three men of God who have most impacted my life:

Rev. D. L. Scott, Sr.,
my father, who taught me that a Christian should be ethical;

Rev. D. W. Durst,
*who dedicated me to Christ and who ordained me to Christian
ministry;*

and Rev. L. H. Hardwick, Jr.
my bishop and friend

TABLE OF
CONTENTS

• • • • • • • • • • • • • • • • • •

INTRODUCTION

WHY THIS BOOK?

This book began 13 years ago in a small apartment on the outskirts of Charleston, West Virginia. I was living there for a few months with my wife Patricia and my one-year-old daughter, Talitha. We were loyal members of a moderate-size Pentecostal denomination, a denomination which strongly discourages interaction with other kinds of Christians. But a strange dream in the early hours, in that peculiar state of mind somewhere between asleep and awake, opened the gates of my closed world.

I say closed world; actually, no one kept me from going anywhere or doing anything. Will Durant says that slavery looks much like freedom when the master is never seen. Since invisible thoughts, not visible men, were my masters, it was difficult to come to grips with the mental and spiritual revolt about to take place in my life. I had been conditioned to shut out people, thoughts and situations that did not conform to the cardinal doctrines of my denomination. Even though my denomination was becoming ever more confining, I wasn't angry about it. I accepted it. I would still be accepting it, had it not been for a bewildering vision which came unsought, unannounced and uninvited.

In the dream, I found myself in a large domed cathedral, filled with mitered and bearded priests, clouds of incense, and an indescribable sense of gravity. Then I, who had rarely worshiped with a Baptist or Methodist, saw tiny bursts of fire come down from the ceiling and rest upon the heads of the priests. They were filled with joy and spoke with tongues. I saw an old priest among them, wearing a long white beard, weeping and saying, "You should have come sooner." Whether he was speaking to God, to me, or to someone else, I did not and do not know. I know only that I felt a great sense of oneness and love for these unknown priests which had been validated in my eyes by a divine sign, unmistakable in its meaning to a young Pentecostal. God was about to anoint ancient churches with a powerful move of the Holy Spirit! (I had no idea that God was also about to instruct evangelicals and Pentecostals in what the church is all about—but we'll save that for later.)

> • • • • • • • • • • • • • • • • •
>
> ## I SAW AN OLD PRIEST . . . WEARING A LONG WHITE BEARD, WEEPING AND SAYING, "YOU SHOULD HAVE COME SOONER."
>
> • • • • • • • • • • • • • • • • •

The image would not go away. For almost 10 years I told no one about it but my wife. During that time, I read everything I could about the history of the church. I visited every kind of Christian assembly imaginable, from Copts and Catholics to Mennonites and Methodists. It is now time to tell what I have seen. I am convinced we are about to drastically reorder the way we perceive and experience the Church of Jesus Christ in this country. The American Church is about to reassert itself, by drawing on the strengths of its varied traditions. Then the fire will fall.

Perhaps, before you read further, I should apologize in advance for my lack of detachment and disciplined indifference.

But I will not apologize, at least not for that. All books are autobiographies—even the most objective, academic and dull ones.

Complete objectivity is unattainable for fallen human beings. And not just to human beings: Even a rock is not objective. It carries, in the very essence of what it is, the history of its being. Within the rock lies the molten core which gave it birth, all the chips and erosion of wind and rain, and the print of the dead moth under its surface. So the rock, which has no conscience and no hidden agenda, cannot tell any story but its own. And neither can we.

I am a man and not a rock. Though I am more eternal than the ageless rock, and have softer skin and an impressionable spirit, I also carry in my being the events of life, and with the events, the ideas that gave them birth. Whatever I write, even if it is a maintenance manual for a printing press, must contain some stain of all the joys and sorrows of my times. So I repeat my claim that all books are autobiographies. That is my justification for the personal nature of this book. I cannot even pretend to be detached from something that is at the very core of what defines me as an American and a Christian believer. It is difficult to speak about such things with apathy.

So that you will know something of my perspective: I am a baby boomer, born after the Second World War, part of the generation that saw President Kennedy take the baton from President Eisenhower and proclaim that a new dawn had risen over America. My generation saw our handsome prince fall into the arms of our American princess in a long, black car on a Dallas street. Another dashing prince fell in Los Angeles, while trying to claim his crown. Then a black man, a flaming prophet calling for equity and justice, fell in his own blood in the streets of Memphis. Viet Nam devoured many of our old schoolmates and crippled those who escaped. Watergate drowned what faith we had left in representative government, as we watched Washington's president, vice president, cabinet members, senators, congressmen, judges, pages and newspaper writers convulse into a feeding frenzy, sharks consuming sharks, until they, and we, were all exhausted.

cated to changing the world, and to leading us into the Age of
Aquarius. Then the answers which were "Blowing in the Wind"
became "Dust in the Wind" as the "Three men we admire most,
Father, Son and Holy Ghost, they took the last train for the
coast . . . singing bye, bye, Miss America pie." No wonder most
American Baby boomers have some sense that the writ of Icabod
hangs over the land (see 1 Samuel 4:21).

I suppose if we are going to talk about an emerging
American Church we will have to define the word American, as
well as the word Church. This will take us down a rather
rambling path of philosophies, theologies, and history. Our age
finds all of that rather tedious. This path contains no car chases
or shoot outs to alleviate the boredom of the ordinary. Nonetheless, the background information is indispensable if we wish to
understand what is about to emerge.

WHAT IS AN AMERICAN, ANYWAY?

The question of American society is complicated enough
by itself. What is an American anyway? What do we mean when
we say "American society"? What language do Americans speak?

Of course, we used to have answers to these questions,
even if the answers did not suit everyone. We knew them even
when I was a child, just 40 years ago. Apple pie, baseball, Bugs
Bunny, cars, cowboys, the Declaration of Independence, Edgar
Allen Poe, Frank Lloyd Wright, girls, hot dogs, hard work, IBM,
jazz, Kellogg's corn flakes, Abraham Lincoln, log cabins, Mickey
Mouse, Norman Rockwell, New York City, Thomas Edison, the
Wright Brothers, and the red, white and blue—all these things
belonged to our definition of "American society."

Our religion was, for the most part, a kind of Christianity
we created by mixing American democracy with the teachings of
Martin Luther, John Wesley, Norman Vincent Peale, Bishop
Fulton Sheen, Mary Baker Eddy, Aimee Semple McPherson,
and President Eisenhower. Those were some of the elements of
our public, common religion. Our various rites of worship,
where we actually celebrated our faith, depended on our ethnic
heritage or social strata— Irish Catholic, Southern White Baptist, African Methodist Episcopal, German Lutheran, Appala-

tist, African Methodist Episcopal, German Lutheran, Appalachian Pentecostal, upper crust Anglophile Episcopal, and so forth. But our allegiance to the common denominators of American Protestantism and democracy most defined our spiritual identity as a nation.

That was yesterday's America. It still exists to some extent in our imagination, and in a more concrete form throughout the rural parts of our nation. It is quickly disappearing, though, both in fact and even as a viable unifying mythology. A new America is emerging from a cultural synthesis that draws from the old paradigm, but which also swallows it up in an unbelievably complex mixture of world cultures, self-help philosophies, mysticism, free enterprise, greed, sentimentality, high tech and nostalgia. The old America has been radically transformed. This is becoming increasingly evident as the generation born before and during World War II surrenders leadership of our nation's institutions to the Viet Nam generation. It is not necessarily what I wish were happening. Actually, I find it rather frightening; but it is, in fact, what is happening.

American Christianity in all its forms is deeply affected by the cultural upheaval. The old European-born and -influenced denominations are in the middle of a social and theological hurricane. The liberal vs. fundamental clash of the past few decades is almost spent. Liberalism is dying because the churches most committed to its ideas are dying. Fundamentalism as we have known it is also running out of steam. Those movements arose in a very different age; now they answer questions few Americans are asking.

Both within and without the mainline denominations are dozens of new movements, resulting from the clashing, merging and synthesis of world views and cultures within our society. Partially because of, and partially in spite of, these movements, an American Church is emerging. It has a definite, foreseeable shape which transcends denominations, and which, I predict, will be committed to historical Christian faith within a modern American culture. I hope in this book to outline the central features of this new American Church.

I will address the nation and the church in four tenses: past, present, future and eternal. I am not at odds with all things new, and I am not enamored with all things old. New and old are both transitory things, and are matters of taste and time. Eternal things are in a category all to themselves. The church, I propose, is the only institution on the planet created as a depository of eternal things, and her unique contribution is desperately needed in the turmoil our society is facing. The restlessness now frothing at the deepest depths of our nation is a war about the meaning of human life. That war is being raged at the foundations of our culture, and whenever we turn off the TV, or take a moment away from making money, we all hear its terrifying din. Nothing, whether new or old, will bring peace from that strife; not some radical revolution—how many more of those can we stand?—and not by trying to recreate the peaceful times of Ozzie and Harriet. Only eternal things, things born in the bosom of God and thrust into our world as a gift from the Father above, will still the storm.

> THE CHURCH . . . IS THE ONLY INSTITUTION ON THE PLANET CREATED AS A DEPOSITORY OF ETERNAL THINGS . . . .

This book is the story of an American baby boomer searching to understand both the past and the future of his faith and country, but searching even more intently to identify and understand things which are eternal. It is the story of a man committed to the person and teachings of Jesus Christ and his church, and who has a passionate belief that Christ alone has the answers for our troubled society. It is a book about how these elements are beginning to come together for an entire generation of American believers, in an unbelievable collage of Christian faith.

One more thing. St. Paul tells us to let the prophet prophesy, and then to allow the others to judge. I am about to tell a vision, a vision I believe to have divine origin. It is the duty of

God's people to judge that vision, to judge it in the light of the Holy Scriptures, and in the light of the history of our faith. In the following pages, I will tell you what I believe is about to happen in the American Church. Whether it really does happen, or whether it even *should* happen, is of the highest importance. Right now it is only the potential future; its actual emergence depends on the whole people of God. I am only the storyteller. The story itself cannot be the property of one man.

PART 1

....

THE ESSENTIAL FAITH

CHAPTER 1
·····················

CONCERNING
CATHOLICITY

You might as well know from the start that I have an embarrassing habit of writing and speaking about things that seem out of sync with the popular mood. That is to say, I sometimes address questions no one is asking. This is an unbearable fault, especially for a minister of the gospel. Ministers are often advised (I have told ministers this myself) to strive to meet the people's needs as the people themselves perceive their needs to be. That advice is motivated by a desire to see ministers address the real needs of people rather than yesterday's controversies. Past struggles were, of course, important enough yesterday, to the parents of those we now serve. The present population, however, usually has forgotten the issues that moved their parents (or, for that matter, the issues that moved them the day before yesterday). I am aware of all of that, and am as afraid of being irrelevant as the next guy.

Actually, were the truth known, I am probably more afraid of being irrelevant than of being irreverent. Most of the time, hell isn't nearly as frightening as the opinion of my peers. I wish that were not true. It is true, however, and this provides one reason for the difficulties the people of God now face in this nation. We tend to serve the national consensus rather than the Lord of Glory. I sincerely hope to outgrow this common idolatry, because God's men and women are truly shepherds and not hirelings only when they do what is right rather than what is expected.

WORSHIPPING THE GODDESS OF RELEVANCE

I have only recently concluded that when the times are out of joint, it is the Christian's moral obligation to resist the times—not in superficial ways, such as in music and dress and other things that may cause discomfort only because they run against some cherished cultural preference, but to resist the spirit of the age at the absolute depths, at the spiritual foundation, from where all that we think or do springs.

I have concluded, too, that the reason we ministers are so often running ourselves ragged to keep up with the times is because the goddess of relevance, whom we Americans serve with unceasing high and reverent honors, changes her mind almost daily. She is a fickle and bitchy goddess. Those who serve her cannot find her, even in the day they seek her with all their hearts.

The elders of many of the great denominations have rushed to the temple of relevance to worship her over the cries of their own parishioners. These church leaders have no idea how ridiculous they have become, even in the eyes of the pagans and the godless. They seem unaware, bowing to their goddess, that she laughs as their calamity comes.

The joke is cruel: The bowing elders are, horror of horrors, irrelevant. Why? Because the masses of American Christians, the same Christians that the elders were supposed to be leading to a relevant faith, are actually seeking the ancient faith, the same faith the elders abandoned in favor of progress!

Meanwhile, the American Pentecostals, charismatics and other representatives of the free church tradition find these older churches amusing. Much of their amusement comes from their ignorance of the issues. They have no idea what is at stake and, unfortunately, if they knew they might not care.

They are, however, facing the same battle on a different front. They collect new material for worship every few months, change the decor, change their sermon topics, go to this meeting and that, and whirl around every bit as much as their liberal counterparts in the same mad struggle to keep up. They sanctify this obsession with novelty by making it into a theology, always waiting for the "next great move," or the "next wave," or the "new thing God is doing," worshiping that nebulous something called "the next thing."

At its worst, this attitude produces a movement that reinvents itself every few years. This allows the tele-evangelists—some of whom are sincere about reaching the nation for Christ—to lead their followers to worship glitz, glitter and sequins. The local churches follow suit with constantly updated theatrics.

So we now demand sensation, even if the sensation is based on nothing but sensation. This is the difference between the old Pentecostals and many of the newer, more popular brands. In made-for-television Pentecostalism the sensations have become the end of the spiritual search rather than its by-product. Early Pentecostals shook because they were convicted of sin, or because they were rejoicing that their sins had been forgiven. The newer Pentecostals tend to shake because shaking feels good.

CREDO, CREDO

I *am* a Pentecostal myself (or was, I'm not sure). I am still a Pentecostal in that I truly believe in the charismatic gifts and the contemporary work of the Holy Spirit through miracles and guidance and so forth. I don't believe that he is a retired author. At the same time, however, I hope that I have become more than simply a Pentecostal, that I am becoming accountable to the whole people of God, as well as an heir to the treasures of the whole Church. I hope for that more than I hope for life.

The whole Church, which to be whole must include those of other times and places, on both sides of the grave, contains within itself, in all the human variety that it embraces, a stable witness to eternal truth or, as Tertullian put it, *"that which has been believed at all times and in all places."* We call this invisible something that binds together believers across denominations, time and space *catholicity*.

I was raised outside what is considered to be the mainstream of American Christianity, but I became a minister because I believed in God. I believed, too, that a gospel was sent down from heaven, and that God was calling me to witness to its message. Though I did not know all its implications for the human family, I believed that the contents of that message could save a human soul from eternal damnation. I still believe it.

You have probably notice the number of times I have said, "I believe." In Latin, one of the ancient languages of our faith, the words "I believe" are one word: *credo*. I can almost hear this word being chanted from some dark, dank catacomb, a shout of life in the midst of death: "credo, credo"— "I believe, I believe."

The earliest creed of all is called The Apostles' Creed. I was raised without it, but when I first heard it I could say nothing but "Amen" because I believed what it said. I grew up without the great hymns as well, but when I heard them, I sang them with conviction and passion because I believed their words. I didn't understand all the complicated historical arguments about the Eucharist, but when I was offered bread and wine I bowed low, with tears. I read Thomas a Kempis, Augustine, Wesley, Luther and Chrysostom like one who had been subsisting on berries and roots who suddenly finds himself invited to a feast.

So I am now a Christian who has come not only to the Lord, whom I met long ago in power and glory at a Pentecostal altar, but to his Church. The Church is the natural home where my soul was created to breathe, to live and to grow. It is, as G. K. Chesterton said, the "natural home of all human spirits."[1] I believe in the Church.

Ironically, I have come to believe in the Church at the very time that many of its former guardians in America are embarrassed about the Lord, his Church and its treasure. They seem to believe that all this stuff is too old, that we are too modern and the world is too advanced. "The smart people are all running to the temple of relevance," our leaders say. But I don't want to go. I just got here, and I came from a long way. It is my personal story, but it is also the story of millions of American Christians.

THE CHURCH OF THE POOR AND THE ORPHANS WHO FLEE TO IT

It is a simple story: While the elders of the American churches were arguing about how much of the faith could be jettisoned, while they were falling over one another to be the "church of the poor" or the "refuge for the disinherited" or whatever notion the great goddess of relevance was suggesting that decade, the poor and the disinherited themselves gathered in large groups to shout and sing under tents and brush arbors. I was born of God among those people. We were so filled with joy at being accepted into God's family that we came to believe we were the whole family. We led ourselves into faith; the teachers of the mainstream Church, embarrassed that anyone could be so happy at finding eternal life that they would weep and dance, all fled to their ivy-covered buildings.

In many of those ivy-covered temples of learning, little by little, future leaders of American Christendom turned away from the Holy Scriptures and toward whatever current philosophies happened to be in vogue. When some of these individuals finally came out to minister, their people were noticeably bored at what they had to say. The people wanted to hear from heaven, from some rushing mighty wind or from a still, small voice. They didn't like the whine, the confusion, the heresy that broke from the lips of the enlightened. But many of these "enlightened" ones became bishops, teachers and high potentates anyway, mumbling endlessly about their cherished "church of the poor." While they were chattering, their people joined the real church of the poor, churches like ours, churches led by people so backward and ill informed that they still believe in a physical resurrection, in the Holy Scriptures, in the effectiveness of the sacraments, in the immutability of God's law, in our Savior's virgin birth and in the literal truth of his promised second return. The people excommunicated their bishops.

• • • • • • • • • • • • • • • •

WE WERE PREPARED TO LEAD AS OUR FATHERS LED—BY THE SEAT OF OUR PANTS.

• • • • • • • • • • • • • • • •

Now what were we to do, we who made up this motley collection of Pentecostals, charismatics, independent Baptists, and those who endlessly and ignorantly insist that they have no denomination or religion? We were not prepared to lead the people left orphaned by the elders of the old churches. We were prepared to lead as our fathers led—by the seat of our pants. They led small churches where our cousins, sisters and uncles led the singing, prayed with the discouraged and painted widows' houses on Saturdays. They had no liturgy, no creeds, no real answers for the problems people of their socio-economic level would never face anyway. We took for granted that our generation would do the same. But now we are called to pastor those who govern society, who run hospitals, who teach children and who manage the affairs of the nation.

The leaders of yesterday's power club—the reporters, the seminarians, the conventions of great, old denominations, the writers of magazines and journals—often jeer from the sidelines. They say we are trying to keep alive a corpse, that we are not bowing to the inevitable, that we are knee-jerk this or that. They say things like, "you can't be serious." But we are serious; we are believers, believers of the most obstinate kind.

American Christianity took a long time to notice us. We worked and worshiped on the edge of the nation, we and our fathers, rejoicing in God, loving his Word, wanting to serve him. We were in almost complete darkness about the so-called "mainstream" heritage of faith from which we felt excluded. We did our best. In the process we did many foolish things. We abandoned society, as our critics charged, but most of us had never been a part of society anyway. We were mountaineers, immigrants, black sharecroppers and tenant dwellers. We had no idea about the problems of society, the complexities of philosophy, the glories of high art and other issues that concerned our affluent and learned brothers. We were worried about our souls and eternal life. We still are, God helping us, but we find ourselves suddenly thrust into the public arena, charged by the faith we hold dear to answer to the hope that lies within us. Our elder brothers who could have done the job well, who were prepared to do the job well, have abandoned the task, so timid are they in the face of the goddess of relevance; and they left us with their orphaned children.

So here we are, fumbling, staggering, saying things that often make onlookers laugh; things about values, morals, an eternal law of God and a certain queer notion about a resurrection from the dead and eternal judgment. We understand that we are ill prepared, but we will not quit. When we appear foolish, it is our style that is at fault, not our faith. We will remain, because we are not the children of yesterday, we are the children of eternity. Our message is not dated, it is eternal. It will survive even the destruction of heaven and earth, and it will survive when all the relevant things are long forgotten.

This brings me to the issue of catholicity. The believers who have been fleeing the gentle and mild-speaking heretics and apostates who now lead many of the old churches in our country have come to us, pastors and elders who are often far beneath their socio-economic and educational level. No doubt we often say and do things that make them grimace. They have demonstrated a preference for truth over social standing. The proper name for that preference is humilty, an extremely important Christian virtue. They have won the heart of this pastor and others who have been willing to listen to our adopted children in the Lord tell how our faith appeared in history, great as an army with banners, clothed with the glory and majesty of her risen King. They have taught us much about our heritage. In God's name we have pledged to defend and proclaim this heritage, which we are only now investigating fully.

THE AGELESS DANCE

The old churches lived with continuity, and took it for granted. They had rites, they had histories and they still have old buildings, all of which breathe a fragrance of antiquity. They believe this antiquity is killing them. They are wrong. Their new goddess of relevance is killing them. This relevance does not ask for adaptations in things like music and architecture, something we have always been ready and willing to accommodate, but asks us to bend eternal things toward fads, to exchange truth for false and short-lived ideas. This sort of accommodation we cannot accept.

We will not accept it, and the American people will not have it. They are not hungry for a religion that dances to every new tune of the age. They desire the ageless dance, the dance that is a response to music composed before the world was, and which will continue when time is no more. I am longing to claim that antiquity and the treasures it contains. "The gifts of God are for the people of God," as the old liturgies say. Well, they are, and if the people of the old churches have been abandoned to our care, then the goods that were given by the Father to sustain them are now ours to guard by default.

We are trying to take our new responsibilities seriously. We have pledged ourselves to earnestly contend for the faith once delivered to the saints; but we need to hear from those saints to whom the faith was once delivered. They will teach us: the Bible writers, of course, always first and foremost, but also Aquinas, Augustine, Calvin, Clement, Irenias, Luther, Pascal, Wesley and the all the fathers of the Church. Their hymns and sermons, their counsel and wisdom, will educate us for the struggle of our time. Why do I believe this? Because what has endured of their teachings has endured because it was not written for their own time alone, but for all times. By putting their roots down in the soil of catholicity, into a faith that is good for the ages and not just for an age, these saints showed that they belonged to the Church that honors and teaches what "has in all places and in all times been believed by the people of God."

I am claiming a place in that Church. I am claiming that place for myself and for the aimless and wandering American believers who have been lost in a far country. That country is called modernity, and there we have spent ourselves in foolishness and have eaten the corn husks meant for swine. We are weary and long to go home.

CATHOLICITY: A DEFINITION

Catholicity is what binds together all God's people in all places and in all times, the living with the dead. Sectarianism, on the other hand, is something which separates some of God's people from the rest by emphasizing something which has *not* been at all times and in all places believed. Sectarianism is the essence of a group out of sorts with the Church of its time, as we seem to be, but also of a group out of sorts with the Church of the ages, which we are not.

In our youth, many of us believed we should strip the church of tradition and ceremony. We believed that we should be a pure church, that we should return to the simplicity of the apostolic age, unencumbered by disciplines, teachings, doctrines or even buildings. Each year brought us a new revelation, a new piece of the puzzle, a new "wave" of charismatic ecstasy. Our people helped us: they brought us tapes, papers, prophesies and interpretations.

Now we are tired. We are willing to admit that while we have been led by God, we have also often been led by self. We are beginning to face the truth of our own mortality, the cruel fact that even baby boomers get old and die. Most of us are tired of fads, whether they come from the right or the left. We are tired of politics and politicians who have used and abused our God-given roles as shepherds of God's flock. We are weary of the goddess of modernity whom the liberals worship, but whom we often worship, too, in a different form. We want to prepare to come to old age and be gathered to our fathers in peace, knowing that we have done what our Master called us to do, and that we have passed on the faith once delivered to the saints.

BRANDISHING THE TOOLS OF THE WHOLE CHURCH

To be specific, we must now accept the inheritance of the Church in this nation. We must rebuild its foundations. We must accept the multitudes of disillusioned American Christians who have been disinherited by mainline madness. But we cannot be under the illusion that our spontaneous, happy-go-lucky, antiestablishment attitudes will be equal to the task. That attitude works for those in rebellion, but not for those who must lead. We must lead because we are about the only ones left to lead. Our great denominations have lost their way, and their wonderful heritage is guarded by godly remnants under siege. So if our nation is not to fall into the most serious kinds of apostasy and wickedness, it is up to us to shepherd God's people.

We need the tools of the whole church to do this work. We need Pentecostal power and passion, and we need the evangelical proclamation and teaching of the Scriptures. But we need as well the orthodox—dare I say catholic?—reverence for God and that tradition's long heritage of wonder and humility.

We need to rethink the issue of catholicity for many reasons. We live in a different world from our fathers, a world we never anticipated. To face these times, we need the advice of the whole Church, past and present. As we study the church through history, looking for strength and wisdom for our times, it is natural to take another look at churches which have endured the ravages of time.

When we look at ancient churches in our own nation, those American churches which value catholicity, our eyes first light upon the Episcopal Church, which is the Anglican tradition in America. We received its life as a gift from our mother country; its torch helped to light our own flame. But at present the insanity of the times has captured many of the bishops of that church. The younger priests seem to be hearing the ancient music again, and God willing, will erase the heresy of their fathers as they come to power, but they will have to completely rebuild their church. At present the spiritual state of the American Episcopal Church looks like Europe after the war. Their stepchildren, the Methodists, are also between two opinions, and cannot say for

• • • • • • • • • • • • • • • •

WE MUST BEGIN TO REBUILD THE ANCIENT FOUNDATIONS IN OUR COUNTRY.

• • • • • • • • • • • • • • • •

sure where they are going. As for Rome and Constantinople, our differences with them are real, and though we must learn from them and respect them, they do not represent a viable option for most of us.

In short, we who comprise the Pentecostal/charismatic movement, as well as the broader stream of independent evangelical churches in the United States, must grasp for the spirit of catholicity without much of a tangible institutional example to lead us. We must do what is right to do, what is in harmony with the Church of the ages as we understand it, hoping that our example will be a beacon to the hundreds of thousands of believers now wandering across the American landscape in search of a spiritual home. We must not become a new sect—nothing could be more repugnant— but we must become accountable to one another and to the Church of the ages. We must begin to rebuild the ancient foundations in our country. We must do this based on nothing more than this: It is the right thing to do.

I do not mean to imply that we should give up our own heritage for ritual. Nothing has more wearied the people of God than tradition without passion. The old churches come dangerously close to the scriptural warning of "having a form of godliness but denying its power" (2 Timothy 3:5). But is formless worship the answer? We know that it is not. There is a holy combination of form and power that the New Testament assumed to be the norm. If it is possible to have a form of godliness while denying its power, then we must assume that there is something that can be recognized as a "form of godliness." That form comes from our Jewish roots, through the New Testament, through the church fathers, through the history of the faith, and should live among all who are part of the people of God. It contains the sacraments, the doctrines and the disciplines of our faith. It is the repository of all that the people of God have done and taught up to our very day. We do not have to give up anything in exchange for these things which belong to us already as the people of God.

RECONNECTING WITH THE ROOTS

To be concerned with catholicity, we must understand two things: our relationship with Christians of other denominations, cultures and nations, and our relationship with the Church of the ages. We must bridge the gap of denomination, culture and of time. I have been talking mostly about the gap of time, because I believe that the American church in all its expressions is nearly cut off from the past. Indeed, we have rejoiced in our severance with the past. But like all living things which get cut off from their root systems, we are dying as a national church. That is why a new generation of believers is feverishly searching for its roots.

There is hope, though, that we will reconnect with those roots. People have enormous interest right now in hearing what the saints of ages past have said. But time moves in the other direction, too; we must be concerned about transmitting the gospel to a new generation of American leaders. We desperately need to recover the lost art of mentoring, of sharing not only information but character with the next generation.

I am assuming that our seminaries will not do this; I'll even say that alone they cannot do it. They cannot do it because most of them no longer believe the gospel, for one thing. But they cannot do it for another reason: The seminary is created to produce scholars, not pastors, missionaries and evangelists. I do not say this in opposition to the seminaries—I believe in them. Let them teach people how to translate the Bible, how to interact with world philosophies and all of that; they will rarely produce men and women of action and daring, people consumed with a zeal not to do the thing right but to do the right thing. We need visionaries and church planters right now, and we need shepherds and godly leaders. Only visionaries and church planters can produce visionaries and church planters; only shepherds and godly leaders can produce shepherds and godly leaders. Each must produce after its own kind.

I suppose the bottom line is that I believe most of the mainline denominations to be so nearly apostate, so far removed from what has "at all places and at all times been believed," that there seems to be little hope of their redemption. (Notice I said "little hope"—we do serve a God who often resurrects the dead!) I believe the thousands of non-aligned, independent assemblies across the nation have become our best hope for the continued presence of a vital Christian witness in our nation. However, I also believe that the frontier culture which produced these churches is dead, and that the present climate will not sustain them. We must draw on the strength not of the disappearing culture of the American frontier (though some things our fathers gained there will help us) but on the eternal truth which lives in the historical faith. Catholicity must put on new clothes. We cannot ignore our responsibility now—we have to assume the place left vacant in the town square. We must grow up.

THE CIVILIZATION BUILT ON ANCIENT FOUNDATIONS

Our life on the edge of national culture cannot survive. We know that instinctively. But the answer cannot be to politicize our churches. Part of the reason for the decline of the great American denominations was their idol worship of leftist ideology. Their allegiance to their politics took precedence over their allegiance to their faith in Christ and His Church. So the answer cannot be to worship the idol of right-

wing political ideology: Republicans are probably no more
concerned about our faith than the Democrats; they have just
found us convenient.

No, the answer cannot be to worship the right or the
left, to be obsessed with issues which rise up today and will be forgotten tomorrow. If we are to move from the edge of national life and into its heart, we must proclaim the eternal gospel and the implications of that gospel for everyday life. We must draw deeply from the old family well, from the heritage of faith that has been the alternative civilization, that civilization which moves through history in opposition to Ninevah, Babylon and Rome.

> WE MUST DRAW DEEPLY FROM THE OLD FAMILY WELL, FROM THE HERITAGE OF FAITH THAT HAS BEEN THE ALTERNATIVE CIVILIZATION . . . .

This is the civilization that St. Augustine called *The City Of God*. That civilization has a rich culture that is ready to assist those of us who feel estranged from the values of our own times.

On that ancient foundation we must build an alternative to both the religious mainstream which has abandoned historical Christianity and that "National Enquirer" religion we tolerate in the name of spirituality. We have to train a new generation of leaders. We have to encourage excellence and entrepreneuring. We have to assume the mantle of catholicity that the great denominations have discarded, and which the sectarian groups have yet to recognize. We have to claim legitimacy, and then we must take our own claim seriously. We have to insist that while being the Christian Church involves all sorts of cultural diversity, that name cannot cover a disbelief in the resurrection, a redefinition of the nature of God or the inclusion of Hindu piety into the liturgy. It also cannot cover theme parks and snake oil salesmen. We have to draw the line. A denomination's retaining the buildings of its ancestors and demonstrating an unbroken historical line to great saints of God is no proof of its legitimacy or catholicity.

We must respond with more than protest. God knows we have always been able to protest, but the times call for more. We must develop alternatives. That means we must be willing to learn about those parts of Christian heritage which may be foreign to us, and incorporate any part of our heritage which seems helpful to our claim to be alternative churches for the discouraged members of the great American denominations. We must pick up their discarded torch.

RESPECT

A concern for catholicity should involve respect for church groups whose culture is not our own. I must be careful, for example, not to rage against a church simply because its style differs from my own. The issue is not about cultural preference, about whether a church allows dance as a part of its worship, or incense or drums. These things are important to our sense of comfort, but have little or nothing to do with "that which has at all times and in all places been believed."

Having been a part of a legalistic system, I know how cruel and hateful a crusade for righteousness can be. I hope never again to be led to a battle against those whose only crime is speaking a different theological language. I don't want to be guilty of treating even a heretic in any way other than as a man or woman made in the image and likeness of God. We must respond positively, quietly attempting to build a place for God's people to go instead of merely tearing down those places not to our liking.

Many of the liberal leaders of American Christendom have never had the chance to hear a real gospel presentation. They were raised in churches that were little more than social clubs, and moved on to seminaries which have lost a gospel witness. They have fashioned their doctrine after the philosophy of the age because they thought that there was no alternative. In many cases, they have never been exposed to an orthodoxy linked with intellectual integrity. So if orthodox

Christianity in America is to survive, it must have scholarly defenders as well as popular pulpiteers. It must have also prophets of truth who demand that we not halt between two opinions. When people see the truth set on fire, just as in Elijah the prophet's day, many of our countrymen will return to the God of their ancestors. Let us build our altar, and let the God who answers by fire be God (see 1 Kings 18:16-39).

If we are to be true shepherds who love the flock of God, if we are to proclaim truth out of a desire to exalt Christ rather than a desire for conflict for conflict's sake, then we must anchor our churches to the Church. We must lead our churches to that multitude of pilgrims who are moving from Egypt to Canaan, led by one who chooses to be counted with the children of God rather than be called the son of Pharaoh's daughter.

We have to be concerned about eternal things, to speak of things that belong to the ages rather than things that belong only to today. We have to absorb the words and deeds, the songs and emotions of the fathers; we must gather them, like the bones of Joseph; we must carry them gently and lovingly until we place them into the hands of our children and our children's children. That is catholicity, and that is what our times, indeed what all times, demand. Without it, the emerging American church will not be a Christian church at all.

PART 2

THE NEW AMERICA

CHAPTER 2
THE POT AND THE STEW

Like most Americans, my family history disappears into the mists. Three generations back, it turns to fog. Most of my ancestors came to this continent in the second half of the eighteenth century, mostly from Northern Ireland and Scotland. They were wild, wandering Celts, boarding floating coffins in which a third or more of the passengers usually died en route. I know even less about a smattering of other ancestors who included Huguenots, Germans and Native Americans. I have found at least their names after years of searching moldy books in old court houses—names like Minerva Toney, Nancy Surret and Richard Scott. Beyond the names, I don't know much about them. Most of them were running from something in the Old World and running toward a new life in this new continent. Here they longed to find land, hope and human dignity.

They came here a long time ago. We have done a lot of work since then. We conquered a continent and tied it together with a railroad. We created toys that let us talk to one another over long distances, and then added picture to the sound. We fought a war to free men we had enslaved, and then spent another hundred years trying to figure out whether we should allow them to join us in this new society. We built cities, dams, highways and chariots that move under their own power. Then we went to the moon. From coffin ships to space ships, it has been a fast-paced ride.

We Americans are the children of wanderers. All of us came from somewhere else, even the Native Americans who beat the others by several thousand years. We descend from people who lost sight of some familiar shore in order to reach a place about which they knew next to nothing.

Now we have run out of geography. If we become disenchanted with our present company, we cannot, like our ancestors, wander to some new place to start a new society. We are stuck with each other—with a spectrum of human beings as wide as the human race—all of us claiming to be Americans!

It is shocking that this news should shock us. After all, we grew up here. But we are just now noticing, in a way that our grandparents never noticed, the many conflicting claims on what it means to be an American. My neighbors' roots are in Russia, Nigeria and South Vietnam. So who are we really, we Americans?

ETHNICITY AND CULTURE

We used to call our country a melting pot. We believed that all the world's societies and peoples came here to "melt down" into a new, American culture. Our melting pot ideal was the old Anglo-Saxon culture, modified to meet the needs of a new age and a new world. It was defined mostly by the upper classes, and it exerted its influence downward with various degrees of success.

Then, in the 1960s, the upper crust lost its grip on the nation. Our old cultural norms, born and nurtured in Europe, began to be quickly displaced. Now a true meltdown has begun, and it is taking a much different course than we would have expected a few decades ago. Each distinct culture of the nation is adding to the whole a flavor of its own, but without being completely assimilated, contributing its distinctives to an emerging culture whose shape is only dimly recognizable. For good or evil, our melting pot has been filled with a chunky stew.

Back when we were trying to be a simpler sort of melting pot, we used to say that England was our mother country, even though descendants of English people in the United States comprise only thirteen percent of our total population. In the first centuries of our existence, first as colonies and then as a nation, that percentage was, of course, much higher, though it was never a majority. In those foundation decades, though, English people made up the ethnic group which most defined our "American" culture.

As other peoples came from other nations, they attempted to absorb the Anglo-Saxon values of the ruling class. Why? Because English Americans were the respected nobility, the founders of universities and the fathers of the nation. As the country pushed its boundaries west and south, however, it incorporated other ethnic groups like the much older Spanish-speaking communities, the French-speaking peoples of Louisiana, the African-American slaves and the Native American tribes en masse. For them, the process of assimilation was not so complete, probably because they were absorbed not as individuals but as entire functioning societies in their own right.

The Native Americans came first. Some of them intermarried with the sons of Europe to become our ancestors. Others fought to the day of their extinction. Still others converted to our religion and were then destroyed in some of the most heartless acts ever committed by a nation claiming the name of Christ. The Cherokee nation for one, with its capital city and government, was seized. Its inhabitants were rounded up and taken to camps in the West. Its lands were added to the wealth of the United States based on no more a provocation than the gold which Caucasians had found on Indian land. The eastern tribes were mostly converted and assimilated; the Western tribes were systematically wiped out or quarantined in camps called reservations.

Despite this abuse, the ways and words of Native American peoples influenced the nation. Robert Pirsig argues that the cowboy, America's favorite icon of itself, was essentially a white Indian, a frontiersman who learned how to survive by adopting Native American ways.[2] Those who came after hated the Indian but loved the Caucasian who acted like one. The cowboys copied the Native American style of life and attitudes toward authority, land and freedom, allowing Americans to learn Indian culture secondhand.

● ● ● ● ● ● ● ● ● ● ● ● ● ● ● ●

SO MANY OF THESE GERMANS CAME TO AMERICA THAT BENJAMIN FRANKLIN ONCE FEARED THAT GERMAN WOULD REPLACE ENGLISH AS THE NATIONAL TONGUE.

● ● ● ● ● ● ● ● ● ● ● ● ● ● ● ●

The Germans came, settling mostly in Pennsylvania, but also in the Shenandoah valley. From there they wandered West. Most of the early Germans who came to these shores were pietist Protestants, seeking, like the earlier English, a place to pray in peace. Among these was a man named Jacob Kirfna, who went to the western counties of Virginia where he married the daughter of a Scotch-Irishman. They began a lineage from which came the author of this book. So many of these Germans came to America that Benjamin Franklin once feared that German would replace English as the national tongue.[3] That didn't happen, but Germany did replace England as the place from which the greatest percentage of Americans descend.

Our nation absorbed Florida, Northern Mexico's rebel state of Texas, California and then Puerto Rico. These additions gave the country cities that were twice as old as most of those founded by the English. The geographical names, food, music, language and pace of life in Spanish America were very different from the old thirteen colonies. By the 1700s, travelers to California were already writing to their families in New England about how relaxed life seemed there compared to home. By the middle of this century, however, one could hear English-speaking Floridians complaining about how their state had been overrun by Spanish speakers! Currently, Hispanic peoples outnumber African Americans, making Spanish speakers the nation's largest minority group.

Senator John Quincy Adams vigorously opposed President Jefferson's purchase of Louisiana. He claimed in a passionate speech on the Senate floor that the "Gallic" character of the wild, half-naked people of New Orleans would drastically change the character of the nation. He said that the original character of the constitution would not stretch far enough to cover the gap which existed between the two peoples. The president responded that it would take "a thousand generations" to fill up the distance between "us" and "them." He bought the land. So the French and Spanish settlers there, together with the refugees the English had gathered in French Canada and dumped in the Southern swamps, joined the expanding country.

Then came Hawaii. The monarch of the island decided it was better to be an American than a king. With no links of land to the continent, the native peoples opened their plot of paradise to the nations of the Pacific. In an amazingly short time, Polynesians, Japanese and native Hawaiians welcomed the lingering tourists who could see no good reason to return home to mere earth. These peoples joined together in planting the stars and stripes in the middle of the great ocean.

Alaska, too, first settled and evangelized by the Russians, passed into American hands because Alexander the II, head of the Russian empire, was hard pressed for cash. The American people called the purchase "Seward's folly," a frozen wasteland of perpetual ice and polar bears. But barely half a century later the native Alaskans and descendants of Russian settlers watched gold-crazed men from the South who were just learning to walk on snow shoes invade what became our largest state.

Meanwhile the nations of the earth poured forth their sons and daughters. These people made their way to the Americas, looking for land and opportunity. Opportunity was here

for everyone except the peoples of Africa, who had come first
as indentured servants, but who, unlike the others, were not
released after their seven years of labor. Generations came and
went while the black man poured out his sweat and blood on
the fertile land. In the 300 years of slavery, African blood so
mingled with Caucasian that fully eighty percent of all Louisiana families that were there before the civil war, and who are
now classified as white, have some African ancestry. (In the
rest of the South it is merely forty percent, including, no
doubt, Klansmen who shout stupidities about the purity of
the race.) Now virtually no full-blooded Africans are left.
Almost all American blacks have European ancestors, proving
that the rules of the plantation could not suspend human
nature. The half-breed slave children labored on, building a
nation in which they had no stake. Their trials gave us a
national music, a folklore and inner cities boiling with rage.

By the early twentieth century, the sons of Britain still
ruled American society; but their value system had become a
thin veneer coating a melange of Hispanic, African-American,
oriental, Native American and Appalachian subcultures. Underneath that veneer, each group was influencing the birth of
a cultural syncretism that was, and is, astounding in its scope.
By mid-century, the new America was piercing through the
old.

The new Americans selected new kinds of presidents:
first a Roman Catholic Irishman, then a Texan, a peanut
farmer from Georgia, an actor from California, an ivy league
president who ate pork rinds and told us he was from Texas
and a saxophone player from Arkansas. To be from the "Eastern establishment" became a political kiss of death. The new
America forced the politically ambitious to spend great amounts
of energy and money assuring the public of their lack of ties
to "the system," meaning the old upper class.

In his quest for the presidency, billionaire Ross Perot
spent millions of his fortune trying to convince us he was
coming from outside the corridors of power. During his first
campaign, President Bush insisted that it had been 10 years
since he had purchased a shirt with a button-down collar; but

in his bid for a second term, even his pork rinds and country music couldn't save him. The new America chose one of its own.

The national complexion changed in other ways. The new America created popular music from blends of Tennessee tunes and African rhythms. Even in rural areas, Americans begin to eat at Mexican and oriental restaurants. As air conditioning became thought of as a necessity instead of a luxury, the center of our population moved into what had been the cultural backwater of the continent. The children of the deprived gained wealth, which won them the right to openly prefer the kinds of music, linguistic habits and dress ridiculed as "low class" just a generation before. The president of the United States could now wear blue jeans in the oval office.

> **EVEN HIS PORK RINDS AND COUNTRY MUSIC COULDN'T SAVE HIM.**

The 1960s brought one social earthquake after another, including civil rights, the fall of colonialism, the women's rights movement, the charismatic movement in the mainline churches and color television. Then there were blue jeans, rock and roll, electric guitars, hair perms and beards. Of course, most of these changes in American culture were simply fads which soon gave way to newer fads. But the underlying causes of the changes were solid, long-term trends, and they will remain with us for a long time. Certainly our country will have its seasons of reflection and recommitment to older ideals, but it will never again be a nation ruled culturally and philosophically from the Atlantic coast. Blacks, Hispanics and "lower class" whites, rising in economic and political power, will continue to mold and reshape the old ways of life, creating an America that is ever less European.

It is not only a matter of ethnicity and culture, however. Changes at other levels are making the new America in many ways a troublesome place for the Christian believer. One trouble spot is the shift in values. We Christians have never done a good job of distinguishing between transitory fads and genuinely dangerous shifts in culture. We must learn. The first is that uncomfortable feeling that comes when we realize that we are getting older and are losing touch with youth. The other is a serious compromise and threat to the gospel.

The new America is here whether we like it or not, and the church has planted its roots deep within the old. If we do not do the missionary work necessary to win the new America to Christ, the American church will disappear with the dying culture. The new America, if that happens, will be a heathen nation.

A PERSONAL LOOK AT THE NEW AMERICA

Perhaps past generations felt little urgency to deal with our differences because the regions of the nation seemed so far apart. My grandfather was born in 1890 on the banks of southern West Virginia's Kanawaha river which meanders around the Allegheny ridge on the western flank of the Appalachian mountains. When I was a child, it was still no small matter to get in and out of our valley, even in a car. The roads one had to navigate to get there wound around almost impassable hills and dales, and when you finally arrived you were almost cut off from the outside world. Right before I was born they built what the natives called the West Virginia Turnpike, which joined Charleston with Virginia and the Carolinas. We were always offended that outsiders thought of it as a road system designed in hell. The truth is, thousands of people have lost their lives on that road, but it was our link with the outside world.

When Grandpa was a boy, before they built the turnpike, the only links with the outside were the railroad and the river. Our ancestors had come over the mountain trails from the Atlantic coast, but they took three generations to do it. It was hard to cross the mountains.

The rivers were easier to travel. A person could float a raft down to Point Pleasant, where the Kanawha joins the

Ohio. From there one could go south, north or west, though hardly anyone did, even in those days when the rivers and canals were the nation's interstate system.

A little later the railroad came through. My mother's great uncle Woodrow, everyone called him Wood, helped lay the first rail into our valley—I think it was the C&O—and lived to show me pictures of himself as a boy laying down steel on the mountain soil of the West Virginia hills.

That was the world into which Grandpa was born. My great grandfather on my mother's side lived about a quarter of a mile down the road from Grandpa Scott. They were very different kinds of men. I mention them because they both said important things that stuck in my mind and won't go away.

As far as I know, Grandpa Scott only left the state once. He went across the mountains into Virginia, but he didn't like it there. Once someone asked him why he never went on trips, and he replied, "What's the use? I'm already here." He just couldn't understand why anyone needed to be anywhere other than in our little valley. In fact, we called it *THE* valley. For us, there was only one valley, and that was the Kanawha Valley. There was no need to define it further.

We called my great grandfather Jordan "Poppy." I can't tell you most of the stories about Poppy, since this book is being published by Christian publishers. I can tell you that he chewed tobacco every day of his life, even as a baby, I think. In his mind, everything that was wrong with the world was the fault of Arabs, which he pronounced *A*rabs. For Poppy, *A*rab was only half a word, because he put an adjective before *A*rab and always said the two words together in one breath. I assumed it was all one word, and it is another thing that I cannot print here.

Now the only "Arab" that Poppy knew was a Lebanese peddler named Mr. Haddad who came through Chesapeake periodically with a backpack selling cooking utensils and blankets when Poppy was a boy. There weren't any real Arabs within hundreds of miles. Poppy liked Mr. Haddad, too, so it wasn't anything personal. Mr. Haddad was one of the good ones, Poppy thought. It's worth a laugh that Mr. Haddad's descendants now own at least half of the southern part of the state.

Anyway, the story continues and is longer than I can tell here. My other grandfather had to move to Ohio to find work. He stayed there for 12 years. At every family reunion, he would tell us, with tears in his eyes, "If I die in Ohio, don't bury me here, take me home." It worried him a lot. As soon as he could he did return home. He died there and was buried on Marmet hill, along with our ancestors who discovered *THE* valley.

MY MOTHER TOLD ME, "THIS IS A WICKED PLACE, A REAL WICKED PLACE."

The generation of Americans born before the Second World War lived in a large world filled with strange, exotic places and people. Going to Florida was a long, long trip. Calling someone on the telephone in another state was a very rare thing, something you told everybody about the next day. (When I was a child we would say, "We talked to someone in California last night." The response was always, "Could you hear them OK?" Usually we could reply, "You could hear 'em pretty good.")

We went to New Orleans once when I was a boy to attend a Pentecostal conference. I heard people speak French, or what passes for French in Southern Louisiana, and was amazed. We ate a strange food called gumbo. I heard music on Bourbon Street and saw pictures of scantily clad Cajun women on big posters. My mother told me, "This is a wicked place, a real wicked place." She was right—it was a wicked place. All the same, I remember wondering if we could go again sometime.

When I was fourteen, a friend of mine took me to a Chinese restaurant in Charleston. People drank tea from cups without handles. They served no mashed potatoes. They had no fried chicken or hot dogs. I thought I had gone to heaven. My dad thought he had landed in hell.

About 1960, that old world just fell apart. The Second World War had shrunk the world, and a new generation began to adjust to a smaller planet. For my generation, Chinese food is not at all exotic. We eat it for lunch. I don't go to New Orleans to get gumbo now; I get it at the Red Lobster at Hickory Hollow Mall. The cable shows me on television what is happening in Moscow and Mogadishu, any hour, day or night.

It is still possible to live in the old America, the America of my parents, but it is getting harder. You have to shop at old stores, drive on the back roads, and limit your television watching to the Family Network. Some people do it, mostly evangelical Christians. But as we cocoon, the new America is not disappearing. It is growing.

The tension between the old America and the new is sometimes unbearable. People who still live within the perimeters of the old culture insist that we should buy American products. Most of us would like to do that, but there are few truly American products left; there are just products with American names. One kind of Ford and a Chevy are made here from start to finish. The rest of the so-called American cars are made, at least partially, abroad. Four other automobiles are made here in this country from start to finish, but they all have foreign names like Nissan and Mitsubishi. It has become difficult to distinguish domestic from foreign cars. Is an American car a Ford made in Mexico or a Nissan made in Murfreesboro, Tennessee?

We live in a world of reshuffled categories. The old America assigned a place for every language group and every race to live, but that world fell apart. We are now all mixed together in huge metropolitan areas. These great cities define the culture and the products of the world.

My generation has to work at it if we want to live in the disappearing old America, and my children will have no choice about it. They will live in the new culture. The future has arrived. So the Church must learn to minister to this emerging world. It can't insist on ministering to a world that has disappeared everywhere except within our own church walls.

My great grandfather could rage about Arabs because he didn't know any, and would never see any. I have to live in a different world. There is a real live Mosque in our city and thousands of Muslims. Every day I talk to people in other states and even other nations. We fax information back and forth, to and from all points of the globe. I must live with diversity.

Today, learning about other races, customs or languages is not an academic exercise or some strange hobby. Such skills have become important simply to survive in the world. They will become increasingly important for our children, important in business, diplomacy, and the work of the Lord.

THE FALL OF COMMUNISM

The 20th century came to an end on August 21, 1991. Properly speaking, of course, the century had eight more years to live. The spirit of the old century, however, died with the fall of communism. We have entered a totally new age. American liberals were shaken by the event; they now have no worker's paradise for us to emulate. American conservatives are in no better shape; they have no evil empire to hate. The implications of the fall of the Eastern Bloc are profound for our entire nation and for the entire world.

We could see it coming. Three years before, Poland elected its first freely elected President since 1932. Hungary followed, and then Czechoslovakia. The eastern part of Germany, cruelly divided from the rest of the nation by an evil and misshapen wall, first relaxed its grip and then gave up all pretense of its miserable life. The wall came down in November of 1990. By Christmas, we saw the fall of Romania's Nicolae Ceausescu, a man described by one old Romanian woman as the antichrist. By January of 1991, the United States went to war against Iraq in concert with European allies and a smattering of Arab states, but they were guided in large part by the military intelligence of the Soviet Union!

Then one Sunday at midnight, James Boutwel, an elder of our church, called to tell me that there had been a coup in the Soviet Union, and that the old hard-liners were back in power. We were frightened about new friends we had made there, particularly those who belonged to the church we had just started in Leningrad. The next day, Boris Yeltsin barricaded himself in the Parliament building of the Russian Federated Republic. Later that day the British Prime Minister, John Majors reported that he had been cut off in the middle of a telephone conversation with Yeltsin because tanks were coming to arrest the Russian leader. An hour later, we watched as Yeltsin climbed up on the tanks and commanded the officer in charge to yield to his constitutional authority. To the astonishment of the world, the officer agreed, and turned the tanks around to *defend* the Russian parliament. The Soviet air force then refused to act against him. The Soviet navy followed suit. The coup leaders began to run.

The next day, President Gorbachev returned to an entirely changed situation. Events escalated. The people cast down the statue of the founder of the KGB. In the town square of Tallinn, the statue of Lenin was ripped from its pedestal. The crane swung it round in the air, and mighty Lenin looked like a drunk man, twisting and turning, up and down, torn from his Soviet throne. (Was this the man who troubled the nations?) The man with the power, Yeltsin, closed down the Communist party. *Pravda* had no party news to print for the first time in 74 years. Meanwhile, the flag of prerevolutionary Russia was flying once more over the Kremlin. The Red star shook and fell.

A DIFFERENT GAME ON A DIFFERENT PLAYING FIELD

The world created by the Second World War is gone. Russia is again Russia, and not the Soviet Empire. Germany is again Germany, and not the crippled, mutilated half-nation she was for 40 years. Japan is powerful and rules the economic life of the Pacific rim. The European states, recovered now from the two world wars, are showing their old powerful selves to be very much alive. They are now not only our allies, but our economic competitors. The shotgun marriages, arranged by the western Allies, which united unwilling ethnic partners into artificial nations have filed for divorce, some peacefully, some bitterly and violently. The geopolitical world is now more like it was in 1900 than it was in 1980.

The world created by the Second World War operated along the lines of certain power blocs. The East gathered around the military and political might of the Soviet Empire, and the West followed close behind the economic and military strength of the United States.

The globe was a football field with two great teams playing for all or nothing stakes, while the rest of the world watched and cheered or jeered from the sidelines. Now we are not only playing on a different field, we are playing a different game.

If you were born before the Second World War, your world was the region of the nation in which you were born. (My colleague and senior pastor invariably says, "*way up* in New York," or "*way down* in *old* Mexico.") The next generation began to think in terms of the nation. Baby boomers traveled from California to Woodstock and then back again. The whole nation was ours. Most American baby boomers are not really southerners or northerners now, but just Americans. We travel and live where the pay is good, or where the air is clean.

The new generation of Americans is the first to be globally minded. They see and hear news as it happens on CNN. They watch satellite TV. They buy clothing from China and Korea, cars from Europe and Asia, stereo systems from Japan and Germany. They vacation in Mexico, Brazil and Portugal.

We are witnessing, for good or evil, the emergence of a world culture. Paradoxically, this comes at a time when the great nations are breaking down into bite sizes. Small ethnic groups demand their own state, from Quebec to the north, to the Serbs and Basque peoples in Europe. But these little nation-states are not power brokers and will not be. They are components of a world system, just as our stereo systems have been broken down into components and have been rearranged as parts of a total sound system. The disappearance of communism will produce a growing, interdependent, interlocking network of nations and peoples. Independence has been redefined. Isolationism has become impossible. If Japanese or German banks sneeze, America gets a cold.

The new world order springing up all around us is a complex clutter of conflicting ideologies. The political choice of the nations seems clear: democracy. Their economic choice seems to be free enterprise. The next great choice of the nations will be religious. What will they choose? Islam is still with us. Hinduism and its stepchild, the New Age movement, is still with us. The new world order ensures that Hinduism is no longer something way over in India, and Islam is no longer a strange Arabic sect in a far-away desert. Both religions have become viable options for a growing number of American citizens.

> THE POLITICAL CHOICE OF THE NATIONS SEEMS CLEAR: DEMOCRACY. THEIR ECONOMIC CHOICE SEEMS TO BE FREE ENTERPRISE. THE NEXT GREAT CHOICE . . . WILL BE RELIGIOUS.

We must wake up.

While God's *universal* church is predestined to triumph, it is possible to lose our *national* church. It happened to north Africa. If we keep our eyes closed, it is almost certain to happen here, too. Ignoring the times is one way of helping it happen. Look at Russia again. The old Russian communist guard were so sealed off in the Kremlin that they had no clue of how their people felt about things, nor how the times had changed. They thought that they would do the same thing they had done to Nikita Kruschev in 1965. No one told them that it just wasn't 1965 anymore.

In 1965 there were no personal computers. In 1965 there were no video recorders or fax machines. In 1965 the satellites were primitive and inefficient. But in 1991, video cameras were recording, faxes were faxing and satellites were glaring down on the whole scene from hundreds of miles in space. The people were informed, and chose the charismatic Yeltsin over the prune-faced communist coup leaders. If the coup leaders had looked and sounded good on TV, things may have turned out differently.

The new world we have just entered will demand that the American church come to grips with the implications of technology. Our generation is media oriented. We can no more ignore the new high tech tools than our grandparents could ignore cars. Our great grandparents probably laughed at our grandparents, and told them that people would always need a good horse. They were wrong. Automobiles changed the world, and our new technology is changing the world. We must be familiar with it and its social and psychological impact on our times.

This new world will demand responsible leadership that balances our need for innovation with our paradoxical need for roots and stability. The new Russian government is flying their ancient flag and chanting their ancient hymns. The new technology seems to give a new shine to ancient things. All over the world, the people are crying for both roots and relevancy. National leaders who are sensitive to these needs will win their people's approval. Christian leaders who can hold to both things will lead growing congregations.

We have entered a new age filled with innumerable dangers. Our only option is to dream big dreams and muster the troops for action. It's harvest time and we dare not sleep. We simply cannot go about business as usual. The trumpet is calling the American Church to action. The General of all the ages has begun the countdown to total victory, and we are being called to the frontlines. As the peoples of the world mingle, argue, fight, create, merge, engage and disengage, the local church in America finds herself face to face with the words of the Lord, "And this gospel of the kingdom will be preached in the whole world as a testimony to all nations, and then the end will come" (Matthew 24:14). World evangelism has become our means of survival, and no one tradition of the Church can do it alone. It will take us all—together.

THE AMERICAN CHURCH FACES THE NEW CULTURE

Imagine a little evangelical assembly in the English countryside. Being a missions-minded church, the congregation decides to send half its members to the Amazon jungle. They raise the money and send them out.

The brave missionaries sail away. After many hardships, the English Christians arrive at the place of their calling. They pray. Then they build crude temporary shelters. Their first big job is erecting a church building. It is a little white church with a steeple and a white picket fence, cute as a button. Two people die in the first few weeks, so they start the graveyard behind the church.

As the years go by, children are born and grow up. The missionary children play with native jungle children, so they often speak the Bachi language among themselves. They speak English with their parents, of course. They swim naked, but realize that for some reason dad and mom want them to wear clothes, so they put them on before they go home. The children can use a blow gun, find shata root to make candy and tell when a tiger is around. That is how the first generation of Englishmen born in the jungle adapt. They go to England every four years and enjoy it, but are always ready to go "home" to the jungle. Their parents cry when they leave England.

The missionaries bring their children up in the fear of the Lord. They teach them Bible stories and insist that they put on a tie when they go to church to show reverence to God. The children are urged to bring their native friends to church, but it is always a disaster. They don't reverence God's house. One little Bachi boy comes naked. Even when they get him into pants and a shirt, he will not sit still. He spots a pshat crawling on the back of the pew and leaps over the lady in the hat to get it before someone else. (The pshat make wonderful bait for fishing, but they are quite scarce.) One of the missionary ladies tells him that he is always welcome in God's house, but that he will have to learn to behave if he wants to come back. That was all right with him; he didn't understand a thing anyway. He hated the music and the shirt and tie ate him alive.

What will happen there? My prediction is that when the first generation dies, the next generation will continue with the mission—at least some of them. Most will intermarry with the natives. Some of the natives will marry into the English church and will attend on special occasions. A young man or woman called of God into ministry will bring down the wrath of his fellow believers by coming to preach in a loin cloth and doing half of the sermon in Bachi. The third generation will be naked little blond boys and girls who will grow up hearing grandpa say, "You should cover those kids," and dad and mom respond, "Oh Dad!"

> **OUR NATIVE FRIENDS ARE LOST WHEN THEY COME TO CHURCH.**

Of course that is not the way missionary work is done any more. It doesn't work. Real missionaries would learn the Bachi language, translate the Scripture, win some converts, then allow the Bachi people to write their own hymns and build their own church building, in a style that suits them.

So why do I tell this story? Because it is a parable of the American Church. We Christians now live in a mission field. Baby boomers like me are bicultural. We live in the old America with our parents and in the new America with our children. We understand church language, have some fondness for the old music and know how to dress for God's house. Our native friends are lost when they come to church. They don't understand the language. They detest the music and the sermon seems five hours long. The cultural gap between our children and our parents is often enormous.

We conservative Christians have no intention of changing the message of salvation, but we know that we must change the culture surrounding it. We are in a new country now, and parts of the old church culture—paradoxically not the oldest parts, but the parts to which we are most attached, the accruements of the past dozen decades—hinder the living faith which it contains.

A STONE FROM UNKNOWN MISSIONARIES

A few years ago, I was in the city of Quebec, one of the oldest cities on our continent. While my wife was shopping in the old part of the city, I explored an Anglican church built during the reign of King George III. The church vestibule was all marble, except for one rough stone that jutted out from the rest. Underneath was a small, tasteful brass plate with these words: "This stone was taken from the foundation of a church building in England, built by unknown missionaries in the second century."

I ran my hand over the stone and wept. I thought of my ancestors in Scotland and Ireland, rough people, violent people, uncivilized and uncouth. I wondered how they had received the first foreigners who came to them with the unsearchable riches of Christ.

I wondered why the missionaries had come. I wondered if their home churches in Italy or Greece cared enough to support them, or had they gone in spite of apathy in their home church? Did the leaders in their home church tell them, "We can't send you because our church needs a new roof?" Did the elders argue that it was a waste of money and talent to send people to other lands when so many people close at home were not yet Christians?

No doubt the unknown missionaries did face all of that, just as missionaries encounter that sort of myopia today. Thank God they went anyway. Because they went, there is an American Church today. Someone in Italy, Greece and other nations cared about the heathen in lands far away. Had those early missionaries waited until all of Greece and Italy became Christian, they still would be there. But they had the mind of Christ: reaching all peoples with the gospel of Jesus. Because of their vision, I am a Christian.

We need that vision now. We need an aggressive movement within our American churches to plant churches among the new Americans, as well as in the rest of the world. We

no

need Christians and churches that are brave enough to ignore the criticisms of visionless people.

Some sections of our cities have become as foreign a field as any place on the other side of the earth. They need churches that will revive the human spirit and show people that the way out of misery begins with a change of heart and soul.

Our country needs an aggressive Christian movement in the arts and intellectual communities that will revive the cultural fruit of our Christian heritage. (A good dose of the writings of St. Thomas Aquinas would cure most of the ills of America's colleges and universities.) The American Church can and must respond. We can win our nation back to Christ.

Our children and grandchildren will live in a world that will shrink even more than ours has. Already people crisscross the globe routinely, fax letters around the world, translate documents by the millions and assemble machines from component parts made in a dozen different countries. This trend will escalate. We can't pretend that it doesn't affect us.

The settlers who came ashore at Plymouth rock and Jamestown believed they were founding a new kind of society. They were right. Their influence has been with us all along. Their faith was the core of the melting pot. Somewhere along the way, though, our nation began to ignore the core ideas that gave it birth. New generations arose that had no understanding of them.

A new culture began to emerge. It has now all but overtaken us. The old culture is alive only in a fragmented way in our churches, and under attack even there. Millions of non-Christian immigrants from all over the world have come and raised generation after generation of Americans who never have been evangelized with the gospel of Christ. They are demanding their part of the American dream, but are not accepting the old Christian values, or are not even aware of what they are. The hour is late, and the pot is boiling. The stew is unpalatable. It needs a little salt.

CHAPTER 3

IT'S ALL HOW YOU LOOK AT IT!

*We know that we are children of God, and that the
whole world is under the control of the evil one
(1 John 5:19).*

St. John is known as the beloved disciple. He wrote the
familiar John 3:16: "For God so loved the world that he gave
his one and only Son . . ." So American baby boomer Christians are shocked to discover that this apostle of love also
wrote a verse like 1 John 5:19. It is upsetting for anyone to
claim they know *the* truth. Even worse, claiming that other
opinions, even other human beings, are in error—the King
James Version says in "wickedness"—seems to prove that our
faith is antiquated.

The prevailing reality for our times is the theory of
relativity. What Albert Einstein proposed as new physics has
become a pillar in the temple of modern thinking. His idea
was basically (I'll have to make it basic; my grasp of physics
won't allow otherwise) that speed, time, matter and space are
in relative relationship with one another. Just as the siren of

an ambulance rushing toward me changes pitch as it speeds by, light, time and the perception of reality change with my location, direction and speed. Certain rules of nature rule below the speed of light, others rule above it.

It was just theory. We don't move at the speed of light. It became more than theory, however, when we discovered sub-atomic particles, objects as small compared to atoms as atoms are to us. We took physics even further in a discipline called quantum physics. Many theorists now believe that some sub-atomic particles may move faster than the speed of light, so fast that they move forward or backward in time. Some sub-atomic particles have mass but no weight. Some particles behave differently when they are observed than when they are not.

So while we can't move at the speed of light, we know about things that do. Studying the subatomic world has revealed to us a part of the universe which simply does not obey the rules. We know now that Einstein was right, but that he wasn't radical enough. His theories were relatively true, you might say. All of this has seriously changed the way we see the universe and ourselves. It is as though the rock of Gibraltar has floated away, drifting out to sea as aimless as an iceberg.

RELATIVE MORALS

Human society is adrift, in part because the foundation of thought upon which we built our culture has steadily eroded. Modern mathematicians overcame Euclid, modern physicists overcame Newton, and now the modern Christian has overcome Moses.

Our grandparents were born into a world closer to that of Julius Caesar than M. C. Hammer. Caesar studied geometry, and though he never heard of Newton, he did know that what went up would always come down. This generation has seen things go up that are never coming down, but which will float forever in space. Today's 20-year-olds live in a different universe from their grandparents.

It is not that modern 20-year-olds disagree with their grandparents. They agree with their elders, but also agree with the guy on TV. If the young people are Christians, they agree, too, with their pastors or priests, which does not keep them from agreeing at the same time with people as divergent from one another as Carl Sagan, Norman Lear, Ronald Reagan, Martin Luther King, Jr. and Jay Leno.

Post-modern individuals disagree with no one but the person who claims to believe that some things are absolutely true at all times, in all places and under all conditions. Post-modern individuals are more baffled than angry at such persons. They consider them primitive, as though believers in truth were wild warriors from the Nazarazi tribe of Upper Zamadoch. They think such people are fascinatingly preposterous, until they realize the believer in truth is serious. When they understand that this person thinks some behaviors are unacceptable—that there are standards for art, literature, morals and how one should act on Main Street; that the vows of marriage are serious, even when one "falls out of love"; that being a parent demands responsibility; that one can only eat by the sweat of one's brow—their amused interest turns first to scorn and then to intense anger. A person who thinks this way *is* a wild warrior from the Nazarazi tribe, and a danger to modern society, which will put him or her away.

It's all relative, you see. If George is a modern Christian, on Sunday he will say, with gusto, "I believe in God, the Father Almighty, Creator of Heaven and Earth."

On Monday, however, George will agree with his New Age friend that "the force which guides our existence while we are in this stage of spiritual development is a nonjudgmental, gentle spirit, which moves through the spiritual tradition with which we are most comfortable."

Tuesday, George may go to the erotic dance club with his friend Betty, who enjoys that sort of thing. That night, she and he will have a meaningful relationship that nurtures their emotional selves, without guilt, and without any further complication of commitment.

Wednesday, George may visit his minister, and be reassured that his guilt feelings are the irrational, unreasonable residue of our Puritan heritage.

Thursday, George will misquote a bid for his company, because that is the way business is done. Friday, he will walk around the office answering his portable phone, waiting for the party that night.

Saturday, George will attend the church singles' group, where there is a rather interesting blond who peers deeply into his eyes when he talks.

Sunday, at the service designed for his kind—people who don't get up too early on Sundays—he will repeat again, "He ascended into heaven, and sitteth at the right hand of God . . ."

"Sitteth?" he'll ask himself, "sitteth? Lord, church is so irrelevant."

But he really doesn't mind. This irrelevancy keeps church in its proper place. It's all relative.

I picked up this quote sometime ago that says it all:

> All that is around us, including our own bodies, which appear so substantial, is ultimately nothing but ephem-eral networks of particle-waves whirling around at light-ning speed, colliding, rebounding, disintegrating, into almost total nothingness—so-called matter is mostly emp-tiness, proportionately as void as intergalactic space, void of anything except occasional dots and spots and scat-tered electric charges.[4]

George may never have read that paragraph, but if he ever does, he will know what it means. He lives his life by what he believes to be its implications. Modern morals, like a drifting Gibraltar, have no foundation. George believes, like his ancestors, that where *A* equals *B*, and *B* equals *C*, then *A* also equals *C*. What his ancestors believed, but what he does not believe, is this: When *A* equals *B*, and *B does not* equal *C*, then *A* cannot equal *C* either. That seems bigoted and opin-ionated. *A* and *C* should find a way to get along. George thinks that *A* certainly equals *B* when the situation calls for it, but when *A* is suddenly thrown together with *C*, the rules should be more flexible.

So if Sam and Jane are married, and Mary and Joe are married, this is a good thing. But if Sam and Mary are both out of town on company business, and are lonely, and especially if their respective spouses are not meeting their needs, then the word adultery seems harsh and shows a lack of compassion for Sam and Mary's encounter. After all, they may, by showing warmth and loving affirmation, teach one another to give to their own spouses something they simply did not have to give

IF IT IS NOT A SIN TO LIE, THEN COMMERCE IS IMPOSSIBLE.

before their brief, but meaningful conjunction at the Airport Hilton in Chicago. So Moses is out of the picture. (Who exactly is Moses anyway?) Sam and Mary may find deeper depths of feeling and faith. The encounter may even make them better Christians, and isn't that what it's all about—love and feeling? You may read creeds and commandments in the church bulletin, but what can they possibly mean in real life?

Of course, this kind of thinking is not Christianity at all, modern or otherwise.

Al Akimoff, a missionary for Youth With A Mission, told our church that bridges are collapsing in the old Soviet Union because people are removing the steel undergirding and selling it to contractors for new building projects. It is a pregnant picture of Soviet society, which spent 70 years removing their nation's moral undergirding. Their society collapsed. If it is not a sin to lie, then commerce is impossible. No one can trust a bank, so there can be no banking system. If it is not a sin to steal and cheat, then a taxi driver can set his car up on blocks in the warehouse, keeping the wheels turning so the meter will record the imaginary distance traveled that day, while he plays cards and drinks vodka with his friends. After hearing Akimoff speak, I was left wondering how long it will be until our system collapses from the same cause. What a person believes is important because an idea is the first stage of action.

Our nation can keep teaching us that immorality is just another way to show love, that homosexual behavior is not deviant and destructive, and that adultery should be set free of censure and moral outrage. They can say that the Ten Commandments are part of an antiquated moral code for ancient desert dwellers, hardly relevant to sophisticated urbanites living on the edge of the 21st century. They can keep saying those things all they wish, but the fact remains that the Ten Commandments represent not only God's law, but the way things work. A society can't survive without God's law—its bridges will collapse.

> ● ● ● ● ● ● ● ● ● ● ● ● ● ● ● ● ●
>
> ## THE TEN COMMANDMENTS REPRESENT NOT ONLY GOD'S LAW, BUT THE WAY THINGS WORK.
>
> ● ● ● ● ● ● ● ● ● ● ● ● ● ● ● ● ●

In the same way, our individual faith in God can't survive a lack of knowledge. God said that lack of knowledge destroys his people (see Hosea 4:6). He said that about nothing else. Christian faith has proven God right again and again: Where the knowledge base is undermined and falls, the faith itself follows in a generation or two. Sentiment will hold on to faith for a while, but not very well and not for long.

The early Christians lived in a time when many people were illiterate. Even if they had been able to read, the manuscripts that would later be assembled into the book we now call the Bible were few and far between. Many churches had no copies of the Scripture at all. So they began to recite little poetical statements in their services which contained the essential doctrines of their faith. These were called "creeds" because in Latin the first word of the confession was "credo," which means, "I believe." The earliest is called the Apostles' Creed.

The Apostles' creed begins, "I believe in God, the Father Almighty, creator of heaven and earth." I like the line the Nicene creed adds that says, "of all that is, seen and unseen." This defines *which* god we serve. Our God made

everything. Shirley MacLaine's god and the god of America's
New Age religion is a god that sort of bubbles up from the
earth. In New Age thought, all things are a part of god, just as
all the cells of a body make up a human being. But the God
of the Bible, says this creed, is not the collective consciousness
of creation. He is the creator of all things visible and invisible.

Not only is he the Creator, he is the ruler of the universe. He has laws which he expects to be obeyed. He has
given us a free will, so that we can break his law if we choose,
but we will pay the consequences.

For example, God has a little law called the law of gravity. If we wish, we can ignore that law. We can jump out a ten
story window. But however exhilarating we find the trip down,
at some point we will encounter the law of gravity. If we
break God's moral code, however exciting that may be, we
will face the consequences. No human court, no sociologist,
no psychologist, will be able to overturn that code or the
consequences of breaking it. It is simply the way the universe
works, just as two plus two always equals four, in every country and every age.

Saying that we believe that God is the creator is saying
that we acknowledge his rule over us, and that we are using
his law to undergird our lives and family.

Sometimes we Christians have a hard time with God's
law. We are like everyone else in this regard. I would like to
fly without artificial support, for example. It would be wonderful. But I don't intend to try it because I don't intend to
break my neck. I could possibly convince myself, maybe with
the help of some drug that expands the parameters of my
limited consciousness, that I can fly under my own power.
Then I could jump from the top of the Sears tower. The only
way my brave push against the confinements of convention
can possibly be related to the word relative, however, will be
when my nearest relative comes to pick up my body because I
have foolishly broken my unyielding and inflexible neck.

God's moral law is just as accurate a picture of the way
the world really works as his physical laws. If we screw around,
we will lose our society, bury thousands of friends who die

with AIDS and abandon our children to madness and total
lack of meaning. We will come to old age, if we live that long,
lonely and bitter, and will have contributed nothing to the
future. It brings to mind some more words of the beloved
disciple:

> This is love for God: to obey his commands. And his
> commands are not burdensome, for everyone born of
> God has overcome the world. This is the victory that
> has overcome the world, even our faith. Who is it that
> overcomes the world? Only he who believes that Jesus is
> the Son of God (1 John 5:3-5).

The commandments of the Lord are not burdensome. In
other words, we are children living in a universe ruled by an
all-wise Father. We tell our children, "NO! NO! HOT! BURN
THE BABY! DON'T TOUCH!" because we want to protect
them from harm, not because we delight in keeping them
from some meaningful experience. Our heavenly Father warns
us of the dangers of living in a universe where evil is present,
and he prohibits certain behaviors. Relativity is God's business, outside of the realm he created for us. The universe
where we live, here above the subatomic world and below the
speed of light, is a kingdom of law.

Several ideas now rooted deeply in American life make
that premise very alien for post-modern people. Most of these
ideas began rather innocently, as is obvious in one of America's
most fundamental beliefs: pragmatism.

PRAGMATISM: THE CASH VALUE OF TRUTH

People used to say, "I'm not interested in theory. I'm a
pragmatic person." The statement is American to the core.
Most Americans pride themselves in being "pragmatic." Pragmatism means, in the popular sense, that one has no prevailing ideology behind what one does; one merely does what
must be done. We Americans tend to dislike long discussions
about meaning and worth. We want to get on with it.

I once picked up a paperback book in an airport (unfortunately, I have long ago forgotten the author and publisher) called *How to Conduct a Business Meeting*. It contained a chapter entitled "How to Deal with the Philosopher." It told how to handle someone who gets everyone else off course by meandering down a long road of abstraction and meaningless inquiry into absolutes. Most Americans, particularly most American business people, would wholeheartedly agree. "Just do it! Find the job, describe the job, and do it!"

THE METAPHYSICAL CLUB

At the end of the last century, in the 1870s, an influential group of American philosophers in Cambridge (the so-called metaphysical club) worked this attitude into a formal statement. The club's members included Charles Pierce, who can fairly be called the father of American pragmatism, and William James, its most articulate spokesman and successful evangelist.

Pierce was fascinated with the study of language and human thought. To him, it became clear that thought and belief were dependent upon the symbolic nature of language. Therefore, argument and reasoning is often about words and symbols, which do not necessarily involve practical implications in real, concrete life. For him, pragmatism became a way of clarifying the meaning of symbols. This was important, because all language, even the internal language in our heads, depends on signs and symbols. He once said of his philosophy, "pragmatism solves no real problems. It only shows that supposed problems are not real problems."

William James was less reluctant. He continued to broaden the meaning of pragmatism. His father had been a follower of Swendenborg, an influential pantheist of the eighteenth century, and he, too, had an inclination toward mystical experience. Nonetheless, pragmatism continued to mean for him that "the function of philosophy was to find out what practical difference it will make to you and me, at definite instants of our life, if this word-formula or that word-formula be the true one."[5] Truth, for James, involved finding out a notion's practical use, what he once called the "cash value of an idea."

This is mostly just good old American "horse sense" that one may hear in any barber shop or feed store, dressed up in fine philosophical clothes. It makes obvious sense to most of us, but should it? Is it true? Does it lead to truth?

In a certain sense, it must be true. A question like "Could God create a rock so big that not even he could move it?" is only a dilemma in the linguistic sense. It has no bearing on real life. It's like the drawings of M. C. Escher, where water flowing downhill turns a corner and suddenly begins flowing uphill. You trace the flow with your finger and still can't tell when decline becomes ascent. Escher is a genius at creating problems in the two dimensional space of his paintings. His problems exist only because of the limits of his medium. The "God creating a rock" problem is the same sort of difficulty. It is a problem in the same way that two mirrors facing one another seem to create infinity. Like the mirrors, the mind is able to reflect and communicate the illusion to others. Pragmatism cuts through all of that. It gets to the bottom line.

On the other hand, speaking of the "cash value of an idea" can become an excuse for intellectual laziness and an abandonment of the search for truth. Indeed, as pragmatism continued to develop, that is precisely what happened. Even though today few philosophers claim to be pragmatists in the formal sense of the word, pragmatism became popularized, mutated, and then greatly influenced the way modern Americans think. Consider the statement: "Let's get to the bottom line," and what that usually means.

In Christian circles, pragmatism translates into a disdain for doctrine or theology. We have lost the understanding that an idea is the first stage of action. This is disastrous because we are never really without a philosophy or a theology; we may only have one whose implications we have not considered. When we say, "I am a very pragmatic person, I'm not much for theory" we usually mean, "I don't want to consider the theory I already have absorbed from my environment." We may also mean, "I want to behave in the way I am behaving, and I have no desire to look into the reasons, or what are likely to be the results of my actions, or what would happen to society if everyone acted in the same way as myself."

At any rate, pragmatism, at this popular level, takes James' comment about the "cash value of an idea" at its most crass meaning. What will make money is good; what will work is truth. To the business person it means, "Do what must be done to keep profits rolling in," and "the ultimate impact on society is no concern of mine." To the movie producer it means, "This violence and perversion is what the public will buy. The studies about how on-screen behavior effects real life are inconclusive." To the church leader this becomes, "We must be doing something right, look at our growth!"

> JOHN DEWEY . . . STOPPED USING THE WORD "TRUTH" ENTIRELY, REPLACING IT WITH THE VAGUE TERM "WARRANTED ASSERTION."

Truth and goodness are lost because they are abstract principles, and a pragmatic person doesn't need to consider them.

Although James repeatedly confessed his evidently sincere belief in God, his disciples took his doctrines more seriously. John Dewey, for example (we will examine his ideas more in another chapter), stopped using the word "truth" entirely, replacing it with the vague term "warranted assertion." His philosophy led the nation further down the path of abandonment of truth, of God, of beauty and of glory. Following this philosophy, we are to reconcile ourselves to earth and stop our fanciful flights into the heavens. We are to accept and glory in the achievements of everyday life. There is nothing above to stretch toward.

Evangelicals, who do not see themselves as ever being influenced by secular philosophy, have swallowed this one whole. Utility rules everything. That is why we get metal church buildings, sloppy music and sound systems that are a half step removed from two tin cans connected by a string. Art is not thought to have enough cash value to warrant investment. (On the other hand, popular pragmatism can be used to advance arguments in favor of these things: "The music will draw new people, who will pay for the new stuff and invite their friends.") To argue that we should create and produce good art because it nourishes the human spirit and calls us to a higher plane will not make it past very many church boards, filled as they are with practical, pragmatic people. Artists are so impractical that they are not likely to be on the church boards. Oh well, whatever works!

The downside of this approach to life is that with each succeeding generation truth for truth's sake, beauty for beauty's sake and goodness for goodness' sake, becomes ever more abstract and removed from "practical" life.

C. S. Lewis says that before we say we believe anything we should follow all its thoughts home. If you follow pragmatism's thoughts home, you will find that it lives in a world where there is no truth, no beauty and no absolute good. Sounds like hell to me.

RELATIVE TRUTH

Francis Bacon wrote, "'What is truth?' said jesting Pilate, and would not stay for an answer."[6] Bacon only had it half right. Pilate was a cynic. He didn't believe there was such a thing as truth. He was sneering, not saying, "Sir, I have been looking for what is true all my life, tell me." He was saying, "Truth? There's a laugh. Truth is a meaningless word."

This generation of Americans is a bit different from Pilate. They like Jesus. They believe he is telling the truth. That is, they believe that he is telling the truth for him, at this moment, under these circumstances. Tomorrow, or for someone else, that same truth may not be appropriate. We may need another truth for that circumstance.

This attitude about truth lies behind phrases like "my truth" or "his truth." But we don't hear much discussion about *THE TRUTH*. This generation does not believe something that seemed as certain as sunrise just a few years ago, that truth is true even before it is believed, and that false is false, even when it is believed fervently, sincerely and tenaciously. People today are so tolerant that the possibility of falsehood just doesn't exist for them. Elton Trueblood said, "Complete tolerance makes logically impossible any moral judgment of any kind."[7] He was right, and we are seeing the proof. We are surrendering our corporate sanity.

A few years ago, as a missionary in Latin America, the priests would yell at me, calling me a heretic and a schismatic. They said I should pray to the saints. They said that I did not have the sacraments, and that I would die in my sins. I argued with them. I quoted the Bible. I said that one should pray to God alone. Neither I nor they were very wise, but in our crude way we were all talking about truth. We agreed that the Word of God had authority and that, being Christians, we were bound to follow it.

Some of the new priests are very nice. They do not argue. They do not give me their opinion. This makes life easier. Some of them do not argue because they believe I am a brother in Christ, and they would rather pray with me than attack me. Many, however, have abandoned the battle not because they are more virtuous than the old priests, but because they do not believe what the old priests believed. They don't believe what I believe either. They simply do not believe that truth can be found. For them, no idea, doctrine or faith is worth striving for. The faith of the old priests was much closer to mine than the faith of this new sort of priest.

The fact is, it is very important to me whether or not the Lord Jesus made St. Peter the head of the church, and whether that authority has been passed down through the generations to each successive Bishop of Rome. What Christian is not ready, right now, before taking another breath, to submit to the Lord's chosen representative on earth? I don't want the Roman priest to attack me—I want him to assume that I am sincere in my desire to follow Christ. I am glad for any progress we have made in civility, and for any consideration from him that I am a brother in the Lord, even if a separated brother. However, when all the dust settles, either we should pray to Mary or we should not, and either the Pope is God's chosen head of the Church or he is not. Both the Roman Catholic and I need answers. The questions are far too important to ignore. The search for truth must continue.

That is not happening much these days. The conversation at most ecumenical gatherings does not, cannot, revolve around the Holy Scriptures or our differences in opinion, because we don't believe in truth. We believe in relativity. The Catholics pray to Mary because that is truth for them; the Episcopalians submit to the bishop because that is truth for them; the Pentecostals dance and shake because that is their truth; and it doesn't stop there.

> **THE YOUNG CATHOLIC BOY AT MY SIDE LOOKED HER IN THE EYE AND SAID VERY RESPECTFULLY, "SISTER, THAT IS CALLED APOSTASY."**

I was sitting at the dinner table at an ecumenical gathering with a dear old nun from India. She was kind and intelligent, and I was delighted to be with her and hear her stories. Then she told about the highlight of her spiritual life, an experience in a Hindu temple when the Hindu priest, on some high holy day, had smeared her head with sandalwood. She had felt "one with the peoples of India," she said. She went on to reveal that she represented a group of Catholic missionaries who "read the Upanishads at mass, and paint statues of Christ blue, like Lord Krishna."

I didn't say anything, but the young Catholic boy at my side looked her in the eye and said very respectfully, "Sister, that is called apostasy."

She replied indignantly, "That sort of attitude takes us back to the dark ages."

I confess, I voted for the dark ages along with the young Catholic boy. I don't have all the truth, and neither does he, but we are both closer to it than she because we both believe there is such a thing.

"Buy the truth and do not sell it" (Proverbs 23:23) is useless advice if there is no truth to buy. But there is truth to buy, and it is so priceless that one ought to sell all one has for it, as though it were a pearl of great price. The price we pay to obtain truth is humility and courage. We need to have enough humility to consider all the options available to us, and then, and just as importantly, we need the courage to make our decision. The nun has humility, and humility is a virtue. However, she lacks conviction, and humility without conviction becomes merely a permanent suspension of thought, judgment and action.

Understand that I believe the nun from India to be a good person, but contrary to what a lot of people think these days, just being a good person is not enough. Shirley MacLaine is probably a good person, but what she believes is false. We are not accustomed in our enlightened age to think that anything should be called false, but an engineer who believes two plus two equals anything but four will build bridges that fall down all the same. We build our lives on what we believe, and if what we believe is not true, our beliefs will not withstand the strain of life.

Beliefs have consequences. That is why India and America are so different. India is rich in natural resources, but she believes the wrong things. India is the result of believing like Shirley MacLaine. If you get sick in India, go to a place under the sign of the cross, not to a Hindu shrine. One set of beliefs supports mercy and graciousness and the other simply does not.

That does not mean that I have no respect for India or for Hinduism. India is a fascinating country, and Hinduism is a fascinating religion. Its holy books contain some of the most profound thought in all of human literature. The Hindu priest is not a fool. He may be, and many times he is, more intelligent than I. He may be more devoted than I, too, and pray and fast with a fervency that shames me. None of this answers the question, however. The question is: Are his beliefs true?

Don't patronize the Hindu and me by saying that both of us are right, that we are each following good principles and are simply traveling different roads that lead to God. This cannot be true. The Hindu can say it is true, because he believes that God is in all things and that all things will somehow be resolved into God, including me, my faith, my paint bucket and my mother-in-law. I cannot say that. I follow one who said, "I am the way and the truth and the life. No one comes to the Father except through me" (John 14:6).

What am I to do? Jesus said that truth could be obtained, and that he himself was truth. So I should be kind to the Hindu. I should respect him and his religion. I should even admire his piety. What I cannot do is act as though he has obtained the truth about God. Instead, I must proceed as though I have the cure for a deadly disease, and the one who gave me the cure instructed me to take it in all haste to my Hindu friend.

I am not a heresy hunter. I differ with many of my evangelical brethren about how to deal with the New Age movement in the United States. I don't find it any more dangerous than the humanism we have been dealing with for 300 years. I believe, in fact, that the millions now caught up in this movement are making their way toward God. They don't know how to express their quest in the language of Zion because they have no background in traditional Christianity. In spite of this, I predict that in a few years millions of new Christians will be testifying that they started their spiritual journey as New Agers.

Still, we must warn that New Age spirituality is dangerous, because it is a spirituality without definitions, without boundaries and without a concept of "true" and "false." It is all-accommodating like a madman with an enormous grin who agrees with everything you say. The madman doesn't know that sanity comes from discerning good and evil, up and down, light and darkness, true and false. Neither does our age.

We cannot ignore our age, even if we are conservative Christians. I do not intend to ignore it. Zen Buddhism is so fascinating that I once wrote a paper suggesting that it be the subject of an academic study, not as a religion but as a type of Gestalt Therapy. Touching even the parameters of the philosophy it implies is deeply challenging. Robert Pirsig wrote a best selling novel, *Inquiry into Values: Zen and the Art of Motorcycle Maintenance*, that introduced some central Zen ideas to an American audience. American Christian leaders should read at least that book, which influenced an entire generation of college students. Nonetheless, I press forward again the question of truth.

Either God created the heavens and the earth or he did not. If he did, then he was here before the heavens and the earth, so he cannot be "the collective consciousness of all that is." Either he came to earth in the person of Christ or he did not. If he did, then only he can be worshiped and followed, because he said, "I am the way and the truth and the life."

Christ presents us with the type of choice this generation despises: Either he is the Son of God, or he had a mental illness. He either needs to be worshiped or given lithium. He is not one way among many; he is "the way," or no way at all. He demands that we decide "yes" or "no" to his claims. And that is the truth.

RELATIVE LAW

In the first months of World War II, Germany invaded France. The aging French generals threw up their hands and surrendered. To reward them, the Germans moved the national capital from Paris to Vichy and installed the old generals as the leaders of their puppet regime. France became an ally of Nazi Germany and an enemy of the allied forces.

Then a strange thing happened. A minor French official fled to England and declared that the French government had become illegitimate. He told Frenchmen that Vichy France was an impostor, that it would not be treason to disobey the leaders at Vichy, that in fact it would be disastrous and unpatriotic to follow them. Little by little the French colonies, and then portions of France itself, begin to turn from the Vichy government and recognized the French government-in-exile as the legitimate French government.

The minor official in question, who unilaterally declared the whole French government to be illegitimate, was the haughty, towering figure of Charles DeGaul. He told the French people and the world that the Vichy government had removed itself from continuity with historical French authority and, therefore, the regime was an impostor. Finally the world and the French people believed him.

When our children study the Second World War, they learn that France was an Allied power, and that its real government was headquartered in London during most of the war. History has upheld general DeGaul's judgment that Vichy France was an illegitimate government.

The same issue of governmental legitimacy was raised in the final years of the Soviet Union. The government had to publish studies denying that the communist party had killed the czar and his family. Members of a growing nationalist movement began wondering out loud whether any government that was descended from thugs and criminals should be respected as the law of the land. The Soviet citizens began to wonder if time and habit alone should justify a claim to authority. The communist government had to answer this challenge: A government cannot survive if enough of a nation's citizens reject the legitimate right of the leaders to rule. Perceived legitimacy is critical for any government.

Sociologists are puzzled about why people allow others to rule over them. Since the ruled always outnumber the rulers, why do the ruled obey laws they don't like, pay taxes they do not wish to pay and send their sons to die in wars they did not start? You could answer that the ruler has soldiers who will shoot those who do not obey, but how does the ruler get the soldier to obey him instead of shooting him? It seems incredible that people are ruled at all. Yet, leadership, law and authority are present in any society, no matter how primitive.

A ruler can exercise authority only by convincing the people he leads that he has a legitimate right to rule. A ruler may base his claim to legitimacy on a number of arguments. He can claim that God told him to rule, or that he has descended from a long line of rulers and holds power by the right of legitimate succession. He can claim that the people themselves have elected him. He can claim any number of things, but he has to claim something. No one follows the guy who says, "Obey me just because."

Relativity in the legal sphere destroys legitimate law and sets up a rule of experts (those who know) over those who do not. From the Christian standpoint, it is possible for law to become illegal. We may be dangerously close to that right now in our country. Conservative Christians are terribly upset about the New Age movement, and rightfully so, but are only mildly concerned about the new definitions of law. We have reason to fear these lawless lawmakers, politicians, doctors, lawyers, social scientists, genetic engineers, computer programers and weapons experts. The mechanic down at Joe's Auto repair wants my money. If he is a lawless man he will lie to get it from me. The lawless social engineer wants my soul. He wants to recreate me into a nonaggressive, nonjudgmental, socially adept, post-modern man. While we worry about people wearing crystals, the really bright guys and girls are designing our pragmatic and relative new culture. Now there is something to keep you awake at night!

RELATIVITY IN CHRISTIAN LEADERSHIP

The Church has traditionally claimed authority in several ways. After all, the Church is a society. As such, it has the right to define itself before the watching world. Certainly, in a democratic society one has the right to worship whatever one chooses, even if one chooses to worship Smokey the Bear. I cannot deny such a person the right to practice his or her furry faith. I do have a right to say that individual is not practicing the Christian faith.

Where do I get that right? I get it by confessing the Christian faith as it has defined itself through the ages. The creeds say that the God we worship created heaven and earth, became a man who was born of a virgin, died and rose again from the dead, and so forth. The counsels of the faith have declared the Old and New Testaments to be the canon (or measurement) of Christian doctrine. These doctrines exclude "bearism" as a legitimate expression of Christian faith.

Not starting forest fires is a good rule every Christian should respect, but Smokey's word is not religiously authoritative for us. We are not under his authority. So if a leader of one of our denominations confesses that he prays to St. Smokey—and it might happen any day now—he will by that confession destroy whatever claim he has to my obedience. He will be like the rulers of Vichy France: by cutting himself off from the faith as it has been believed, he has cut himself off from legitimate leadership. The Christian leader who falls into apostasy is like the sergeant who tells his soldiers that he has become an agent for the government of Iraq—no American should feel compelled to follow his leadership under those conditions. St. Smokey is a fine fellow, but he simply doesn't have a place in Christian worship. It's a fairly clear concept.

CLAIMING AUTHORITY—THE GOOD, THE BAD AND THE UGLY

Christian leaders use various arguments to claim legitimacy to speak for their faith. Some claim apostolic succession, asserting that their ordination by a bishop can be traced back to the apostles. If a council of bishops so ordained meet in holy convocation, they may claim a certain authority to speak in the name of Christ.

Leaders may claim authority based on faithfulness to orthodoxy. (Athanasius claimed that sort of authority when he withstood kings and bishops in his day on the issue of the divinity of Christ.) Orthodoxy is how the faith has been believed through history, and a claim to speak on its behalf was powerful in those ages when Christians believed orthodoxy to be important.

Leaders may claim that democratic vote has placed them in office, though the thought is irresistible, "If we put you in, why can't we take you out?"

Finally, leaders can claim, as one hears in some charismatic circles, that the Holy Spirit has appointed them to some high position over God's people.

All of these claims have been used to buttress authority in the church. What is new in our age is the idea that everyone has a right to his or her own opinion, that we can all define for ourselves what constitutes legitimacy and orthodoxy. So we hear Roman Catholics saying the pope is reactionary, and that he is a middle-aged, celibate white man. We read how groups of Catholics are pressuring the bishops to redefine doctrine this way or that. We hear Episcopalians talk about how the church must be dragged kicking into the twentieth century. We hear Presbyterians saying that the Westminster confession needs rethought.

But what in God's name can it mean if bishops are forced to say that the Scripture means X or Y? It means we no longer go to the Scriptures to find out what they say, to learn how to place ourselves under their authority. Instead, we go to the Scriptures having already decided what we believe and how we will behave. We search the Scriptures only to see if any manner of bending or twisting can possibly make a passage reflect the general gist of our preconceived opinion. Someday, someone will have enough sense to see that this approach is not an attack on bishops or pastors (a battle won long ago anyway) but an attack on the very root of Christian authority. The guy lighting incense to Smokey the Bear is in better shape than such foolish people who claim to be Christians but want no part in submitting to what the Christian faith is all about.

In the Pentecostal and charismatic world, the issue of authority really reeks. In that world, it is often those with the richest, slickest road shows who convince the people that they speak for the living God. They are allowed to use people's tithes and offerings to build mansions and buy boats. They can pronounce the most absurd, ignorant, arrogant and baseless doctrines. Eventually, people will see through these acts, but it usually takes years. These leaders leave disillusionment and sorrow in their wake. How can this happen? Because the

God-fearing people believe that the biblical injunction, "Do not touch my anointed ones; do my prophets no harm" (1 Chronicles 16:22) means "Don't require preachers to account for money or their teachings." This is a faulty doctrine of authority.

The American Church, in all its expressions, has had a great loss of perceived legitimate leadership. We do not trust very many who claim to speak for God. Some of that is because we have adopted the idea of relative law, and some of it because the leaders themselves are basing their authority on nothing. In any case the people of God are crying for church leaders who gain the authority to speak for God based on personal integrity, fidelity to biblical orthodoxy, the anointing of the Holy Spirit and submission to authority themselves.

The nation and the Church are both passing through an era much like that recorded in the book of Judges, when "everyone did as he saw fit" (Judges 17:6). We have declined the call to be living stones in the temple of God (see 1 Peter 2:5), and have become instead like subatomic particles, bouncing this way and that, changing course, moving, shifting, purposeless, aimless and out of control. There's not much chance that a watching world will listen to a church like that. There's no real reason why it should.

CHAPTER 4
∙∙∙∙∙∙∙∙∙∙∙∙∙∙∙∙∙∙∙

HAIL, HAIL, THE GANG'S ALL HERE

Democracy is the worst form of government, except for the alternatives.—Winston Churchill (House of Commons, November 11, 1947)

The king had an affair with a captain's wife after seeing her bathe under the soft light of the moon. She was beautiful. He couldn't get her out of his mind. Her husband was conveniently off to war, so the king sent for her. They went to bed.

They never really thought about consequences until she told him she was pregnant. The king was frantic and concocted a scheme to cover up his mischief. He sent a message to the front lines ordering the officer to come home. The captain came, but out of loyalty to his men in the field he refused to sleep with his wife. There was only one thing to do. The king sent the officer back with a note asking the general to put the faithful officer into the line of fire. The deed was done. The soldier was killed. The sin was covered.

Almost. One man knew what was going on, a pesky preacher named Nathan. He made up a sob story about a rich rancher stealing a beloved sheep from a poor neighbor. The king fell for the story. He brashly pronounced that the rancher would die for his gross injustice.

Then Nathan dropped the bombshell: "YOU ARE THE MAN!"

In any other ancient country, the preacher would have lost his head right then and there. But this was not any other country. This was God's covenant nation, where the law did not originate with the king or the state, but came from the hand of God. This was Israel, where rich and poor, high and low, were equal before the law. King David had committed a crime, and King David would pay. Even though the man who called him into question had no governmental position, he stood for the law, and this gave him the stature of a king. The roots of American democracy spring from that concept of equality before the law. (The story of David and Bathsheba is found in 2 Samuel 11-12.)

> IN ANY OTHER ANCIENT COUNTRY, THE PREACHER WOULD HAVE LOST HIS HEAD RIGHT THEN AND THERE.

To the west, a few centuries later, small Greek-speaking cities began a radical experiment in government. All the land-owning males of the city began gathering at special times to consider the common issues affecting them. Each had a vote, and decisions were determined by how those votes were cast. The roots of American democracy reach there as well.

Yet further to the west, the Roman republic was unfolding. Members of influential families elected older men, known for wisdom, to serve in the Senate. As the centuries went by, their decisions were codified, as the Romans grew into a people with a genius for government. American democracy owes something to Rome as well.

Israel, Greece and Rome: American democracy draws something from each. From the Romans, representative government; from the Greeks, governing by direct vote; from Israel, equality before the law. Each concept is an important component of the American system of government.

As the centuries passed, Israel was destroyed, Greece was conquered and, finally, even Rome fell. The ideas remained alive, however. As the Bible was translated into the languages of Europe, the monks copied Greek manuscripts and the church adopted a blend of Roman and Jewish law for ecclesiastical government. In time, some people began to put these ideas together. For example, brief democracies and republics erupted in Italy throughout the middle ages.

Nowhere, however, did the full democratic idea flourish as in Britain. The island of shopkeepers, with its caste system and monarchy, continued to grow away from despotism and toward justice and freedom.

We could talk about the Magna Carta and the gradual growth toward a constitutional monarchy. We could talk of the rise of Parliament, and of the court system. I'll spare you a history lesson and will simply express my overwhelming gratitude to Britain for this amazing gift of freedom and understanding of human dignity.

After the Reformation, English government was forced more and more by its own arguments to justify its actions before the people it governed. *The Book of Common Prayer* and the daily reading of the Scripture in the churches gave the people of England an education like none in the world. Soon they began thinking for themselves. The ground grew fertile for an educated people to have a say in how they were governed.

As the English people began to colonize the Americas, Bible-soaked intellects contemplated how they would govern themselves in a new land, as loyal subjects of their constitutional king. They drew up covenants created from sophisticated, highly developed philosophies of government which were based on Holy Scripture. Their economic structures favored the merchant and his craft. The new government also reflected a knowledge of how ancient societies ordered their affairs.

Until the time of the American Revolution, and well beyond it, Americans drew on this heritage of government and law. It was thought that as long as the people remained committed to the morals of the faith, were literate and kept themselves informed of the issues, they would elect public servants from among themselves who could govern a free people.

Soon after the revolution, however, a more radical version of democracy began to surface. It finally emerged in the presidency of Andrew Jackson, whose administration might well be called a second revolution. This version of democracy was dedicated to the idea that every one in the nation, lettered or unlettered, property owner or pauper, should have a say in the affairs of government.

As time went on, the electoral franchise was opened to all male and female citizens over the age of 21. By that time, the American educational system was the envy of the world. Fourth grade children read Shakespeare from the McGuffy reader system. Finally there was a nation where educated, free people governed themselves by freely electing the most capable leaders to limited terms of office, and who kept control of their government by the periodic review of the elected officials in regularly scheduled elections. This system worked wonderfully until we began to lose our belief in an informed citizenry.

DEMOCRACY AS A CORE VALUE

Will Durant said that there are two Americas: one a transplanted European culture on this new continent and the other an indigenous plant, native to North America. He claims (and he wrote these thoughts in the 1950s) that the transplanted European variety is dying and the native tradition is still in development. He made his evaluation in geographic terms as well, seeing the Atlantic Coast as the most faithful to European tradition, and California and Hawaii as the least European.[8]

I add that the two Americas can also be thought of in terms of age, with older Americans tending toward more European values and younger Americans tending toward a synthesis of world cultures, pragmatism, materialism and sentimentality.

The difference between these two American cultures is apparent in their understanding of democracy. Historically, democracy has been thought of as a way of governing society. It is based on a recognition of the rights of citizens, and allows a person to find his or her place based on merit rather than on the circumstances of birth.

The new culture values democracy in and of itself, not just as the political means to a political end. In the new democratic ideal, all members of the society must have a voice in all matters. They may not be religious, but they can claim a right to denounce the "reactionary" ideas which members of a group voluntarily hold. They may not be students of literature, but they can insist that literature is the domain of dead white men and must be dismantled. If some members of society are not interested in having a voice, then it must be because some deep, structured injustice has robbed them of their legitimate desire and right—so we will give them voice in spite of themselves.

The original notion of modern democracy was rooted in representative government, where the people decide who will represent and govern them. Democracy didn't mean that Aunt Sadie was to elucidate the fine points of an economic treaty with Ecuador. It meant that Aunt Sadie would help choose the men or women who, in her opinion, would best represent her philosophy of government and who would be best qualified to make decisions on matters beyond her personal experience. Democracy meant that Aunt Sadie could get angry at her representatives and vote them out. It meant, too, that Aunt Sadie could run for office, and serve in government herself, if she could persuade enough people to vote for her. It did not mean that she, as a private citizen, would be consulted on every issue.

That was democracy as our founding fathers intended. We would elect the most able from among ourselves, and they would be sworn to rule to the best of their ability. The Senate would consist of two honored statesmen from each state. The house would be made up of representatives chosen according to the population of their home states, and would more directly represent the people's day-to-day concerns. The president would be elected by allowing people to cast a vote for

• • • • • • • • • • • • • • • • •

THE ELECTRONIC MEDIA IS THE FOURTH BRANCH OF OUR GOVERNMENT.

• • • • • • • • • • • • • • • • •

electors, who would go to Washington at the appointed date and elect the person best suited. The president and the Senate together would select and ratify the judges of the Supreme Court, who would sit for life on the bench, free from politics' petty squabbles. Each of the three branches would jealously guard their particular power from the other two, and the states would guard against the encroachment of federal power upon that of the state and region.

What is really happening now is that the nation has overcome the states. The electronic media is the fourth branch of our government. The presidents are elected in beauty contests called primaries, anointed at party conventions which do nothing but stage a show for television, then duke it out on TV for three months while we look on with varying degrees of interest.

Meanwhile, the pollsters continually take our pulse, which causes the candidates to change their positions, redefine their words, and adjust their advertisements to fit our fickle moods. The congressmen are elected and disappear for life. The senators stage TV hearings on various issues. The justices, meanwhile, are prisoners of war, guilty until proven innocent, who must walk through mine fields to get ratified, and are pressured to tell us in advance how they will apply the constitution without bias.

Now there is talk of more democracy. We will participate in the affairs of government by using a telephone or computer to interact with the television, cast our votes and make ourselves heard from our own living rooms.

I can't wait! Electronic town meetings! Wonderful! We will watch the president on TV ask us what we want to do about Cuba. We all will pick up our telephones and dial 222-0001 for "invasion," 222-0002 for "diplomacy," or 222-0003 for "more study." The announcer can tell us the results that very evening: "Fellow citizens, the wisdom of the democratic process dictates that we need more study on this important question." Then we will listen to commentators tell us what it all means. The next night we will vote on aid to Russia.

This is not democracy but mob rule, and is a complete redefinition of American representative government. My question is: We gave up a king for this? Why elect a president at all? Why not put a computer in the White House which can hourly record all the incoming beeps from telephone votes, and continually spit out the accumulated democratic decisions?

I can hear a howl out there from some of you who are reading this. Isn't equality a good thing? Isn't it a Christian value? What the Scripture actually teaches, and what the American founding fathers at least paid lip service to, is *equality before the law.* That means merely that when two people face the judge, rich and poor must be treated equally.

To hold to a theory which declares equality for every individual, in every circumstance, can only mean one thing in practice: bringing down the talented and capable to the level of the untalented and incompetent. C. S. Lewis, as usual, has something to say about this.

> I am a democrat because I believe in the fall of man. A great deal of democratic enthusiasm descends from the ideas of people like Rousseau, who believed in democracy because they thought mankind so wise and good that everyone deserved a share in government. The danger of defending democracy on these grounds is that they're not true.... I find that they're not true without looking further than myself. I don't deserve a share in governing a hen-roost, much less a nation... mankind

is so fallen that no man can be trusted with unchecked power over his fellows. Aristotle said that some people were only fit to be slaves. I do not contradict him. But I reject slavery because I see no men fit to be masters.[9]

There you have, in a nutshell, the bases of two views of democracy. One believes that the exceeding sinfulness of all human beings demands a check and balance to the growth of their power, the other believes that the inherent goodness of all human beings demands a society without moral restriction.

When President Kennedy said in his inaugural address that we believe that the freedoms of the citizen are not a gift of the state but rather an endowment of God, he was appealing to the Christian-based democracy. If there is no God, then of course there is no hand of God and no natural endowment of rights. Freedom, in that case, is a gift of the state to its people. That is the prevailing view of the emerging culture.

THE MYTH OF THE NOBLE SAVAGE

This growing new understanding of democracy has profound implications for the nation and the church. Lewis mentions Jean Jacques Rousseau, who is indeed the source of many of the ideas of radical democracy. The two revolutions, French and American, differed precisely on the question of whether human beings were basically fallen and flawed, or whether the original primitive, noble savage had only become corrupted by social structure.

If a noble, naked, petunia-gathering man is our unspoiled model of virtue and vitality, then we must believe that restraint of any kind is artificial. From that idea flows other thoughts, such as the belief that responsibilities are things unreasonably imposed on us by civilized society, and that it is this which produces our anxiety, stress and dysfunction! This ideology was well suited for Rousseau, who was irresponsible, dysfunctional and completely lacking in ethics. He left his bastard children at birth on the steps of an orphanage. His freedom was compromised by social convention, you see. When you look at modern America, you see the fruit of a man like Rousseau, for a seed always produces after its own kind.

This hunger for the noble savage, for the unspoiled days before social restraints, artificial structure and ceremony, also motivates many American evangelicals, Pentecostals and charismatics. Their distrust and aversion to anything prepared or ritualized; their impatience with pomp and ceremony; their desire for the primitive over the contrived; their demand for spontaneity over structure—all these attitudes among American Christians have been influenced by the same sorts of ideas which motivate those who are dismantling Western civilization.

The truth is, anything made by human beings is artificial and contrived, including hairbrushes, toothpaste and flushing toilets. Rousseau's rantings against artificiality are the product of one who had

• • • • • • • • • • • • • • •

THE TRUTH IS, ANYTHING MADE BY HUMAN BEINGS IS ARTIFICIAL AND CONTRIVED, INCLUDING HAIRBRUSHES, TOOTHPASTE AND FLUSHING TOILETS.

• • • • • • • • • • • • • • •

no intention of being controlled by anything but the impulse of his own glands. I agree with Voltaire, who wrote in a letter to Rousseau dated August, 1761, "One feels like crawling on all fours after reading your work." The truth is, savages are not noble, whether they live in New Guinea or New York.

Civilization itself is contrived, with its marriage oaths, multiplication tables and symphonies. Judges in long black robes, high school graduations, football games—anything that demands learning and rule-following is contrived. Any government based on the idea of the noble savage ignores this and places equal authority over all, in the hands of all, learned and unlearned, reverent and irreverent, cultured and brute. This is like putting players on the football field who haven't learned the rules of the game.

More than any other, the American who is responsible
for this exchanging of the ideas of the American revolution
for those of the French revolution, who helped us finally cast
off the restraints of natural law, Scripture and the quest for
glory, was the kindly old gentleman who captivated American
education: John Dewey.

JOHN DEWEY

In the last chapter, we discussed the influence of pragmatism upon modern America. John Dewey was one of the
shining lights of that school. A brilliant and gentle humani-
tarian, his influence is due to the amazing acceptance of his
thoughts as the guiding light for American public education.
He had a dream—to build a culture based on the American
experience of democracy. Democracy became to him not a
method of government, but rather the central value of life,
and all other things revolved around it.

John Dewey campaigned for many reforms that we all
appreciate today. He cared about education and championed
the teacher as one of our greatest national resources. He was
admirable in a thousand ways. But he asked us to accept
certain concepts, concepts America has in fact accepted, that
are the very points where the emerging culture has departed
from our Christian value system. These points were well
thought out and deliberately presented in such a way that,
once accepted, they would take our country down precisely
the road it has traveled.

Dewey thought that a culture's first stage of development is supernaturalism—a culture of magic, visions, voices,
gods and myths.

Its next stage is a mixture of supernaturalism and naturalism, a culture that is influenced by supernatural ideas but
which begins to make the material world its main focus. He
thought that the America of his day was such a society. People
still loved their church, still held to the dogmas, but no longer
allowed these things to greatly influence them.

Finally, he said, a culture moves to another level, where
the supernatural is discarded all together. We retain, he thinks,

the positive values that we gained in our religious days—our morals, concern for the poor, appreciation for beauty and so forth. But the society must move on. And by the way, in this type of thinking, society is everything. After all, you can't have democracy without society.

To get to the next phase demands that the society realize the importance of education. Education of the young, he said, is far too important to leave to the whim of the clan, the village or the family. Society must actively teach its values so that students can become effective members of the democratic experience. The goal of education is to condition us rather than to inform us.

These were Dewey's ideas, and ideas always have consequences. He was the founder of the National Education Association, so his teachings have become the education bible for generations of American teachers.

An example of how his idea of democracy influences all of life can be seen in modern American art. He felt that in a democracy it was wrong to have art which demands a special environment or a special preparation to understand. He desired an "art of the mass man." He got his wish.

The Christian view of art has been that it ought to be a lifting experience, something that moves you to a higher plane. Art should involve an encounter with beauty and/or truth and be a morally transforming experience.

Dewey, however, did not believe in a higher plane, and our new art professors do not either. This is why we are seeing the general dismantling of Christian culture in the arts. This explains why, as I checked the required reading list for high school literature classes around Nashville, I found lots of D. H. Lawrence and Kafka (both of whom, though they do not represent my values, are genuine artists) but no Christian writers. We now ask our children to read *Sons and Lovers* and the *Metamorphosis*, but no John Milton, John Bunyon or Jonathan Edwards. These writers represent what Dewey and company felt are narrow and marginal religious writers, even though just a generation ago these writers were considered pillars of English and American literature. And on it goes.

I wish that even Kafka and Lawrence represented what we now study in literature. The field has been opened up further, so that any weird, woolly or wicked specimen can make it into our textbooks.

In our new radical democracy, the wizardry of the witch doctor with a bone through his nose is equal to the contribution of a cancer specialist with a stethoscope in his ears at the Mayo Clinic. Even though sick literature professors go to Mayo and not to Mozambique, when then they want philosophy they prefer to read someone who is (what else can we say) more "democratic." They prefer someone close to the ground, someone who speaks to man\woman as he\she\it is, and does not ask him\her\it to consider any higher realm. That would be undemocratic. This is Dewey's fruit, and it has gone bad.

DEMOCRATIC EDUCATION

People are educated when they are humble and respectful enough to submit a portion of their lives to someone more knowledgeable than themselves in the area of their inquiry. A student absorbs material from another, struggles with it, and then synthesizes it with his or her own experiences of life. While teachers must have respect for pupils, teachers and pupils are not equals in the field of study where the teaching and education is taking place.

C. S. Lewis noted that

> This very obvious fact—that each generation is taught
> by an earlier generation—must be kept very firmly in
> mind. . . . None can give to another what he does not
> possess himself. No generation can bequeath to its suc-
> cessor what it has not got.[10]

With all his good intentions, Dewey was dead wrong. He based his entire philosophical system on the belief that there is no knowable God. However, if there *is* a supernatural world, then that fact colors everything. It is as impossible to ignore heaven and hell as it is to ignore France and Finland. They are real places. They make real decisions. They have real ambassadors. They push real agendas. If moral absolutes exist, then ignoring them will destroy the nation. If there is such a thing as knowledge, then five knowledgeable people casting votes together with twenty who are unknowledgeable in the field in which they are voting loads the dice in favor of ignorance.

While we are committed as a nation to equality before the law, and to universal suffrage in the political sphere, extending the notion of equality to all realms of life is ludicrous. It is unworkable and unreasonable.

Dewey contributed to the contemporary accommodation to our fallen nature, to the acceptance of mediocrity, to the willingness to make our place with the animals rather than with the angels, and to revelry in our common "value-creating experiences." He taught us to accept and learn from all experiences, without judgment or preference.

In C. S. Lewis' *The Screwtape Letters*, an old and experienced devil shares with an apprentice demon his thoughts on this sort of "democratic education."

> The basic principal of the new education is to be that dunces and idlers must not be made to feel inferior to intelligent and industrious pupils. That would be "undemocratic" .... Children who are fit to proceed to a higher class may be artificially held back, because the others would get a trauma ... by being left behind. The bright pupil thus remains democratically fettered to his own age group throughout his school career, and a boy who would be capable of tackling Aeschylus or Dante sits listening to his coeval's attempts to spell out A CAT SAT ON A MAT.
>
> In a word, we may reasonably hope for the virtual abolition of education when *I'm as good as you are* has fully had its way. All the incentives to learn and all penalties for not learning will vanish. The few who might want to learn will be prevented; who are they to overtop their fellows? And anyway the teachers—or should I say, nurses?—will be far too busy reassuring the dunces and patting them on the back to waste any time on real

teaching. We will no longer have to plan and toil to spread imperturbable conceit and incurable ignorance among men. The little vermin themselves will do it for us.[11]

DEMOCRATIC THEOLOGY

This idea of radical, all-permeating democracy has been extended to cover a much broader field than what we used to call politics. It must cover all areas of life if it is a central human value. So it was bound to happen that democracy would finally extend to theological issues.

A company of enlightened theologians called the Jesus Seminar meets four times a year to decide what part of the words of Jesus recorded in Scripture we should acknowledge as genuine. They discuss their opinions and then put it to a vote. Colored beads are cast into a box, red if you think, "Yes, these are the words of Christ," black if you think, "No, these definitely are not the words of Christ," pink if "perhaps," gray if "probably not."

The beads are counted, and the results carried to believers around the world who are waiting breathlessly for their decision. The parable of the sower: "probably not." The woman caught in adultery: "yes." The words on hell: "definitely not." And so on.

I just wonder, why can't we all vote? Why not hook our phones to a central computer at the Protestant Vatican on Riverside Drive in New York? Then we all could have a say in what Jesus said and did not say.

Hasn't anybody told those poor souls that this is a stupid way to search for eternal truth? And if it is not an issue of eternal truth, then why bother doing it? This is democracy gone mad, to think one can determine the words of Christ by putting it to a vote. Are we trying to elect a Savior the same way we elect a president?

It does open up limitless possibilities, though. We could vote next on the words of Moses. Let's start with the big ten. Idolatry first: Dial 333-2001 for "Keep the commandment against idolatry," 333-2002 for "No, this is unfair to polytheists," 333-2003 for "Please allow the scholars at Union more time to reflect on this and get back with us."

In a way that is what we are doing already. "Open up the leadership of the church," they say. "Everybody is entitled to an opinion. We need bishops who are sensitive, theologians who understand the human struggle, pastors without a judgmental spirit. Elect leaders who listen to the people, who will not go against the times. Lesbians, loners and lovers of ponies, let them all have their say." When democracy replaces truth as our goal, we begin to search for people's opinion for the sake of getting people's opinion. We stop trying to determine what is right.

> **TO DEMOCRATIC THEOLOGIANS, THEOLOGY IS NOT A QUEST FOR ULTIMATE TRUTH BUT A PARLOR GAME FOR HIGHLY OPINIONATED ACTIVISTS.**

The amazing thing about all this democracy is that no one really believes in it, not even theologians with degrees in sociology. They don't believe in it when the stakes are really high, that is. When theologians need operations on their kidneys, do they demand their doctors include gays and gas station attendants in the decision? And why not? If the bishop can't go against the will of the people and say that historical Christian faith condemns abortion, adultery and avarice, then why should the surgeon decide alone about the theologian's kidney? That isn't very democratic, now is it?

The issue gets real clear about now: To democratic theologians, theology is not a quest for ultimate truth but a parlor game for highly opinionated activists. They see the Church, what many of us still love as "the Body of Christ," as a means to achieve some social goal they think important. They don't have the integrity to admit that they are no longer believers in the Lord God of Abraham, that the god they really worship is called radical democracy, and that they believe we must have no other gods before her.

For we who still believe that a mountain once shook with fire and a man was given tablets inscribed by the finger of God, to that God alone is the kingdom, the power and the glory. The words he gave on the brow of Sinai are his; they are not ours to negotiate. We have a faith once delivered to the saints for which we are commanded to contend. If every Christian denomination tomorrow says that the Ten Commandments have been suspended, then every Christian denomination is to be ignored. "Let God be true, and every man a liar" (Romans 3:4).

Democracy has nothing to do with it.

CHAPTER 5
•••••••••••••••••••

I JUST GOTTA
BE ME

The record shows, I took the blows
and did it my way.[12]

Old man Ramsey loved the bass fiddle. He would go
down to the club on Saturday nights just to watch and hear
the boys play it. He finally bought one for himself. After he
took it home he played it by the hour, day after day. The only
unusual thing about old man Ramsey's playing was that he
only played one note. After hearing this one note, plunk,
plunk, for days, his wife finally asked him, "Why don't you
move your hands up and down the neck, like the boys at the
club?"

"I found what they were searching for," he said.

That is what music sounds like when one old codger
defines it for himself. The same is true for any discipline of
life. If we make our own selves the measure of truth, beauty
and goodness, we will have religion, politics and art of the
caliber of the old man's music.

This is certainly not a new insight. Ancient Greeks figured it out a long time ago. In their ancient mythology, Narcissus was a young man whose greatest joy was peering into the pond at the end of the lane, watching his reflection in the water. "Oh how wonderful and beautiful I am," he thought. He kept staring into the water until he fell in and drowned. The word *narcissistic* comes from that story, meaning someone obsessed with self.

Obsession with self has traditionally been considered a sickness. This sickness takes many forms. A *neurotic* is someone who is so concerned about their own body that every small physical symptom looms large, eclipsing everything else. They always worry about impending death.

Paranoid people believe the whole world is plotting against them. A paranoid kid who steps in a wad of chewing gum while walking home from school says "How did they know I would be coming this way today?"

People who feel they have all the answers for the world, and will be able to provide them as soon as the rest of us move over, have what we call *illusions of grandeur*. The whining *martyr* is another version of the same problem: "I work my fingers to the bone for you and you don't appreciate it. I'll die someday, and you'll be sorry."

All of these illnesses are the same girl in different dresses: ME, ME, ME.

THE DANGEROUS DOCTRINE OF THE AUTONOMOUS SELF

Humanity has always considered obsession with self a disease. In the last few years, however, that notion has been steadily overturned in our country. We now tend to justify and even encourage an obsession with self. We have embraced the disastrous "doctrine of the autonomous self." This modern idea of individual autonomy replaces the family, the clan, the nation, the church, the school, or any other group that was historically the center of our attention, with the self. We used to find fulfillment in playing our roles within a community, but we now pledge to serve our group only as an overflow from our personal fulfillment. The search for personal, individual fulfillment comes first. As a nation we have pretty well rejected the idea that one becomes happy and fulfilled in the process of serving others. We replaced that notion with the belief which says, "I can't help you until I am happy and fulfilled myself."

It doesn't work. Civilization, and all things good which come from it, is based on living for the good of others. The most basic unit of civilization, the family, is built on this truth. Men have to sacrifice time to be good fathers and husbands. Women have to sacrifice themselves to be mothers. For both fathers and mothers, careers must not come first, money must not come first, certainly self and its personal wants must not come first. If the family unit is to survive, and along with it, incidentally, all of civilization, individuals must be willing to pour themselves into their families.

Modern life teaches that marriage consists of two mutually fulfilled, autonomous selves. Not so! Husbands and wives cannot live for self and at the same time practice what we used to call "holy matrimony." When we marry, the Bible teaches, even our bodies belong to one another; they are no longer our exclusive property (see Genesis 2:24, Matthew 19:3-6, Ephesians 5:31). (That's one main flaw with the abortion argument, from a Christian perspective. If you want to own your own body then you should remain single.) When you marry and start a family, you enter an agreement in which you give up exclusive rights to yourself, your body, your dreams and your time. Hopefully, your family encourages your ambitions and gives you time and respect, but you cannot be an autonomous individual and have a family at the same time. Like so many other modern myths, this one inevitably finds itself crashing against the hard rocks of reality.

The most pitiful thing about this notion of the autonomous self is that it cannot live up to its promise. It does not fulfill. Do you know anyone who has embraced these absurdities who is not angry, bitter and mean? Do you know any caring, loving, happy person who believes this stuff? Of course you don't. It remains as true today as it has always been that everyone who serves self becomes sick, hostile and cold. Serving self reshapes men and women into the very image of demons.

Yet another thing to consider in this matter of the autonomous self is that when we believe it, we don't really do what is best even for our own selves. We just do what we want to do right now. The person who makes self the center of life usually does not have a long-range plan even for self. Self-centeredness usually degenerates into an attitude that says, "I want what I want, and I want it now! I want to choose sex now, and not worry about pregnancy. I want rid of this parasite in my body, and I don't want to hear anything more about it. I wanna new TV. I wanna new car. I want, I want, I gotta have, I gotta have it, I gotta have it now!"

> **SERVING SELF RESHAPES MEN AND WOMEN INTO THE VERY IMAGE OF DEMONS.**

This doctrine of personal autonomy gives us amazing new insights. For example, we are hearing horrifying new definitions of old roles these days, things which earlier generations would have called insane. Even motherhood has been redefined. Some radical philosophers are now saying that giving birth is a rape of self, that the infant which tears through his mother's body is committing an act of aggression against womanhood, and that a child nursing at his mother's breast is nothing more than a parasitic intruder devouring a woman. Ideas like these are diabolical. They were hatched in hell. The vast majority of Americans still see them in that light. However, these concepts are only some of the more extreme applications of this sacred doctrine of self that the new America holds with religious fervor.

Contributing to this radical redefinition of traditional roles, at least where mothers are concerned, are the millions of American women who believe they cannot depend on men.

Women can't be sure men won't start families and then run off when they find someone a little more exciting. Women know that they better look out for themselves, because at some point it is very likely they will have to provide for the children men leave them with.

It's time someone said that modern life has gone cuckoo. Marriage is not a baseball contract where if you don't get a good deal you just sign on with a new team; that is the philosophy of the autonomous self. It is incompatible with Christianity, and it doesn't work. Even though this age sees adultery as a misdemeanor, rather like running a stop sign, it is actually what it has always been, a fundamental abandonment of responsibility and honor.

The American people have learned about autonomy from their leaders. They watch movie stars hold out for millions. They see Lee Iococca make seven million a year while he lays off his employees because times are rough. They watch Dan Rather make the screen go black because he doesn't have enough control. They watch Donald Trump restricted by the bankruptcy judge to more money a week than they earn in a year, and then hear him complain that he can't make ends meet on that amount of money. They watch the sports figures strike to make millions of dollars a year playing ball. They watch the heads of our corporations making an average of eighty times the salary of the people at the bottom of their corporate ladder, even when the company is running at a loss.

Some of the people watch all this in the urine-scented, rat- and cockroach-infested, crime-ridden hell holes we call cities. Then, sometimes, the same impulse that causes Lee Iococca to run off with seven million while he is laying off his employees makes a man in the center of Los Angeles cart off a television from a store that is being looted. Some of the savings and loan thieves, who stole billions of American dollars, have already served their time in country club jails. They will soon be on the lecture circuit. The guy who steals the $400 television does not get off so easily. Why is it that we don't get too worked up about crime until the lower classes want in on the act? If the guy who runs United Way can steal, why can't

Jose Gonzalez down in Watts steal, too? That is the question the new America asks itself.

In days gone by, churches, schools, the nation and the family taught people to serve one another. We were taught to play by the rules and not to color outside the lines. Then came the great change. We learned we should look out for number one. We learned that self centeredness is a virtue. We learned that the self is the center of the universe. Well, it has taken a long time for the lowest rungs of society to get the message, but they finally have. Ideas have consequences, and we haven't even begun to see the consequences that will come from believing this doctrine of the autonomous self.

A LOSS OF HISTORY

My college psychology text contained a story of a man who had been in an industrial accident. His head injury had left him with most of his day-to-day ability intact. What had been damaged was his ability to shift items from short-term into long-term memory. Short-term memory clears itself every few seconds, to make way for new incoming information. It dumps items it judges significant into long-term memory, which works on an entirely different system. (Probably, short-term memory is electronically based, while long term memory is chemically based.) At any rate, this fellow had to be institutionalized because every three or four minutes he forgot what had just happened. Doctors would tell him a joke, and if he found it funny, they would tell it to him again ten minutes later. He would throw back his head and laugh again, and again. That is an individual who has no history.

The doctrine of autonomous self is a gigantic head injury for the nation. It makes us think we have no need for the past. The doctrine of the autonomous self doesn't even honor the self we were yesterday or the self we will become tomorrow. Only the present self interests us. This national attitude has made us into a people without a root system, and we cannot survive this way. Understanding our past, knowing how we got here and why, is essential if our society is to exist, much less thrive.

We are what we have become. We did not emerge from the womb of the world thirty seconds ago, already programmed with all the thoughts we are now thinking. The experiences of life produce habits and judgments. We construct knowledge upon the foundation of earlier knowledge, which in turn was constructed from earlier experience. Yesterday gave birth to today, as today will inevitably give birth to tomorrow. We are like onions, each layer peeled from our personality and knowledge revealing another supporting layer underneath.

As with the individual, so with the race. Humanity is challenged and changed by the events through which it passes. Folk tradition preserves the notions of our ancestors through legends and beliefs. History is a discipline that does the same thing in a more formal way, by collecting, writing and interpreting events and ideas so that they will not be lost. We need both history and folk tradition to know who we are. Only they can help us chart our way through the darkness of the future, guided by the light of the past. Progress is impossible without reflection; foresight is impossible to one who has no hindsight. As Anthony Harrigan said, "To try to escape the past is to attempt to bypass all the achievements of mankind. What we do today, what we are capable of tomorrow, depends on the giants of the past, on whose shoulders we stand."[13]

The past never really dies. It continues to exist within the present.

In Nashville, where I live, there is a Roman Catholic church, called the Cathedral of the Incarnation, which is a replica of the old Roman bath houses which were transformed into churches after the dawn of the Christian era. A few blocks away stands the only replica of the Parthenon, complete with a gigantic statue of Athena. In my own church, I perform weddings, using old words birthed in England hundreds of years ago. We use candles, in spite of the fact that we pay our electric bill and have electric lights. We sign registers with plumes, even though a simple bic pen would do the job better. What is all of this about? It is the simple recognition that continuity is a sign of mental health for individuals and societies. Drastic changes in personality and habits are not healthy signs, for individuals or cultures. We instinctively know that we need these relics, and we are right.

C.S. Lewis says

> [W]e need intimate knowledge of the past. Not that the past has any magic about it, but because we cannot study the future, and yet, we need something set against the present, to remind us that the basic assumptions have been quite different in different periods, and that much which seems certain to the uneducated is merely temporary fashion. A man who has lived in many places is not likely to be deceived by the local errors of his native village. The scholar has lived in many times and is, therefore, in some degree immune from the great cataract of nonsense that pours from the press and microphone of his own age.[13]

Without a doubt that is true, and yet, progress is our great American obsession. We are constantly urged to let go of the past, to move on to the next thing, never stopping to think that "progress," as Elton Trueblood once said, is a concept that involves judgment. Someone has to decide what is "progressive."[14]

A real understanding of democracy ought to include an appreciation of history and tradition. G. K. Chesterton put it this way:

> Tradition means giving votes to the most obscure of all classes, our ancestors. It is democracy of the dead. Tradition refuses to submit to the small and arrogant oligarchy of those who merely happen to be walking about. All democrats object to men being disqualified by the accident of birth; tradition objects to their being disqualified by accident of death.[15]

Will Durant said it this way: "One man is rarely wiser than the accumulated wisdom of the race."[16]

The autonomous self is a self cut off from that which gave him birth. It is like being introduced to a character in a novel in chapter ten, and then insisting that all ten chapters which came before him are superfluous and can be cut from the book without loss of significant content. This popular American attitude toward history is a sickness, and our churches have caught the infection.

RESTORATION, A THEME OF AMERICAN RELIGION

If there is a constant theme in American Christianity, it is the idea of restoration, of getting back to the apostles, or to Jesus himself, back to the point before Christianity was corrupted. This persistent notion motivated many an American revival, particularly from the last century to the present. It help give birth to the Churches of Christ, Adventism, Mormonism, Jehovah's Witness, Oneness Pentecostalism and the segment of the charismatic movement that longs for the renewal of modern day apostles and prophets.

The motivating idea for them is always the same: The church was once glorious and grand, but she fell victim to a Satanic plot. The church was highjacked. Centuries came and went, millions went to church, but they were in wretched darkness, nonetheless.

The point where the church is thought to have gone astray varies with the group wanting to restore it. In my group, it involved baptism incorrectly administered. The Churches of Christ believe the high point of wickedness came with the introduction of musical instruments. The Adventists think that worshiping on Sunday and eating bacon were the culprits. The newer charismatics blame the institutional structure of the church itself. All of them blame liturgy and sacrament as a perversion of the original truth.

Now, in these enlightened times, God has sent Joseph Smith, Mary Baker Eddy, Ellen White, Alexander Campbell, William Brahnam, or (fill in your favorite restorer here), to lead us back to primitive purity.

It is no surprise that every one of these groups has an extremely weak understanding of the history of the church. Members of these churches rarely know about outstanding figures who rose up during the centuries of the desperate darkness which they believe lies between the apostles and their restoration of truth upon the earth. There is no St. Francis of Assisi, Basil, Cyril, Wycliffe, Tyndale or St. Patrick for these people. Some of them do not even revere Martin Luther, and if they do, it is only a grudging tip of the hat to someone who helped get the ball rolling back into the court of real Christians like themselves.

These restorationists have no understanding of how we got the canon of Scripture, how the gospel reached Europe and America, how manuscripts of the Holy Scripture were preserved and protected and who did it, or how millions died with the Lord's name on their martyred lips, even though they did not know the four spiritual laws, were not baptized correctly, did not keep the Sabbath and allowed a flute to be played in church. Charles Spurgeon smoked a pipe—that leaves him out; Luther drank beer—too bad; St. Francis used prayer beads—oh well; and Chrysostom—who was he anyway?

The restorationists believe that the church was lost for all those years, but was resurrected in the good old USA by people who, curiously enough, sang songs like we do, built buildings like ours and who spoke English in our very own dialect. So we don't have to deal with those centuries of incense sniffers, bell ringers and chanters after all. Surely the apostles, who were almost post-modern Americans themselves, wouldn't have gone for all that stuff.

Pardon me for hitting this a bit hard. To me, this loss of history represents a poverty of spirit beyond words. The American church desperately needs the history of the faith now. Both the liberals and conservatives are trying to rewrite history from their own angles, and the Pentecostals and charismatics are trying to throw it away as meaningless. We need the lessons of the past. People become wise as they learn to reflect on their mistakes and successes. We Christians, if we are to be wise in our times, must learn from the pages of our past. We must study the anti-Semitism, the purges, the Inquisition and all of that, so we won't repeat those terrible mistakes; we also need to study our historical victories, so we can take courage from the examples left for us by the heroes of faith. If we ignore our history, we will have no foundation to engage the culture around us. We will be swallowed up.

To say that we believe in the New Testament church, but not in what the church became afterward, is to say that we like the roots of the tree and its leaves, but that we totally reject the trunk. Impossible! The roots produce the trunk, and the trunk upholds the branches and leaves. Another way of saying this is that the New Testament is the theory of faith, and the history of the church shows us how the theory has been fleshed out in real lives of individuals and nations, century after century.

> •••••••••••••••
> **[THE GOSPEL] TELLS US UP FRONT THAT THE KINGDOM WILL BE A MIXED BAG; TARES AS WELL AS WHEAT WILL GROW IN ITS FIELD . . . .**
> •••••••••••••••

If we say that the Inquisition was carried out by people who were not real Christians, we are fleeing to the same defense that the communists used to justify atrocities in Russia—"that wasn't real communism." They said it again about Cuba, China and Albania. Communists always asked us for just one more chance. Why? Because the communists were reading books about communist theory, and communist theory is wonderful. Its rottenness only becomes apparent when it is applied to real life.

The communist theory doesn't take into account fallen human nature, and that is its fatal flaw. The gospel does, which is one of its great strengths. It tells us up front that the kingdom will be a mixed bag—tares as well as wheat will grow in its field; good as well as bad fish will be caught in its net; and that all manner of fowl will lodge in its branches.

That is the history of our faith. The Inquisition happened because some good men believed bad doctrine and because some bad men pretended to be good Christians. Albert

Camus claims, "When they were burning John Huss, a gentle little lady came carrying her fagot to add to the pile." Good people, particularly when ignorant of the real issues, sometimes do bad things, and bad people sometimes do good things, particularly if it seems advantageous to them. We don't really know which is which, and we will not know until the end of the age when the Father himself reveals it.

Pope Alexander was a wicked and evil man, but St. Francis walked so much like his Lord that poor peasants thought he was Christ himself. Every manner of pervert has lived in the monasteries, but so have monks who spent their entire lives copying the words of life. Liars, cheats and thieves have occupied the seats of abbots, bishops and deacons, but these positions have also been occupied by those of whom the world was not worthy.

The light has been shining, even when the windows have been smudged, and, in fact, it has been that very light which revealed the smudges. I will not refuse the light because it is sometimes distorted by human flaws. I, too, am a man, and I am flawed. The church has never said we are otherwise. On the contrary, it exists in order to deal with that flaw.

We are justifiably proud to acknowledge Johann Sebastian Bach, John Milton and Mother Theresa. We must also acknowledge the crusades, the burning of Servetus, and the selling of indulgences, because those sorts of things exist in the American Church today, in every denomination. What are the "blessing packets" the tele-evangelists peddle, if not indulgences? What is the war in the Southern Baptist Convention, if not a crusade? Pretending that only Catholics or Methodists (or any group other than our own denomination) deals in evil is dishonest and is itself evil.

Roman Catholics have, as we say these days, a paper trail. They have kept records for a long time. How many little denominations exist in our country, out of the public eye, where every sort of authoritarian abuse, financial impropriety and promiscuous escapades are tolerated at high levels? In those very denominations, of course, walk naïve and incredulous men and women, woefully ignorant of the mess around them, gently going about doing the work of the kingdom, turning the other cheek, and doing good to those who despitefully use them. However noble, this naïvete is killing us. We must learn the landmarks if we ever hope to find our way.

A loss of history is a loss of identity. The nation is forgetting who it is. The American church must not do the same. We will forget who we are, however, if we accept the doctrine of the autonomous self, because embracing that doctrine involves focusing on trends, trying to accommodate every shift and hue of the constantly frothing sea of autonomous selves we are trying to direct toward the door of the Church. If we are not careful, we will finally forget why we wanted them there in the first place. If we insist on maintaining our modern doctrine of autonomy, we might as well realize this up front: forgetting comes with the territory.

THE NEED FOR COMMUNITY

Perhaps no title given to Jesus is more meaningful to us than *Savior*. Our most cherished hymns, our greatest sermons and our most meaningful religious holidays all revolve around Jesus as Savior. Evangelicals often ask believers from other traditions of the church, "Do you know Christ as personal Savior?" But what did that word mean to the early believers? What does it mean to us today?

The idea of salvation is hardly new. Even in first-century Judaism it was a familiar term. The entire Old Testament revolves around the Exodus, Israel's national salvation from Egypt.

For the Israelites, the Exodus colored everything. It provided a model for every oppressive situation. The God of Israel was a God of deliverance, a God who saves. The Israelites remembered it in annual feasts. They sang about it. They retold the story again and again. It became the center of national life.

The Exodus is the most prominent story of salvation in the Scriptures, but there are many other salvation stories: Abraham from Ur; Lot from Sodom; David from Saul, Goliath,

66666

108 — THE EMERGING AMERICAN CHURCH

and Absalom; Elijah from the prophets of Baal and Jezebel; Jehoshaphat from the Midianites; Esther from Haman; Daniel from the lions; Nehemiah and Ezra from Persia; and the incredible Maccabees from the Greeks. All of these reinforced the same story, of how the "God who saves" steps into history on behalf of his covenant people. These salvation stories were often strung together as a sort of "national litany."[18] When the Israelite farmer, in thanksgiving for the first fruits of the harvest, came to the temple with his offering, he first rehearsed the ritual litany of his people:

> "My father was a wandering Aramean, and he went down into Egypt with a few people and lived there and became a great nation, powerful and numerous. But the Egyptians mistreated us and made us suffer, putting us to hard labor. Then we cried out to the Lord, the God of our fathers, and the Lord heard our voice and saw our misery, toil and oppression. So the Lord brought us out of Egypt with a mighty hand and an outstretched arm, with great terror and with miraculous signs and wonders. He brought us to this place with milk and honey; and now I bring the firstfruits of the soil that you, O Lord, have given me" (Deuteronomy 26:5-10).

This was the Israelite creed. Notice how the theme of salvation focused on the nation, followed only then by the individual act of worship. This creed can be found throughout Scripture, updated each time to include the more recent acts of the Savior of Israel. We find it in Psalms 78, 105 and 106. Stephen uses it before the high court of Israel (see Acts 7). Paul uses it in the synagogue at Pisidia before his Jewish audience (see Acts 13:14-42).

IN OLD AND NEW TESTAMENTS ALIKE, SALVATION IS A COMMUNITY AFFAIR.

The God of Israel was "one who saves," and his message was enshrined in the history of his people. If a pagan asked his Jewish neighbor about the nature of his faith, he would hear, "Our father, Abraham, went out by faith from Ur of the Chaldees. He wandered, following the promises of God. Isaac, his son, was after him, also in covenant with the Lord of the earth. Jacob also, who had twelve sons," and so forth. A Jewish theologian was essentially a historian, making sense of the acts of God through his people. To "witness," for ancient Jews, was to tell what God had done among his people.

In the New Testament the theme of salvation within a community continues. St. Paul writes to the Corinthians:

> For I do not want you to be ignorant of the fact, broth-
> ers, that our forefathers were all under the cloud and
> that they all passed through the sea. They were all bap-
> tized into Moses in the cloud and in the sea. They all
> ate the same spiritual food and drank the same spiritual
> drink; for they drank from the spiritual rock that ac-
> companied them, and that rock was Christ (1
> Corinthians 10:1-4).

His point is obvious: Jesus had led his people out of the kingdom of darkness. He had led them through the baptism of water and baptized them in the "cloud of glory," that is to say, the Holy Spirit. He, like Moses, had given them a new food and drink. In Old and New Testaments alike, salvation is a community affair. Moses lead the Israelites out as a people, not one by one.

This is what Tertullian meant when he stated, "Outside the church there is no salvation." The church can save no one, nor keep anyone from salvation except to the extent that it refuses to proclaim the gospel Jesus saves. But we must be reminded that Jesus is a king. He has a kingdom. He invites all those who are lost into his kingdom. He wants them to be fellow citizens with the saints. Salvation is primarily a corporate affair; if we want to be redeemed, we must become a part of that community that is being redeemed. The doctrine of the autonomous self leads to eternal autonomy from God.

CHAPTER 6
....

WHO OWNS THE FOUNDATIONS?

As I was going up the stair
I met a man who wasn't there.
He wasn't there again today.
I wish, I wish, he'd stay away.
—*Hughes Mearns,* The Psychoed

Sam was out for a Sunday drive, moving at a leisurely speed on an old country road. He was just about to follow a sharp curve around the hill when a car, weaving almost out of control, came cruising toward him. It barely missed him. Sam was upset enough about the possibility of wrecking his car, but what really ticked him off was what the woman yelled at him as she sped past: "Big pig! Big pig!"

He could hardly contain himself. He shook his fist and yelled back, "Fat Cow!" He was so upset that when he turned the curve, he almost ran into the big pig.

What we hear and understand, what we see and inter-pret, and what we think and believe, is always based on something. That something is called a presupposition. The lady was trying to warn Sam about a real pig in the road. The man presupposed that she was trying to insult him. His presupposition did not allow him to hear and interpret what was really being said.

Thought has a foundation. Everything we believe is an interpretation of data or sentiment, based on a prior understanding of how the world works. If Sam believes in God, and believes that God speaks to human beings, and hears that God has spoken to his uncle Charley, he will go ask uncle Charley what God said and evaluate if, in fact, God has spoken to uncle Charley. If Sam does not believe in God, or does not believe that God speaks to human beings, then he will want uncle Charley to get psychiatric help.

The doctors in the Soviet Union sent believers in God to asylums, where they were given shock treatment and drugs. What else could they do? When a society that believes only in the material world confronts believers who talk of heaven, miracles and conversations with the Almighty, therapy is the only humane thing it can offer. Such a society doesn't consider this persecution. It thinks of it as mental health treatment.

THE NEW COMMON SENSE

All the members of a society will tend to share certain accepted presuppositions. Individuals born into that society absorb these ideas and build their mental lives upon them. Our country has believed certain presuppositions since its birth. Now we are in the middle of reassessing them. We are struggling over who or what will guide our national soul. The struggle involves how we define reality, how we answer the all-important question: *"What is real?"* Our answer is crucial because this question and the answer we propose forms the fundamental core of our culture's values and beliefs. Everything else depends on it.

Although every human being thinks about the nature of reality at some level, the study of the issue in a formal sense is called philosophy. All hocus-pocus aside, philosophy is nothing more than the formal study of thought. When we adopt a certain philosophy, we are choosing a collection of interlocking ideas upon which we will base our lives, ideas we believe best describe the way things actually are.

Most people never critically examine their philosophy of life. They receive it from their parents and the rest of their environment, making whatever minor adjustments they feel necessary to meet the changing conditions of life. It's sort of like inheriting a grandparent's house. As a family grows, or as modern appliances and building materials become available, the house is adapted to meet the new conditions.

PARADOXICALLY, MOST ARGUMENTS ARE BETWEEN PEOPLE WHO HOLD SIMILAR PHILOSOPHIES.

Just as our house determines how we organize space for ourselves and our family, our philosophy determines to a great extent what we hear, what we are willing to examine and how we react to new information. Very few people tear down their house in order to build a new one, just as few people ever really change the philosophy central to their lives. When that does happen, we call it conversion. Much of American society has been converted; that is why we can speak of a "new America." Americans have built a new house, or perhaps it would be better stated in the plural: Americans have built new houses.

Another way of saying this is that Americans no longer share the same common sense. *Common sense* means, after all, the shared, or common, ideas that people agree to live by. Common sense is the social cement which holds a people together. The greater the difference between their philosophies, the more difficult it is for people to carry on meaningful community. Paradoxically, most arguments are between people who hold similar philosophies, just as most arguments take place between people who live in the same house.

Maybe your mother said something like, "No house is big enough for two families." Like all mommyisms, this one is almost always true. People trying to live in the same house argue about how to use the space. Likewise, those who hold a common philosophy argue about how to apply it to daily life. If your philosophy of life differs too much from your neighbor's, you probably won't argue; you likely will not communicate at all. When you do disagree, however, the disagreement is more likely to turn violent.

> ● ● ● ● ● ● ● ● ● ● ● ● ● ● ● ● ● ●
> # IF THE BUDDHIST SAYS, "THE JEWEL IS IN THE LOTUS!" I ALWAYS AGREE WITH HIM.
> ● ● ● ● ● ● ● ● ● ● ● ● ● ● ● ● ●

I have argued with Baptists, charismatics, and Campbellites. I fuss with Baptists about baptism, with charismatics about charismatic gifts and with Campbellites about nearly everything. I have never had an argument with a Buddhist. There is not enough common ground between me and a Buddhist to argue.

If the Buddhist says, "The jewel is in the lotus!" I always agree with him. It's not that I'm so easy to get along with. I agree with him because I don't care. If he finds a fellow Buddhist to argue with him, they can have a real discussion. They can decide between them whether or not the jewel is in the lotus, how to get it there, or whether it belongs somewhere else. The Baptist, the Campbellite, the charismatic and I have no idea what the jewel, or the lotus, is all about.

An argument, like any kind of battle, demands common ground. Both argument and agreement presuppose common interests. The more different our philosophies, the less we can interact in any fashion, friendly or otherwise. If my mother-in-law moves from my house to one across town, we will not have as much to argue about. On the other hand, we may cease to communicate at all! That is what is currently happening in American society. We are losing common ground. We do not all live in the same house anymore.

This is why many of us are noticing that when believers disagree with unbelievers these days, both sides seem to be more frustrated with the other than in times past. When we and unbelievers debate abortion, adultery and homosexuality, we speak two different languages. They see these as issues of individual freedoms; we see them in terms of corporate responsibilities and the law of God.

Secular Americans, including many church-goers, are genuinely bewildered by those who take seriously the Holy Scripture and the traditions of Christian faith. We both may agree that "religion is a good thing," but they mean that religious sentiment is soothing, and we mean that religious teaching is truth. They are horrified that one would order one's everyday life by such ancient, and obviously archaic, principles.

So while I may enter a spirited argument with a believing Baptist or an orthodox Roman Catholic, ours is a family feud. Loyalty to common history and Scripture will give our arguments certain boundaries. We know what we are arguing about and realize that the stakes are high. The increasingly frustrating struggle with the unbelievers is due to the fact that we don't even agree about what is at stake. We doubt one another's sanity.

WORLD VIEW

Every house has to be built on something—it must have a foundation. Philosophies, too, are built on something. A philosophy's foundation is called a cosmology, or, to use a more popular term, a *world view.* As the term implies, a world view means "how one views the world." We get our world view from our answer to one central question: "What is the nature of reality?"

Some people are shocked that there are different ways of seeing reality. As my Uncle Harry used to say, "Simple. What is real is real, what is not is not." It doesn't seem very complicated to most people. But a study of different world views, such as those held by Hopi Indians or Zen Buddhists, shows how differently human beings define reality.

Consider, for example, the color spectrum, a graduated band of hues rather arbitrarily divided by human beings. At what time does blue become green? Cultures define that separation differently. Some cultures make no distinction at all between blue and green. They have one word for what we see as two colors. In the same way, some cultures do not separate time and movement as we do. Rather than past, present and future, they deal with "potential being" and "actualized being." That means a dead person will be spoken of in the same way as someone who has moved to another continent!

We are learning that what human beings see, and what they do not see, depends to a great extent on their world view, just as what one can see from a house depends on whether the house is built high on a hill or low in a valley.

THREE AMERICAN WORLD VIEWS

Forty years ago, C. S. Lewis said that the gulf between Christians and non-Christians was increasing. He did not attribute this to their differences in relatively superficial values and behavior, but to the fact that their respective world views were becoming so widely separated.

In his day, Western culture offered two major world views: materialism (or, to use his term, naturalism) and Judeo-Christian religion. He understood even then that our Western culture would soon be debating the merits of *three* major world views. He was right. Today American Christians face not one, but *two* major rivals. We are having to understand what our faith has in common with, and what separates it from, two opposing world views— materialism and pantheism.

Perhaps it would not be an oversimplification to say that these three world views can be ultimately traced to three ancient civilizations: Israel, Greece and India. These cultures first constructed formal answers to the question: "What is the nature of reality?"

Over centuries, the issues were debated within those cultures in a written form, so that they were absorbed by younger civilizations. In this way, the ancient arguments and ideas gave birth to the great world philosophies including, of course, the ones under consideration in modern America.

Israel defined reality theologically: "In the beginning God created the heavens and the earth." The Jewish scripture does not tell us *why*, or *in what manner*, or *when* God created, but just informs us that everything began at a point called simply "the beginning." In philosophy, a beginning point like that is called a *given*; it is the hook upon which all other thought hangs. Genesis 1:1 is the given of the Judeo-Christian-Islamic family of religions and philosophy. Those who accept that given will develop from it their scripture, law, worship, literature and moral code.

HUMANISM

Aristotle, the Greek philosopher, became extremely influential in the development of the modern Western mind. He answered the question of reality in a naturalistic, nontheological way. His influence in Europe finally resulted in the popular belief that all reality can be apprehended by the five senses. In other words, if something exists, you can hear it, see it, taste it, feel it or smell it, perhaps with the aid of instruments.

We call this world view many names, depending on the context. Writers often call it naturalism, or materialism. American evangelicals call it secular humanism. Its followers call it common sense! I'll call it humanism, because it is materialism that has been influenced by Christian concerns such as care for the poor, the brotherhood of man and the dignity of the individual. These have been the centerpiece of secular Western thought for several centuries.

But however influenced by Christian values, the core value of humanism is materialistic, which means simply that the *material* world is all there is. In humanism, the hook upon which all other thoughts hang is this: The universe either gave birth to itself, or else the creator (whoever he/she/it may be) is for all intents and purposes absent.

Western culture was formed by the interaction and tension that exists between Judeo/Christian theism and this materialism with a human face. Our academic communities have represented the humanistic side of the balance. The churches have represented the theistic side.

PANTHEISM

This old paradigm of American culture is now rapidly changing. The modern mind has become a post-modern mind. Materialism is now in decline. Humanism is regarded by the emerging culture as spiritually sterile. Post-modern men and women cannot live with its denial of human spirituality.

As a consequence, the Western world has been shocked by the growing influence of a third family of philosophies, called by many names, and ranging from the very silly to the very sophisticated. Its popular name in America is the New Age movement—a hodgepodge of Druidism, Native American folk medicine, free enterprise and Eastern Religions. Its proper name is pantheism, and its most thought-out form is Hinduism, the ancient philosophy and religion of India.

Ancient India also answered the question of reality in a theological way. But Hindu theology differs from Hebrew theology from the very first presupposition. The Hindu world view may be stated something like this: "All things, seen and unseen, are parts of One Entity. That One Entity probably has a collective consciousness. We may call this intelligence God, if we wish."

In Hinduism, conscious things are thought to be more in tune with that divine connection than nonconscious things. A chicken is more aware of its divinity than a rock, but less aware than a man. We are all a part of a great chain of being, linked to all other things. The separateness we feel from nature and from others is an illusion. The hook upon which all other thoughts hang in this world view is this: All things that exist are parts of God, as human cells are a part of a larger organism called the body.

Hinduism can accommodate any form of spirituality that accepts this basic world view. In India, Hindus worship different gods from village to village. It makes sense. If all things are parts of God, then one may worship anything. The issue

CHAPTER 6: WHO OWNS THE FOUNDATIONS?

CHAPTER 6: WHO OWNS THE FOUNDATIONS?   **119**

becomes not *what* you worship, but only *that* you worship. It is a most open and tolerant way to look at religion. The New America loves it, since it prizes tolerance and openness above all things.

Hinduism, in the formal sense anyway, is not all that widespread in the United States. However, numerous ideologies are here that share its underlying world view. The proper name of that world view is *pantheism*. C. S. Lewis believed pantheism to be the natural religion of human beings, the one into which we are most likely to drift. Most religion is some sort of pantheism.

Jews, Christians and Moslems are exceptions because they believe in *revealed* religion. A revealed religion does not believe God is a composite of all things. It believes God *made* all things, *rules* all things and reveals himself in his own terms. There is an enormous difference between the two world views, just as there is a difference between whether my Uncle Harry *made* the living room chair or whether "Uncle Harry" is just my pet name for the living room chair. It makes a difference in how I treat Uncle Harry, how I define Uncle Harry and how I address Uncle Harry.

No wonder, then, that worship of nature is a constant earmark of pantheism. Pantheists do not respect nature as God's creation. They revere it as God's body. The pantheistic revival is the force which energizes modern environmentalism. Christians, too, should be ecologically minded. We have a mandate from God to dress, till, cultivate and subdue the earth. We are the stewards of creation, and someday the Lord will require an account of how we have treated his earth. So we share many of the goals of the ecology movement. We are far removed from Pantheists, however, on the *reasons* for our ecological concern.

I once had a cup of tea with a favorite author, Thomas Howard, when we were both attending a literature symposium at Oxford. He told me that one of the things which had bothered him as an Episcopalian, in the days before he converted to Roman Catholicism, was a prayer in the new prayer book asking God to help us to reverence creation. I thought he was quibbling over a trifle. As I thought about it, however, I saw what he meant. G. K. Chesterton says that to the Christian, Nature is never *Mother* Nature. She is *Sister* Nature. We share the same Father, but she is not our goddess. We should respect her, not venerate her.

Another feature of pantheistic thought throughout history, and a major component in the current revival of pantheism, is the worship of the life force. Sex. Ancient pantheists worshiped sex, and modern pantheists do, too. That is why temple prostitution was so common in ancient times. Sexual acts were part of pantheistic worship, because sex was the very thing being worshiped. The temples of ancient India, as well as the Inca ruins in South America, are full of statues of gods, men and animals in all sorts of sexual configurations. Modern American pantheism, even the Christianized version, is no different.

Not long ago I saw a picture of an altar which "Christian" feminists had built in a meditation chapel. On the altar was a sculpture of the human vagina. This artwork was supposed to remind us that we have come from the womb of God. I laughed out loud! My thoughts were not turned toward heaven, but rather decidedly earthward.

I wondered if these feminists were aware that millions of Americans already worship at this altar, even though Christian faith has for centuries insisted that one must learn to turn from the worship of sensuality to the living God. We humans don't need help focusing on our reproductive organs. We need help learning how to get our minds off of them long enough to face eternity and the law of the Lord. Excuse my lack of sophistication, but some of this is just plain stupid. It poses a real danger to Christian faith, though, because the people who propagate such foolishness are not honest enough to tell us they are leading us back to Baal and Aphrodite. Christians they are not.

Our churches are reeling from the effects of the spreading revival of pantheism. The so-called mainline American denominations are wrestling with these sexual notions which have deep roots in the world view that sustains them. It doesn't seem to bother us too much. Maybe the ground was prepared by the popular belief in the sexual self as the fundamental core of the human being and the deeply held American truism that sexual fulfillment is an essential component of mental health. The new America is soaked through with these influences. As baby boomers become our spiritual leaders, we are likely to see increased pantheistic influence.

HOW WORLD VIEW AFFECTS ART

One's world view colors not only everything one perceives, but also everything one propagates. This is especially true of artists, who reveal their soul through their art. This is very obvious in art such as painting and sculpture and also, in a less obvious way, in other types of art, such as architecture.

FRANK LLOYD WRIGHT

For example, pantheism clearly influenced the work of America's greatest architect, Frank Lloyd Wright. What he believed produced a very different sort of architecture, and that architecture deeply affected the way modern Americans build the places in which they sleep, work and worship. The buildings, in turn, have molded the way we interact with our environment. The pragmatic person tends to think that ideology has rather limited application, and is an intellectual plaything for bored academic types. Such a view could not be more wrong, as we see in Wright's life and career.

Consider his famous *Unity Temple and Parish House* in Oak Park, Illinois. It is a wonderful display of his talent and an unveiling of his ideology. As he was creating Unity Temple, he asked himself and the congregation which employed him some very important questions. He started by telling them a story.

> There is a tale of the holy man who, yearning to see God, climbed up and up . . . to the highest relic of a tree upon the mountain. Rugged and worn, there he lifted up his eager, perspiring face to heaven and called to "God." [Wright's quotation marks.] A voice bade him get down . . . go back!

Is not that "finger" the church steeple, pointing on high, like the man on high to see him? Perhaps it is a misleading symbol.

Is it not time now to be more simple, to have more faith in earth and less anxiety concerning heaven about which one can know nothing? Concerning this heaven we have never received any testimony from our own senses.

So, "Why the steeple in the little white church"?

Why point to Heaven?[19]

Wright answered his own questions. He would build a temple, "not to God in that way—more sentimental than sense—but a temple to man." He set out to build a "natural building for a natural man." Even Voltaire had dedicated his chapel to God. Wright was proposing to dedicate the temple to man. It was startling that the architect should decide to whom the church should be dedicated, but this is a democracy, and in the radical democracy of secular America the architect has as much to say about it as the priest.

> • • • • • • • • • • • • • • • • •
> ## IT IS A TEMPLE, BUT IT IS NOT A HOUSE OF GOD.
> • • • • • • • • • • • • • • • • •

Wright succeeded in his plan. Unity Temple is wonderful. The church keeps one focused downward, toward other men and women. Nothing causes the eyes to wander upward. It is a temple, but it is not a house of God. It is, rather, a house of Man, dedicated to the mythical "everyman" so beloved by modern thinkers. This so-called "everyman" could not have created it. Only a Frank Lloyd Wright could have created it, and he was far from being an "everyman," but who demands that modern ideas be consistent?

So the question is: Where did Wright get his ideas?

It is puzzling to students of Wright how often he denied the oriental influences upon his work. He denied them even in the face of his own admission to kinship with the East:

". . . it is true that when we speak of organic architecture, we are speaking of something that is more Oriental than Western. The answer is, my work is, *in the deeper philosophical sense*, Oriental."[20] [Emphasis added.]

How could Wright both admit and deny this influence? Well, there was his famous ego. He didn't like to acknowledge any influence on his work. He wanted to be thought of as creating something brand new. He was not entirely dishonest about his sources, however. His oriental influences were indirect, for the most part. (Even though he was deeply influenced directly by the Japanese pavilion at the 1893 Colombian Exposition in Chicago and thought then that ancient Eastern structures could provide a model for his famous Prairie House.)

Wright's father was a Unitarian minister. So Unitarianism provided the ideological soil in which his early life took root. Unitarianism, though it springs from heretical Christian roots, is an eclectic faith which seeks to find universals in world religions and to synthesize them into a pragmatic framework. It is American heresy at its best.

From the mid-nineteenth to the early twentieth centuries, American Unitarianism was deeply influenced by Ramnohun Roy's Indian reformist movement, the Brahmo Samaj. Roy's successors, in fact, traveled widely through the Unitarian congregations in this country in the 1880s and the 1890s.

During this time Wright was internalizing his values, when the air was filled with the scents of the East. His parents were Transcendentalists, who early in life introduced their son to Emerson and Thoreau, writers also heavily influenced by Eastern thought.

Wright's architecture is a window into his soul. Notions about the "TAO," or finding the grain of things (going with the flow, as we said in the 1960s), Hinduism, Buddhism, democracy and plain old American pragmatism all came together in the flash of genius that was Frank Lloyd Wright. Later in life, through his last wife, he became involved with theosophy (Krishnamurti). It was, in many ways, a homecoming.

In Wright's work there is an obvious spiritual connection between himself, his materials, the site and his ideological influences. He wanted to pass this on to the American culture. He used popular magazines, such as the *Ladies Home Journal* and *Life Magazine*, as well as the professional journals. He was a communicator, and he wanted to spread his architectural philosophy. He believed that the common American man and woman would fall in love with his art. They did. He wanted to free American architecture from the "tyranny of the past." He did that too. He helped the nation's culture drift away from Europe, by drawing on models from the Orient, from the Aztec and Mayan civilizations, and from native American designs.

It must be obvious that I admire Wright's work. I regard him as a national treasure. One does not have to agree with an artist to recognize that he or she is gifted. Yet, it bothers me to realize that America's homes, offices and houses of worship have been so influenced by ideas like those that motivated Wright. Not that all of these influences on American architecture were bad. I am moved by his work with cinder block, for example. Yet the influences that are particularly pregnant in a work like Unity Temple draw us earthward, toward nature, inward, toward ourselves—toward utility and function rather than grandeur and glory. It encourages us to make peace with the earth as it is. Such architecture rejects the notion that nature has fallen, and it blocks the way to heaven.

I contrast this with my visit to Notre Dame in Montreal. My wife and I went there to hear Handel's Messiah, just a few days before Christmas. The inside of the building declares the glory of God. One can't help but look up at the wonderful ceiling. But you see, looking up is the *right* thing to do. Didn't king David say, "I lift up my eyes to the hills—where does my help come from? My help comes from the Lord . . ." (Psalm 121:1). So as the orchestra played and the tenor sang "comfort ye, comfort ye my people, saith your God," I looked up, first to the beautiful ceiling, and then through it to see the face of the Father, and I was comforted.

Wright was wrong about this matter of looking up. As a Christian, I cannot truly see the face of man until I have seen the face of God. I have nothing to give my neighbor until I receive it from the Almighty. So the architect of Notre Dame and Handel, together with all the workers who constructed the church and all the musicians who gave their years and talent to that wonderful night, came together to lift my heart to God. Perhaps that could happen in Unity Temple, but it wouldn't be as easy. Art should help us get to God, not put a roadblock in our path.

HAGIA SOPHIA

I wrote a paper in college comparing Unity Temple to the great Hagia Sophia (Holy Wisdom), the seat of the Patriarch of Constantinople. In 532 A.D., emperor Justinian chose two architects, Anthemius of Tralles and Isodrus of Miletos, to design the world's greatest church. Together they conceived of one of the grandest structures of all time. The many domes of the church look like a sea of heads bowing in the presence of a great king. One's eyes move from the lesser domes, up, following the contours of the roof line, until one is staring at the central dome, 184 feet high. The lesser domes serve the greater and distribute its enormous weight on their shoulders. One can't help looking up; the smaller domes themselves call us to look toward the reason for their existence. Hagia Sophia was built to evoke feelings of grandeur, elegance and reverence.

Inside the great church, the eyes again are pulled upward. The space above one's head dwarfs the awed worshipper below. The windows at the base of the dome, still far above one's head, allow the sun to shine through the clouds of incense.

What a fascinating place it must have been in the days before the Muslim invasion. The priests would enter, wearing their beautiful robes, chanting psalms and singing the rich musical heritage of the Eastern Church. The incense floated upward, carrying the believers' prayers to the Almighty. As the worshippers looked up, they would see a haze of smoke and light floating over them like the cloud of God. Kneeling and rising, singing and praying, eyes opening, then closing, the pious could enter a world different from everyday life. Every human sense participated in the drama of glory enacted in that house of God.

It was a fitting place for the ancient manuscripts of Holy Scripture, letters of saints and apostles, and the burial place for servants of God. We who speak English got our King James Version of the Bible indirectly from there; as the invading Muslims conquered the city, nameless monks fled with precious portions of the Scripture and took them West, just in time for the awakening of European Christian scholarship.

In the days of the building's glory, the Slavs from the north arrived there, looking for God. They returned from Constantinople to tell their prince that they had seen a place that was more like heaven than earth. They had visited the Hagia Sophia, watched the drama of worship, and sensed the invisible participant for whom the building had been built. Ancient Christians constructed buildings with God in mind; we build them for men. One can tell the difference.

Thousands travel every year to see both the Hagia Sophia and Unity Temple. They are each magnificent buildings in their own way. Each represents breakthroughs in architecture. Both are invaluable treasures of art. The difference between them is nothing less than how one views God and his world. Worshippers inside them learn very different things.

Why devote this much space to a consideration of art? Am I getting away from the theme of this book? Not at all. I chose my illustration from architecture *because* it seems so far from the subject. If we can see how a person's world view influences the way they construct buildings, then surely world views must mold other disciplines. "For as he thinketh in his heart, so is he . . ." (Proverbs 23:7, KJV). The foundation one builds upon always imposes its form upon the building which rises from it.

CHAPTER 7
·····················

TIME FOR
SESAME STREET

It was the Sunday before Christmas in Montreal, Quebec, where I pastored a little French-speaking assembly on the south side of the St. Lawrence. Right before I brought the message, the members of my church presented me with a black and white television set.

I was flabbergasted. I had no idea what to do. I was a member of a religious group which forbids its ministers to own a television.

Living without a TV wasn't a great impoverishment, but my parishioners felt sorry for me. They thought that I was too poor to buy a TV, which was also true. Besides, I never told them about the television rule, because they were both new converts and French, and had the annoying habit of not swallowing the preacher's every idea as though it just fell from heaven. To make a long story short, they bought us a television, and I graciously accepted it.

We watched our little black and white television for several weeks. All went well until we had a visitor from our denomination's headquarters, a nice Christian man who happened to be responsible for payroll. He was in Montreal to assess our work.

On the third day of his visit, while we were eating break-fast, my three-year-old daughter ran frantically into the kitchen.

"Mama, Mama, it's time for Sesame Street, and I can't find the TV! Where is that television?"

My wife, whose emotional level doesn't move up or down a degree a year, calmly replied, "It's on the porch."

"The porch? The porch? The television is on the porch?" my daughter asked incredulously.

Our visitor was a real gentleman. He sipped his coffee without saying a word. That was amazing, because that group considered television ownership only two-and-a-half pegs down from adultery and bank embezzlement. I wanted to die and get it over with, but my visitor gently went on to other matters. I have always been grateful to him for that, but I kept my television all the same.

> • • • • • • • • • • • • • • • •
>
> ## WE ARE THE FIRST GENERATION IN ALL OF HISTORY THAT HAS BEEN SOCIALIZED BY A MACHINE.
>
> • • • • • • • • • • • • • • • •

"It's time for Sesame Street." If you are a baby boomer parent, you've heard that before. In another chapter I'll talk about a song we used to sing in West Virginia about the "all-seeing eye." For American baby boomers, the all-seeing eye is the great electronic eye in the living room. We are the first generation in all of history that has been socialized by a machine. We have watched wars on television. We saw two presidents shot on television. We saw China before we were allowed to cross the street. If we are not careful, our children see actors pretending to have sex before they reach puberty. Jock itch, hemorrhoids, tooth decay, therapy, rape and pimples—we talk about it all on TV.

From the standpoint of cultural change, however, the content of television is not such a drastic shift. The sheer act of watching television is the real social change. We Americans have changed the way we process information. We have moved from being a society that processes information primarily through the written word—books, magazines, newspapers, etc.—to become one which uses nonliterary symbolism as its primary means of exchanging information. Half of all American college graduates do not buy one book a year. Of those who do buy a book, 60 percent purchase popular fiction. Serious literature, in all its forms, now reaches a very small percentage of Americans.

This change from a literary to a nonliterary culture challenges American Christianity to its core. Evangelical Christianity especially demands reading skills, because its entire religious focus is on a book and books about that book! The highlight of an evangelical service is the sermon, which almost always assumes a literary audience. Television preachers, primarily Pentecostals and charismatics, discovered years ago that the medium for conveying information in our society has changed. Evangelical churches still haven't got the message. The fact is, the literary culture upon which evangelicalism draws its membership is disappearing.

The role of electronic information media on the American culture and church, and increasingly on the cultures and churches of the world, has become pivotal. Sometimes it works to our advantage. One day, in our local church in Nashville, we received a fax message that a Filipino pastor stationed in Saudi Arabia was to be executed in 48 hours for possessing anti-Islamic literature. We began to push all the political and ecclesiastical buttons we could. In a few hours we had contacted several major religious and political leaders. We were not the only ones doing this, of course. So in a half a day a ground swell of concern mounted across the nation. Congressmen began calling the Saudi embassy and sending telegrams to Ryaad. The execution was changed to deportation.

Sometimes the media works to our disadvantage. The innumerable shows where the pastor, priest or evangelist is a buffoon, womanizer or drunkard creates a constantly reinforced impression on the minds of the public. This impression is difficult to overcome, despite the millions of honest, hard-working, dedicated men and women of God around the world. THE SOURCE has spoken, and its verdicts cannot be easily overturned. It is not the information on TV, per se, which really affects us. The real issue is the social and psychological change which electronic media has effected on our process of perception.

HOW THE CHANGE IN INFORMATION MEDIUM AFFECTS US

I pastor several people who are much better known than myself. Sometimes that is a blessing, sometimes not. A while back, one of the tabloids, the kind in which green spacemen inhabit the basement of the Smithsonian, did a feature story on the Judds, the mother-daughter country singing performers. In the article, the paper mentioned my name as their pastor. I received a number of fascinating calls because of that article. One was from a lady in Pennsylvania who wanted to inform "a man of God" what was happening up there.

"The communists are buying up everything," she said.

"Really?"

"Yes, and tomorrow they are going to buy Independence Hall, and nobody cares! Do you care?"

I had to think fast.

"Well, yes, if this is actually happening, I would care very much."

"You don't believe it is happening, do you?" she demanded.

"Well, ma'am, I guess I don't," I replied.

Furiously she shouted, "My God, you're one of them!"

She hung up the phone, and I didn't hear from her again.

During the next few days, I heard from several other colorful folk from around the country. Naomi and Wynnona had a lot of fun watching me deal with something they wrestle with constantly. These papers, and the people who read them, are a world to themselves. The best-known tabloid is the best-selling newspaper in the country! Why? Sensationalism. What

respectable newspaper could hope to compete with CALI-
FORNIA HERMAPHRODITE IMPREGNATES HIMSELF!
I saw that one in a little corner grocery in northern Maine. I
laughed so hard the shopkeeper came around to see it for
himself, and we both had our laugh of the day. Unbelievable!

Why do you think I put that story in this chapter? I did
it because I thought it would get your attention. My publisher tells me I should find "arresting illustrations" to prove
my points. I hope that is one of them!

Modern man lives from one high to the next. Regular
"news" just isn't exciting. What kind of regular news could
possibly excite us, anyway? We saw the Berlin wall come
down. We saw communism fall. We saw the bombing of
Baghdad. We saw Woody Allen accused of carrying on with
his lover's daughter. We saw the Duchess of York sunning
topless by a swimming pool. We saw the president puke. What's
next? The tabloids are getting further and further out because the
mainstream press has been cutting in on their territory.

The driving force behind this is money. The advertisers
push their products on television programs and magazines
that sell. The television programs and magazines that sell are
those that grab the public attention. The self-impregnating
HERMAPHRODITE gets attention. It got mine. I'm guess-
ing it got yours.

Can I tell you one more? This one happened many years
ago, when Tiffany, my youngest child, was about three years
old. She's very smart (I'm sure yours is too). She could read
already. We were standing in the check-out line of the super-
market, with our cart full of groceries. Tiffany was sitting in
the cart. Suddenly she shouted, loud enough for everyone to
hear, "Dad, Dad, look!"

I looked. She was pointing at the tabloid rack. "They've
caught the Devil!" she shouted.

Sure enough. A bold headline proclaimed: SATAN CAP-
TURED! Below the headline was a picture of a beastly, hairy
man behind thick bars. The world was safe for three-year-
olds. A small-town policeman in Apple Orchard, Alabama,
had captured Satan.

What happens to a generation constantly bombarded by "arresting illustrations," sensational news, hyped events and outright lies? Just like any other drug, the dosage must increase.

The man on the street works all day, watches lights flash, hears noise and battles tensions at work. He doesn't want to come home and read an editorial by William Buckley on "The subtle effects of Nietzsche on American Consumerism" or the Book of Romans, for that matter. So he switches on the TV, finds the remote control, flops into the easy chair, and flips through all 46 cable channels, one after the other. Dan Rather (10 seconds is enough, click); animals of the Sahara (3 seconds, click); Opra talks to mothers against heterosexual cross dressers who love ducks (ahh, that's interesting, 6 minutes, click); starvation in Africa (too depressing, what can I do? 10 seconds, click); "Today in Brussels" (click); "A NEW CAR" (click, click); naked people dancing to a new Madonna hit ("Oh how disgusting! who watches this stuff?" 5 minutes, click). "Lord, there is just nothing on TV," he sighs.

In an age like ours, as attention spans get shorter and shorter, the need for sensation grows greater. Those are the people politicians must get through to, and it is also the audience we face on Sunday morning.

POLITICS AND THE GREAT EYE

Numerous books have been written about how electronic media have changed American politics. We see it in televised congressional hearings where actors who play the role of physicians in some soap opera are interviewed to get their informed opinion about drugs. We see it in presidential debates where the candidate feels free to ignore the question at hand in order to slip in a carefully rehearsed sound bite. Before the debate, Senator Devonshire will be groomed and dressed for his televised "debate" with Governor Hornplayer. The make-up people will put on the final touches. The handlers will also be at work.

"When he asks you about Russia, Senator, hold your head like so, lean into the camera, and say, 'Governor, I am concerned about St. Petersburg, Russia, but what really concerns me is the poor lady in St. Petersburg, Florida, who can't get a job. What are we going to do about that?'"

The handlers know that Johnny Six-Pack will be watching, sitting in his favorite chair, wearing his T-shirt, sipping his favorite beer. When he hears the remark about Florida, he'll holler to his wife in the kitchen, "Hell, yes! Ethel! Come 'ere! They better stop a-worryin' bout all them foreigners! I like that guy!"

That one sound bite, which will be repeated dozens of times on "news programs" and carried on the front of *USA Today*, may well capture the Bubba vote for the good senator. The governor, too, will try to insert his share of magic sound bites.

Both candidates know that without the approval of the electronic media, no one gets elected in America. I don't mean that no one can get elected without the approval of the media establishment. A really charismatic person can bypass their control. I mean rather that the election will go to the one who best understands theater in a media age. This person doesn't have to be handsome; he can be rich, like Perot, or outrageous, like Madonna and Rush Limbaugh. He can be cruel, stupid or intelligent, but whatever he is, he must be that in a superlative way. Moderation doesn't play on the Great Eye.

Joe McGinnis wrote years ago in *The Selling of the President*

> It's not the man we have to change, but rather the received impression. And this impression often depends more on the medium and its use than it does on the candidate himself.[21]

In a media age, style and perception are more important than substance and policy. The candidate has to be noticed, not necessarily respected. In fact, it is far better for a candidate to be attacked, even viciously, than ignored. If he is attacked too much, a swell of sympathy will roll across the fruited plain. He can look into the camera with eyes full of moist hurt, shrug his shoulders and say, "I just wanted to serve my country."

("That's great, Senator! We'll run that on a thirty-second piece, with Ray Charles singing 'America the Beautiful' in the background. We'll fade with the shot of the little boy in Kansas saluting the flag. They'll love it in the midwest, where we are trailing a bit in the polls.")

Does this sort of thing give us any more information to help us select our president? No, it doesn't, but the battle is no longer fought on that front anyway. Educated people can make it to the White House, but they have to be media smart also or listen very carefully to the handlers. Intelligence and leadership ability alone won't get you there.

A quote by a certain Karl Kraus in a 1909 book called *Aphorisms and More Aphorisms* says it well: "How is the world ruled and how do wars start? Diplomats tell lies to journalists and then believe what they read." For our age we might rephrase that to say, "Handlers tell lies and select video clips that make their lies seem reasonable, and then the politicians watch TV and believe what they watch." The name of the game is staging sensational news and views, and building on the resulting public opinion.

The first modern politician in this sense was Hitler, a media genius. Someone, I forget who, called the Nazi rallies "the first rock concerts." Everything was planed for visual and emotional effect. Colossal crowds, a monstrous flag, momentous music, lights, smoke and dramatic production all led to a sensational speech full of sound bites. Hitler had it right. It is the age of Wagner; the candidate who studies foreign policy and endless pages of facts is going to lose to the guy who masters the screen and the stage.

That is no less true for the pulpit than for the political podium. The masses will choose a preacher who understands theater and production over one who knows the Bible. We shouldn't be surprised. Scripture told us that a time would come when there would be ". . . a famine through the land—not a famine of food or a thirst for water, but a famine of hearing the words of the Lord" (Amos 8:11). It doesn't say

a famine of the "preaching" of the Word of God, but deliberately uses the word "hearing." People raised in a media age
have difficulty *hearing* the Word of God, particularly when
presented in the format we have been using to proclaim it.

THE CHURCH IN A MEDIA AGE

The people who go to church on Sunday morning are
not different from the people watching the screen. They are
religious, but they are still the children of a media age. The
younger they are, the more media-conscious they tend to be.

For the last few years, the church growth movement has
encouraged American churches to view themselves as competitors in the media marketplace. They tell us that while we
are reaching for the attention of the masses of American people,
AT&T, Taco Bell and the Democratic party are, too. Therefore, according to this philosophy of mission, we also must
think in terms of the product we offer and the market we
serve.

I have been sympathetic to this idea. The church tends
to live in a culture that is two or three generations behind the
contemporary society around it. This makes it difficult for
people raised in a non-Christian environment to even approach the gospel. They don't understand the language, music
or social structure of the people who preach it.

On the other hand, there have to be limits to this notion. When the rock concert comes to our town and puts on a
laser show, do we follow with one the following Sunday? To
do that do we cut out the public Bible reading? To pay for it
do we cut out benevolence or missionary support? Should we
try bungee jumping from the church roof? How about gour-
met bread and vintage wine for communion? How about
accepting Mastercard, Visa and American Express for tithing
and missionary offerings? Wouldn't that appeal to upwardly
mobile baby boomers? At what point do we miss the point?
At what point do we turn into an entertainment center pointing to nothing but entertainment? There is, after all, an offense to the gospel. Many forsook Jesus when he pressed
forward the demands of discipleship.

Today, of course, we should know that his decline in membership was plainly unnecessary. Any good consultant could have helped the Lord repackage his message or taught him to take a poll to find out whether the people preferred discipleship teaching or bread multiplication for Sunday morning worship. Perhaps we would suggest that Jesus should have held two services, one for those who wanted to hear about loving your neighbor as yourself, and the other for those who prefer miracles and signs.

I am not really cynical. I truly believe that God himself has raised up the American church growth movement. In my opinion, it is one of the movements being most used in our country to bring together the body of the Lord. Many of its leaders and thinkers are real men and women of God. Nonetheless, I believe there is a danger in grasping too tightly a philosophy of growth organized around giving the people what they want.

I'll come right out and say it: The Church of Jesus is not a democracy, and what the people say they want is not always what the Lord says they need. No one wants a cross, but the Lord says that if we are his followers, we must carry one. No one wants to die, but Jesus says that to find our lives, we'll have to lose them. No healthy person enjoys rebuke or correction, but St. Paul says that Scripture has been given to use ". . . for teaching, rebuking, correcting and training . . ." (2 Timothy 3:16). An escape from these very "media negative" doctrines is an escape from the real gospel. We must at least consider that if media hype is a drug habit we need to kick, will the use of that drug help deliver us from it?

Much of what we hear from God's Word is counter culture. It simply doesn't fit this age, no matter how we try to package it. "Turn the other cheek," is understood by all, and practiced by almost none. And what is so hard to understand about "Thou shall not commit adultery?" That, too, is understood by all. It is offensive, and we have no authority to make it any less so.

Yet coming to grips with a media-conscious society is unavoidable. It is a part of the language of the new culture.

An effective missionary simply can't ignore it. The biblical pattern seems to suggest a balance. The Jewish temple had a Court of the Gentiles, but it also had a Most Holy Place. A church that has no "Court of the Gentiles," no place where the heathen can come near to God's presence and God's people without partaking of the rites and ceremonies, will become insular, myopic and old. But a church that has no Holy Place has no center, no heart and no soul. Such a church has no purpose to exist. In the biblical sense, it is no church at all. A Court of the Gentiles has a purpose—directing the heathen toward the Holy Place at the center, toward holiness, where they can experience and submit to the God of Israel.

THE MEDIA AND LEARNING

Electronic media does not encourage sequential thinking. Sequential thinking is stating a premise, then the major points, illustrating those points with examples, then stating a conclusion. After all this, one can advance to the subject's next stage. If one is in a course of study, one will work from simple to complex ideas, along the way building one's vocabulary, grasp of abstract material and proficiency in the actual practice of the discipline. A is followed by B, and then C. One cannot make sense of X until one has understood A through W.

Most of our sermons demand sequential thinking. The minister lays the foundation, derives points A, B and C from the premise, tells stories to illustrate the points, and concludes. The sermon may even be continued next week, or three weeks from now.

But post-modern Americans are just not plugged into that sort of thinking. A is forgotten well before C is considered. Television sometimes has a mini-series, but it has to be powerful enough to bring viewers back night after night, and they can't last more than a week. In regular serial drama or comedy, episode 15 will rarely refer to past material. (Every episode in the life of the Bunker family was a slice of life unconnected with past or future, except for the continuity in the development of their characters.) New viewers watch every week, and we don't want them to be lost. Also, regular viewers can be absent from the program for three or four weeks, and they want to understand what is going on when they return to the show. Even the soap opera, which has some sense of continuity, must be constructed to pull in the one who is seeing it for the very first time. Television knows no history and no future.

We should accommodate the nonsequential learning style to the extent that it does not take away from the gospel. Jesus told parables because the people liked stories. He was a wonderful teacher, even though he never preached an expository message!

WHY JESUS DIDN'T PREACH

Now I love expository preaching, and I mean no disrespect, but Jesus didn't use that method. He told interesting stories. That is why we remember his teaching all our lives, because it is wrapped inside wonderful stories. I learned the parable of the shepherd looking for the one lost sheep before I knew the alphabet. I still remember it. But I have forgotten all three points of the message I heard three weeks ago.

We need to wise up! Object lessons, slides, banners and dance are all methods that we may use, and should. Many times we don't give people what would really help them simply because we are too lazy and sloppy to work at it, or too stubborn to learn new ways to communicate. We need to remember that teaching doesn't take place unless someone learns something. Lecturing may take place without anyone learning anything, but never teaching. Our Lord was a teacher, not just a lecturer. We need to learn how to teach, too.

Above all, the sacraments are God's show and tell and, when they are approached by faith, they communicate divine insight and grace. This generation *will* respond to living sacraments when they are carried out with dignity and are not allowed to become perfunctory. A new generation will have to be taught what the sacraments are all about. Sacraments and rites are letters of a language that has to be learned, but it can be easily learned by those who hunger and thirst.

The masses of pagans must be made welcome, but they must not direct the church's spirituality. While we must attempt to speak their language, know their taste in music and accommodate them in every way possible that does not compromise our faith, we must continually ask ourselves, "Where are we leading these people? Or are they leading us?" If they are leading us, it cannot be toward the Holy Place. They don't know where it is or even that it exists. In time, if we accommodate the culture but do not strengthen our understanding of what constitutes the Holy Place, even the leaders of the church will become secularized and will finally abandon the quest for holiness.

If a church is to successfully balance the Court of the Gentiles with the Holy Place, then it must teach its leaders the doctrine and mission of the church, and it must be sure that they personally experience God. If we produce a generation of leaders who are media-smart but do not know the history of our faith, the Scriptures and what the mission of the kingdom is all about, what will we gain? The Lord told us that a person can gain the whole world, but lose his soul (see Matthew 16:26). Can a church lose its soul? What is it after it has lost its soul, but saltless salt, good for nothing but to be trodden under foot (see Matthew 5:13)?

We need not be dismayed. This is not really a new situation. Preaching to a literary public has been the novel situation, a parenthetical time between nonliterary eras. The church survived hundreds of years in a nonliterary environment, where information was exchanged orally and by ritual. Christian history provides us with examples of what to do. The answers involve ritual, storytelling, an appeal to the senses and a demonstration of spiritual gifts.

We will need one another. We need to draw on the faith's liturgical roots. We also need to learn from the Black and Pentecostal churches how the people of God can truly celebrate faith in Christ. The fragmentation of the church has caused us to be suspicious of one another and the things each of us emphasize. We can't afford that anymore. If evangelicals are going to get an audience to listen to what they claim to be the Word of God, then they will have to be willing to share it in a place where a choir may do Black gospel, and where the message can be followed by taking the bread and the wine in holy celebration and enactment of what has been proclaimed by word and song. The days of dry lectures are over. No one is going to be there to hear it but three old deaf ladies and the kids you punish if they don't stay awake.

WHAT'S COMING?

I have been talking about media, but we only think that we live in a media age now. What is just around the corner will so transform human perception that it staggers the imagination. Three dimensional television is coming. Portable telephones are already here, but soon they will link up to satellites that will reach any other portable phone anywhere in the world. *Anywhere.* Arctic circle to Antarctica, Amazon to Africa, Mongolia to Manhattan. Long distance will be a thing of the past because it will cost the telephone company more to determine the difference between a long distance and a local call than to just eliminate the difference.

Three dimensional, computer-generated cyberspace is coming. You will put on a helmet and body suit and feel all the sensations of an artificial universe. This is not fantasy, it already exists. If you are in St. Louis you will be able to meet a friend from Hong Kong in cyberspace. Shake hands. Sit at a table that exists nowhere on earth, a table that only you and he see, made of bytes and bits. Interactive drama, where you join the show and help determine its outcome, is coming. Virtual Reality is its name.

How about the combination of robotics and telepresence? A woman will drive to work, walk into a nice office complex, go directly to the lab and don a body suit and helmet. The suit will be electronically linked to a huge robot at the bottom of the ocean hundreds of miles away. First, she will get the feel of things. Then she will raise her right arm. The robot will mimic her move. She will close her hand as though grasping an object. The robot will simultaneously grasp a large anchor on the ocean floor. She will feel the anchor in her hands, because pressure sensors in her glove allow her to feel exactly what the robot is handling. Her eyes will follow everything through her three-dimensional visor. It will be a real question whether she is at the bottom of the sea or in the office. She may not be sure. Can you imagine the difference in the way human beings will think of reality in such an age? Can you imagine how we will preach?

GOD'S "VIRTUAL" REALITY

I was pondering all of this awhile back, and our senior pastor asked me, "Is virtual reality really different from the idea behind the tabernacle of Moses?"

"What do you mean?" I asked

"Well," he said, "Moses built a place in the desert that would reproduce what he had seen in the heavens. When the Israelites went into the tabernacle to worship, they were no longer in the desert. They were in heaven. In the tabernacle, all the senses were challenged to move the worshippers from earth to heaven. Then they went back out into earthly life, having been exposed to a bit of heaven. That little bit of heaven challenged the people of God to colonize earth, to work toward bringing what they had experienced inside the tabernacle to the rest of life."

I began to look at the Scriptures. I found that one of the objects of worship is to move us into the presence of God—into heaven, if you will. The question seems to be, "Which realm is the 'virtual' reality, the desert or the tabernacle?" Once you have tasted heaven, you will know that what we experience here is at best only the simulated heaven. Worship simulates the other world.

So the aim of the church gathered for worship is not to reproduce secular culture within the church—though we may use it to communicate to unbelievers—but to take people to another reality altogether—into heaven. The singing, the praying, the preaching and the sacraments should communicate to our senses that we are in a different place. For the life of me, I don't know what else we offer a society like the one now emerging.

PART 3

THE AMERICAN CHURCHES

CHAPTER 8

THE AMERICAN FAMILY ROBINSON

Walt Disney ensured that *The Swiss Family Robinson* would become a part of every American child's life by adapting the book to the silver screen. The story, written by Johann Wyss, tells of a Swiss family sailing to a colony in the Orient. On the way, they become victims of a terrible shipwreck in which all passengers except themselves perish. The family survives on a small island in the South Pacific by quickly adapting to their new environment. They reshape odds and ends from the old ship, and by joining them together with new materials found on their island, they "make do" in a splendid way.

The story strikes a chord in the American heart. We, too, brought much of our culture from Europe, but were forced to adapt it to very different circumstances. Our European fathers borrowed from their new surroundings, learning about food, language and games from the natives. They gave their children in marriage to Native Americans and other peoples. Little by little, we created a culture in America that was both new and old.

The great Protestant denominations share this story. Tenderly and carefully, European believers carried their faith with them from the old continent to their new home. The American Protestant denominations were born from that concern, and generations of their descendants have lived and died within those denominations.

As the twentieth century gives way to the twenty-first, however, it is becoming apparent that the faith of many of the descendants is not what their European ancestors brought with them. The forgivable, and even delightful changes in religious life, changes that have resulted from a new environment—changes in architecture, music, social structure and so forth—should not be condemned. After all, we are Americans now, not Europeans. But other sorts of changes have afflicted the great Protestant denominations, changes which so radically alter the nature of the faith that it can justifiably be said that it has become another faith altogether. American Protestants have suffered a shipwreck, and the damage is grievous.

The Americans are not totally to blame. They have shipwrecked in part because they have been receiving erroneous information from their European cousins. The heresies of Europe seemed so much more sophisticated than our homespun orthodoxy that our seminaries were often shamed into their betrayal of the gospel.

Consider the story told me by a roommate at a retreat last year. He was a minister of the Disciples of Christ denomination. He holds a doctorate in theology from a mainline seminary. He is, in every way, an intelligent man whose gifts would grace the pulpit of any assembly. He was distressed that when ministers of his denomination get together, there is increasing openness to every heretical foolishness ever hatched from hell. One minister has been learning to channel the spirit of a medieval doctor and has performed this feat for his fellow ministers. However, when my roommate rebuked an evil spirit in a woman who was raging incoherently in the worship service—even though he did it gently and in order, and even though the woman herself confessed that she was instantly delivered from a long-standing oppression—he was reprimanded by the same colleagues who had found the channeling session so fascinating!

Many mainline pastors can tell similar stories. From the standpoint of a conservative Christian of almost any tradition, our great denominations are flirting with total apostasy. This is sad. Our nation drew its life from the Protestant reformation. The people who were touched by its message of grace and of the believer's priesthood, who learned from it a devotion to the Book of Books, and hence to literacy and to the free discussion of ideas contained in them, who believed that a common per-

> **ONE MINISTER HAS BEEN LEARNING TO CHANNEL THE SPIRIT OF A MEDIEVAL DOCTOR . . . .**

son could wrestle with his or her own conscience and take a stand against the world if necessary—these people created America. The good and the bad extremes of our country spring from the Protestant seeds sown on the western banks of the Atlantic. Very simply, the old American culture was Protestant.

Seeing the spiritual devastation of what we call the mainline denominations, one is tempted to look for the roots of today's consuming corruption in some of the central ideas of Protestantism. This can be done, and is being done, but I'm not sure we are right to do it. What may seem to be the inevitable flow of history as one looks backward would certainly not have been evident to earlier generations.

The stories of sacrifice, scholarship, piety and passion displayed by the founders of American Christendom are many and grand. I cannot criticize modern American Protestantism without first showing honor to the brothers and sisters in Christ who "fought the good fight," "kept the faith" and labored in unknowable distress to bring Christianity to our American shores.

HOW MAINLINE PROTESTANTS
CAME TO AMERICA

The ferment of the English and Scottish Reformation formed the foundation of our country. While it did not take England long to begin using her colonies as a dumping ground for undesirable people (paupers, pilgrims, political losers, bigamists, liars and thieves), the founders of the colonies were individuals who came here out of conviction. They did not come here because they had been convicted by some court, as did many later colonists. The first Europeans in our country were deeply religious people driven by their dream of creating a new world patterned after their view of Scripture. America would be a "shining city on a hill." These pioneers and their children controlled the colonial culture for an amazingly long time.

Their emphasis on universal education, their desire to instill in the hearts of their children and the new immigrants their values of civic responsibility and radical Protestant ideology, was strong and nearly unshakable. Of the first fourteen colonists in Virginia with a university education, twelve were clergymen who poured their lives into teaching Americans how to read and reason. This was an extremely radical act. England had a cast system, and however influenced by democracy and parliamentary procedure, it did not for a long time aim at the ambitious goal of educating all its citizenry. The American colonists did, and this desire was due to their religious convictions. They wanted their children and fellow citizens to read the Word of God and to be conversant with the great doctrines precious to English Protestants. This religious impulse continued to be a central guiding principle of the American people well beyond the Revolutionary War. As we will see, other visionary ideas joined this religious desire as generations went by.

(Oh yes, the other two university-trained colonists, the ones who were not clergymen, returned home. They had no public agenda. Education in the colonies was closely tied with the cultural mandate that grew out of Puritan theology. What other reason would have attracted educated immigrants to early America?)

As noble as it was, this drive toward education and universal literacy became major factors in the mainline denominations' loss of the frontier, and thus contributed to the loss of Christian influence on the emerging American culture of the twenty-first century. It was not inevitable that a concern for education be linked to a decline in religious sentiment, but unfortunately, that was the path things took in the centuries following our national Independence.

THE CHURCH IN EARLY COLONIAL AMERICA

The three major church groups in the early colonial era were the Congregationalists, the Presbyterians and the Anglicans, the groups we would call today "mainline denominations."

The Congregationalists were Puritans who settled in New England. They were the community churches located on the town square of most villages of the American northeast. The Congregationalists descended from several English congregations that packed up and sailed for America because they were unhappy with the way the mother country dealt with those who did not conform to the Church of England. Once here their congregations formed loose federations, but church government was strictly a local affair.

The Presbyterians were influenced by Scotland, where the bishops had been replaced by committees, called presbyteries, during the Scottish Reformation. Their guiding theological light were the writings of John Calvin, John Knox and the Westminster Confession, all of which had been important to the English and Scottish Reformation. These had exerted strong influence both inside and outside the Church of England. The Presbyterians, however, as well as the Congregationalists, believed that the Church of England was not breaking quickly enough with the past.

The Anglicans were the official representatives of England's national church. England was one of the few places where an entire national expression of Christian faith was swept into the Reformation. Because of this, the English church retained its medieval structure and much of its ceremonial life. Its so-called "middle way" rested, in both theology and practice, between Roman Christianity and radical Protestantism. Although the Separatists first established viable settlements in America, and did so in order to nurture a more radical form of Protestantism here, during the colonial era the officials who represented the king and Parliament in North America were almost always Anglicans.

They were the most conservative of all religious groups in the colonies, almost always opposed to colonial self-rule, and certainly opposed to independence. The Revolutionary war almost destroyed Anglicanism in this country because so many of its priests and influential lay people returned to England or fled to Canada after Independence. The Anglicans who remained were discouraged and aimless for some time. However, in due course, the church was reorganized under the name The Protestant Episcopal Church. It steadily regained much of its former influence, especially among the upper classes.

THE RISE OF THE BAPTISTS AND METHODISTS

The period following the Revolutionary War was crucial to the advance of the Baptists and Methodists, the Holy Rollers of that era. The Baptists took an especially accommodating view of democracy. They had dispensed altogether with the historic office of the bishop and placed ordination, communion, baptism, and matrimony, as well as the temporal issues of the church, under the control of a voting church constituency. Preachers were raised up, sent out, hired and fired by the members of a congregation duly assembled.

This sat well with post-revolutionary Americans who felt hostile toward hierarchy and protocol. (This attitude remains influential in the nation today, and continues to mold the way American Christians govern their churches and view Scripture.) The Baptists, perhaps more than any other religious expression in this nation, tend to view Christian faith through the lens of the American democratic experience.

The Methodists (we will examine them more fully in a later chapter) retained the office of bishop as well as a high view of sacramental grace. They were much closer to the Church of England than were the Baptists, to the extent that their founder, John Wesley, hoped against hope that Methodism would remain a society within his beloved Anglican church. Wesley believed in order, and he was no democrat. But he did organize his societies into a highly flexible army of small, well trained, bite-sized groups.

> **THE MINISTERS OF THE METHODIST CHURCH IN AMERICA WERE MUCH LIKE MEMBERS OF A MONASTIC ORDER . . . .**

Bishop Francis Asbury, one of America's most influential souls, organized an independent American Methodism, which he called The Methodist Episcopal Church. Under his long and able leadership, American Methodists used the small group concept well. These groups developed into small Methodist churches, which in spite of their belief in an ordained clergy could carry on weeks or months without an ordained minister. The ministers of the Methodist church in America were much like members of a monastic order, who, under the direction of bishops and superintendents, traveled from church to church ministering the sacraments and giving instruction; they left practical church management in the hands of local laypeople.

Baptists and Methodists were deeply resented by the older three groups (Congregationalists, Presbyterians and Anglicans) that preceded them. Gradually, however, Methodism took its place with the older groups at the heart of the nation's religious life. The Baptists, in spite of being many and powerful, have still not fully accomplished this. The Baptists are still, to a great extent, a church for lower-middle-class Americans. It is interesting to note, however, that they remain strong and continue to grow, either in spite of or because of this social liability.

THE RELIGIOUS STRUGGLE FOR THE AMERICAN FRONTIER

As we will see in a later chapter, the religious struggle for the American frontier narrowed into a rivalry between Baptists and Methodists, the former making the most gains in the south, the latter in the north. This happened because the older churches would not consider using uneducated or marginally educated lay leaders.

The Presbyterians made a great head start in the Appalachians—Scotch-Irishmen tended to be nominal Presbyterians —but they simply would not allow even the temporary use of nontheologically trained leaders. The problem was the older denominations' concern with universal literacy, which they believed was necessary for the American experiment to succeed. The Methodists and Baptists, who came from lower socio-economic strata, did not see this as an issue. They felt simply that men and women were lost and needed to be saved, and that the broader issues of culture and enlightenment were not religious concerns. The American Protestants' dichotomy between secular and religious life had begun.

In retrospect, we can find fault with both sides. The older denominations demonstrated more than a little snobbery and lack of concern for the poor settlers on the frontier. (The Congregationalists by this time had been infected and divided by the serious heresy of Unitarianism, a doctrine that denied the divinity of Christ. Evangelism was the least of their concerns.)

The Baptists and Methodists, in contrast, cared for the souls of the frontiersmen. Still, their tendency to narrow the concerns of the church to the emotional and moral lives of its people left us with the great chasm that now lies between the churches and "secular" culture. Secular and religious culture went separate ways, giving us a spirituality that does not nurture our arts and does not participate in the marketplace of ideas. Today the Church must beg to be included in the mental and emotional care of its own people and even when allowed to do so must operate on secular terms. But despite this cultural legacy, I affirm my belief that the frontier revivals were sent by God, and I rejoice that they swept hundreds of thousands of people into the kingdom of heaven.

The older churches, which had been attempting to build a biblically-based culture, rejected their new frontier brothers and sisters in Christ, even though they would have gained much from being included in the original colonial vision. If the Eastern churches would have had enough patience and foresight to accept the unlettered joy of the newly converted heathen, the passion and youth of the frontier Christians could have reenergized the Puritan heritage. That did not happen. Instead, the head and heart of American religion divorced and have not been on speaking terms since. As often happens, the new Christians were from the wrong tribe, and the old Christians would not share their social reproach, even for the sake of the kingdom.

Meanwhile, as the decades passed, the Baptists and Methodists carved out their respective territories on the constantly moving frontier. They consolidated their gains by establishing seminaries, hospitals and churches.

OTHER CHURCHES REACH AMERICA

As immigrants from the nations of the world poured through the ports of the coastal cities, the original Anglo-Saxon stock was joined by Germans, Irishmen, Swedes, Russians and Italians, and then by every other nation on earth. With these immigrants came their churches.

The Lutherans came with the Germans and other Nordic peoples. They made Pennsylvania almost a German speaking state for a hundred years. Throughout the rest of the nation, they found their niche as foreign language churches serving ethnic sub-cultures. They were more tolerated than most other new groups, because Protestants respected Martin Luther, the Wittenburg monk who had excommunicated the pope.

As the decades went by, the Lutherans—Swedes, Norwegians and Germans—became part of the American mosaic, becoming yet another expression of American Christianity.

The Pietists, who were also Lutheran, recharged the American churches. As they came to this nation, they challenged their new countrymen to seek that heart-warming experience which later generations of evangelicals would call the "new birth." All over the colonies, Presbyterians, Anglicans and Congregationalists responded to the Pietistic challenge and sought for the assurance of a "personal relationship with Christ."

● ● ● ● ● ● ● ● ● ● ● ● ● ● ● ● ●

AMERICA'S CHURCHES WERE ESTABLISHED BY PEOPLE WHO CARED ENOUGH TO FOLLOW THE IMMIGRANTS TO A NEW LAND . . .

● ● ● ● ● ● ● ● ● ● ● ● ● ● ● ● ●

Dozens of varieties of dozens of denominations came while established communities of faith split, merged, changed affiliation, influenced other communities, were influenced by them and in general added their understanding of the gospel of Jesus to the mosaic of American religious life.

That last sentence hides thousands of stories of sacrifice and devotion to Christ. America's churches were established by people who cared enough to follow the immigrants to a new land and to nurture their faith in this new soil. Their bodies are buried in ten thousand American churchyards, mostly in unmarked graves. They are unnoticed for now, until the great gettin' up mornin', when what was done in secret will be shouted from the housetops. All American believers owe an enormous debt to these people of God. We are Christians because of them. They are not to blame for the current mess of contemporary Christianity in this country. And it is a mess!

The story of the century is that the American Church in all its forms has been deeply affected by the growing confusion of American society, a society that is now redefining the

core of its own being. I believe, however, that a national
church is emerging, rising to meet the challenge of cultural
change. The character of that church is beginning to take a
definite and recognizable shape in the many transdenominational movements now influencing the future of
American Christianity.

This emerging church, for which we fervently pray and
for which we anxiously wait, is called to rebuild our religious
life on the foundation of the saints who brought their many
varieties of Christian faith to this continent. If the doctrine of
the communion of the saints means what I believe it means,
then their prayers are with us as we wait for the reemergence
of a viable and faithful American Christianity. We are their
children; their prayers are welcome.

THE SECULARIZING TRENDS

The great Protestant denominations that evangelized our
country made it, like Russia and India, a god-intoxicated nation. In one sense of the word, few countries are more religious than the United States. Yet few nations wrestle with an
energetic movement like the one we have here, whose central
aim is the radical secularization of our public life. Few Christians around the world understand why this militant secularization finds some of its most enthusiastic support among the
leaders and thinkers of the great Protestant denominations.

THE ENLIGHTENMENT

Conservative Christians should remember that from the
very beginning this country has held at least two mutually
incompatible visions of itself. We believe in the idea of the
national covenant—a country with a special divine
calling—which the English colonizers on the Atlantic coast
and the Spanish on the California coast brought with them.
But we also hold to the deistic humanism of Jefferson and
some of the other founders who longed for a nation based on
the Enlightenment, birthed in an age of reason, free from the
prejudices and superstitions of the old world, a home for the
North American friends of Voltaire. Each of these, in its own

way, is a defining myth for our country and aims to make us an example to the world.

Both American visions have found supporters in every generation, people who seem completely unaware of the existence of the other dream. Decade after decade, these people are amazed at the strength of their counterparts on the other side of the aisle.

This explains why today the established media marvels again and again at the entrenchment of religion and religious sentiment. The media seems to sincerely believe that some new surge of fearful fanaticism from the outer reaches of what they delight in calling the "far right" is poised to overwhelm our enlightened piece of earth.

The religious people, on the other hand, are ignorant of America's other side. Every generation of Christian believers fancies that the humanist expansion is coming from somewhere else, and piously calls us back to our roots, back to the time when we were founded in godliness.

The loss of history robs us all of perspective. These two streams both flow from at least the time of the American revolution, and every American has been influenced by some of both.

The secularists are right when they say that during some periods in early American life relatively few people went to church. While early Americans were almost always nominally Christian, at times those who gave the faith more than a respectful nod were neither numerous nor powerful. However, the first and second Great Awakenings, national revivals that brought huge numbers of Americans back to church, drastically redirected social trends that were taking the nation toward rapid secularization. Without the great revivals, these trends would have left us much like modern Europe in terms of viable Christian faith.

There is no doubt that the colonies were founded on deeply held spiritual convictions. But the War of Independence was almost entirely an economic affair. All the pious patriotic reasons for the uprising grew out of economic concerns. The English monarch was no Hitler. He wasn't even a

czar. The English people, including the American Englishmen, had the most protected rights of any people on earth.
The revolution was fostered by merchants and land owners
who were ready to rule and
trade without the interference
of a government far away in
London, a government in
which they had little voice.

> **OUR CORE
> NATIONAL VALUE
> IS PROBABLY
> THE INDIVIDUAL
> CONTROL OF
> CAPITAL . . . .**

American Christians of
every persuasion prayed for
their king, as Scripture com-
mands (see Romans 13:1-7,
2 Peter 2:17). They were per-
suaded slowly and with great
difficulty to rebel against their lawful sovereign. (It has been
said that a third of the population favored revolution, a third
opposed it and a third were indifferent.) Since Independence,
American politics have revolved around economic concerns.
Our core national value is probably the individual control of
capital, not, as we might wish, individual freedom of religion.

So the Enlightenment strain of thought in our country,
epitomized by people like Jefferson, Franklin and Hamilton,
has molded our public life and influenced us all at the core of
our souls. The cherished and often discussed wall of separation between church and state was a Jeffersonian doctrine,
suggested by him in private correspondence. He submitted it
as a doctrine that would keep the state from interfering in
religious affairs.

It seems reasonable, however, that Jefferson and his fellow travelers fully expected that the gentle spread of Enlightenment philosophy would in time erase the tenuous hold that
religion seemed to have over post-revolutionary America. Those
in the humanistic tradition continue to be frustrated that this
has not happened as predicted. Nonetheless, each generation
of Americans is subjected to the cherished notions of our
humanistic tradition, including the "fact" that thinking men
and women reject religion. (This, by the way, is the main
cause of fundamentalist hostility toward higher education.)

Immigration continued during all these decades. The early settlers had come looking for a place to pray, but many of the new immigrants were tired of praying and were ready to make a living. They pinned their high hopes and aspirations on our democratic and capitalistic ideals. For them, America was a land of opportunity, where one could rise from economic slavery to unthinkable heights.

JEWISH PEOPLE AND THE AMERICAN RELIGIOUS SCENE

Among these immigrants were the Jewish people of Europe, long burdened by terribly restrictive prejudices on that continent. Most of them quickly became secularized, with little or no religious sentiment except for what religion provided them in terms of cultural cohesion. They appreciated the humanistic American attitude toward religion, which tolerates all and takes none very seriously. They were, understandably, terrified of any religious revival that makes religion a quest for truth rather than a sentimental escape into one's ethnicity and sub-culture. They still are.

These truly brilliant and industrious people are a major force among the intelligentsia. They have, for example, a powerful influence within the entertainment media, to name only one arena where they have excelled. While they have enriched our nation's intellectual life, their fear of orthodox Christianity is often apparent in their artistic and scholarly offerings.

This is true not only of the Jews but also of the many European members of state churches who, had they been asked, would have claimed Christ's name but would not have identified with the passionate vision of the earlier settlers.

AMERICAN HUMANISTS AND THE DANGEROUS FAITH

As generations passed, American humanists became ever more convinced that religion as a definition of truth and behavior (as opposed to religion as soothing sentiment) disappears as the population matures. They have become quite willing to actively participate in the fulfillment of their own prophesy. The early unbelievers who helped found our country respected their fellow citizen's faith, but the new unbelievers are often militant against faith—not against all faith, for humanists are very tolerant people, but against the truly dangerous one, the one that will not go away: orthodox Christianity. The mainline denominations have swallowed so great a dosage of this philosophy that not only have they been secularized, they are themselves a source of this national secularization.

Beginning last century, one by one our great universities, almost all founded as centers for religious instruction, were shamed into accepting the inevitability of humanistic triumph. Once they accepted it, they sent wave after wave of ministers into the pulpits of America to prepare our Christian people for the inevitable decline of orthodox faith. However, the persistence of numerous educated but nonetheless faithful American Christians has perplexed them. (This perplexity has provided many a student with a vast reservoir of inspiration for research and analysis, particularly in the sociology departments of our great universities!)

Meanwhile, a fundamentalist reaction to the secularized and secularizing American Protestants has given birth to a nation of culturally isolated believers. These people escape into their church and believe what it teaches, but cannot connect that teaching with the rest of life. They worship God fervently and fearfully, but cannot see how the gospel of Christ has the potential to transform and mold a culture. They do not know St. Augustine, Pascal, Aquinas or even Tolstoy. They are shell-shocked by the apostasy of their brethren, and, moved with fear for the saving of their own households, have cut themselves off from Christian civilization. They cannot accept the emerging godless civilization, so they earn their living in a hostile world and retreat to the church on weekends, trying to hang on for dear life until the end of the age.

So American Protestantism is now represented by secularized Protestants who have capitulated to Caesar, and by rootless fundamentalists who have lost the knowledge of how to disciple their nation, and even the knowledge that this is a worthwhile goal. How did the vision of a "city on the hill" become so twisted?

Like the Swiss Family Robinson, our mainline churches didn't intend to land on the deserted island where they now find themselves. At the advice of their navigators, the mainline captains made many turns of the wheel which brought them to their present state. We will consider a few of the most important.

A SHIFT IN WORLD VIEW

An earlier chapter examined the importance of one's definition of reality, or world view. I contended that our country has become unsure of which world view should serve as our society's foundation. Now I will suggest that the same is true of many modern Protestants: They are unsure of how to define reality. How in God's name could Christians have become so confused?

NEOPLATONISM AND THE WORLD TO COME

It started a long time ago. Early pagans who became Christians converted to a Hebrew world view. They accepted the Jewish scriptures and the approach to life they taught. But by this time, much of Hebrew religion had undergone a major modification. First century Jews, and therefore first century Christians, were influenced by a revival of the philosophy of Plato, which, a century later, would be called neo-platonism. This philosophy served as a bridge connecting Greek and Hebrew thought, making it possible for early Christians to evangelize Greek-speaking Jews and pagans. The New Testament itself makes ample use of Platonic ideas and vocabulary. You might even say that there was a marriage between Platonic philosophy and early Christianity. This union endured until medieval times for Western Christendom, and endures still for Eastern Orthodoxy.

Very simply, Neoplatonists believe in a higher world than this one, and that all things here are imperfect copies of things there. The New Testament borrows this language when it speaks of Christ as the *true* light, or the *true* bread, meaning that the light and bread of the Old Testament tabernacle were only replicas of the light and bread in heaven's true tabernacle, both of which came down to earth in the person of Christ. (See Hebrews 8:1-7, 9:1-11, 23-24.)

The New Testament presents Christ and his Church as the way human beings may step beyond the shadows and imperfect copies of this world, until they have *"tasted the good word of God, and the powers of the world to come"* (Hebrews 6:5, KJV).

In its Christian form, Neoplatonism centers on the Christian belief that by becoming a man, Christ became the bridge between time and eternity, between matter and spirit. Neoplatonic Christianity is sacramental, because sacraments are thought to mediate, or act as channels between, the higher world and our own.

ARISTOTLE AND THE NEW PHILOSOPHICAL HOUSE

Western Christianity held this Neoplatonist view until the late medieval era. By that time, the religion of Mohammed had conquered much of the eastern Mediterranean world. His followers had assimilated the literary riches of the old Greek culture. Manuscripts of old philosophers, and especially of Aristotle, began to circulate among the Muslims. The writings made an enormous impact on the thinkers of that culture. When the Muslims took the writings north, they had an equally powerful impact on Christian thinkers.

Aristotle was Plato's pupil, but he had little time for Plato's mysticism. He was concerned with investigating tangible things, with categorizing the things he found, and with considering the implications of his categories. As the Christian thinkers of the late medieval era began to read the old Greek writings, they became alarmed. They saw in his ideas a serious challenge to the philosophical underpinnings of Christian civilization.

A number of writers attempted to harmonize Christian doctrine with Aristotle, as a sort of vaccine against the new danger from the East. The most successful was St. Thomas Aquinas, author of the *Summa Theologia*, who almost single-handedly convinced the Western world to turn from Neoplatonism to an Aristotelian view of reality. In so doing, he built Europeans a new philosophical house.

MATERIALISM, THE ENLIGHTENMENT, AND SECULARIZATION

As the centuries went by, the Aristotelian revival lead to even more radical departures from traditional Christian philosophy. Soon new generations were reacting against Aristotle as their fathers had reacted to Plato. Only instead of returning to Plato, they kept drifting further toward materialism, the view that "what you see is all you get."

During the colonization of America, the philosophical ferment in Europe had produced a blossoming secular counter-culture. That secular culture became full grown in what we call the Enlightenment.

The great thinkers of the next few centuries built all their philosophical systems on the Enlightenment, which, as we have seen, preached that the material world contains all that we can directly experience. Little by little, secular Europe drifted far from its religious past. Its churches were blown first this way then that, like boats in a furious storm.

These philosophical changes in Europe affected the Roman Church, of course. After all, the writings of Thomas Aquinas were the definitive statement on Roman Catholic doctrine until Vatican II. But Roman Catholic liturgy, and the popular piety of its people, were just too mystical to succumb completely to secularization.

The newer Protestant bodies, struggling against what they perceived to be superstition, fell the hardest for secularism. Accordingly, the Protestants stripped their worship services of awe and mystery, and made them reflect the university. The people sang, heard a lecture about the Bible and went home. Their spiritual world view began to take on the complexion of their rationalistic worship experience. Their theology followed. Protestantism simply had no ingrained habits strong enough to resist the implications of the Enlightenment, so it began to secularize the faith.

THE BIRTH OF LIBERAL PROTESTANTISM

We could mention a number of intellectual movements which have weakened Protestant faith. One of the most influential has been higher biblical criticism. This movement was patterned after a secular trend launched in 1795 by G. F. Wolf with the publication of his *Prolegomena*. In that influential work, Wolf attempted to prove that the poet Homer had never lived, and that all the persons, places and events cited in the Illiad and Odyssey were wholly mythical. The book helped popularize the trend of "debunking" ancient documents. Soon Socrates was declared a myth, Plato's writings were cast in doubt, and even a writer as recent as Shakespeare was declared not to have been the real author of the famous plays and sonnets associated with his name. This movement had a real impact on Christian scholars as well.

A small but energetic Christian group of thinkers began calling into question the trustworthiness of the biblical text, especially Genesis and the rest of the Pentateuch. The so-called higher criticism or historical-critical method of biblical interpretation was born. Its roots, however, went back another hundred years, to the mid 1700s.

Jean Astruc (1684-1766) startled the world of biblical scholarship by theorizing that the Pentateuch (the first five books of the Bible) had been compiled from two separate traditions, a so-called "J" and "E" source. These two traditions were based on the names of God used in the Hebrew text, *Yahweh* (Jehovah) and *Elohim*. According to Astruc, these demonstrated that two separate religious traditions had been reconciled to produce what we know as Judaism. By the nineteenth century, further speculation had increased the sources of the Pentateuch to four (beside the additions, deletions and mistakes of compilers and copyists). Liberal scholarship also concluded that the text was of much more recent origin than the ancient Hebrews claimed.

Liberal Christians have continued to interpret the Bible in the light of these beliefs. They remain convinced of the untrustworthiness of the text, believing as they do in the ideas born from the anthropological and archeological views popular in the eras we have just discussed.

Higher criticism rested on three basic presuppositions:

1. Writing was unknown in the days of the Patriarchs. Their teachings and the stories of their lives must have been passed down by oral tradition. Hundreds of years must have passed before the stories were committed to writing.

2. The names used for places in Genesis were found only on the pages of the Bible, being mentioned nowhere else.

3. Any ideas expressed in the earliest stories of the Scriptures are much too advanced for the primitive ages the Scriptures attempt to describe.

What happened to the secular side of this story? Well, in 1874 a half-mad German named H. Schliemann—a man who worshiped the ancient Greek gods, used ancient Greek as his family language and raised his children as members of that bygone culture—set out for Turkey.

He and his family lived in a tent as he dug for Troy, the ancient city mentioned by Homer in the Illiad. In 1876 Schliemann found the tomb of Agamemnon, King of Mycenae (the king Wolf had declared to be nothing more than a myth.) Schliemann turned Wolf's myth into a mummy.

The next few years saw astounding progress in archeology and anthropology. The ancient city of Elba was found with its archives fully preserved—tablets that pre-dated even conservative estimates of the age of Abraham by 200 years! Names began to surface on old documents which had previously been found only in the Hebrew Bible. Diplomatic correspondence and monuments uncovered from three and four thousand years B.C. recorded ideas approaching those of Rome and Greece in their days of glory. Secular scholars began to treat the writings of antiquity with much more respect than before.

It is worth asking if those involved in last century's biblical studies would have laid the same philosophical foundations and reached the same conclusions if they had known of the discoveries which have come since. Had they known that writing predated Abraham by hundreds of years and that the places named in Genesis were once well known throughout the ancient Middle East, would they have dismissed so quickly the historical trustworthiness of Holy Scripture?

We cannot answer those questions. We do know that through movements like biblical higher criticism, Protestant Christians learned to live their lives in two components: a real world where they worked and lived, and a religious world where they learned about ethics and celebrated the passages of life. Protestants were not insincere about their faith. History shows that the faith of Protestants was fervent and steadfast. But as generations came and went, the implications of some of their humanistic presuppositions grew ever more clear.

DEMYTHOLOGIZING—THE MAINLINE DENOMINATIONS' SHIPWRECK

By this century, the mainline denominations really began to hit the rocks. The winds of the Enlightenment had finally blown their old boats into destruction. Some Protestant theologians frantically began to reinterpret the great doctrines of the church, trying to save whatever they could salvage of their old and dear faith. They called this endeavor "demythologizing."

The theology which justified demythologizing was as complex as it was misguided and disastrous. The guiding idea behind it was that the spiritual values of the Bible and tradition were in danger of being discarded by modern man because of the language in which they were originally communicated.

Their argument went something like this: "The ancient world had used authenticating myth to communicate important ideas, and the Bible writers had done the same. In this context, mythology is a symbolic language which often communicates great truth. Whether or not the stories are literally true is beside the point. The stories of the Scripture were wonderful examples of authenticating myth, but probably not useful for modern peoples."

The demythologizers suggested that those who wish to communicate the truths contained in the Bible should lovingly lift those truths out of the fantastic stories surrounding them. Responding to this advice, ministers of the gospel soon demythologized the Bible of the Resurrection of Christ, the Virgin Birth and the divine inspiration of the text itself.

> **"SOME THINGS FROM THE GOOD SHIP COVENANT MAY BE USEFUL ON THIS DESERTED ISLAND CALLED MODERNITY," THEY THOUGHT.**

The demythologizers, like the shipwrecked Swiss Family Robinson, salvaged many usable articles from their abandoned ship. "Some things from the good ship Covenant may be useful on this deserted island called modernity," the demythologizers thought. They figured that the Sermon on the Mount may be useful, along with the story of the woman caught in adultery, the thirteenth chapter of St. Paul's first letter to the Corinthians, and a few other odds and ends from the old boat. Most of the old stuff, alas, could serve no real purpose on their new island. And it is an island. They are separated by oceans from their own Protestant past, from other believers in Christ, and even from the spiritual perception of the vast part of all humanity.

Poor deserted, dejected, marooned modernists! They wanted to heal what they saw as a schizophrenic Western Christianity, a religion that earnestly professes to believe in supernatural things while claiming that materialism makes more sense in everyday life. What the demythologizers actually did was to rewrite the very meaning of faith, moving

Protestantism yet further away from the world view of early Christians.

This capitulation came to full flower at the same time that secular society was growing weary of humanism. So the emerging American society no longer looks to the Church for spiritual guidance. Is it any wonder? One would hardly seek spiritual enlightenment from an institution that has serious doubts about the very existence of a spiritual world. Christian believers in America, for the most part, have come to accept the same world view as their secular friends.

Today American Protestants come in two types: those who accept the implications of the Enlightenment and have reinterpreted their faith in light of that movement's presuppositions, and those who compartmentalize their philosophical lives by ignoring Athens on Sunday and Jerusalem during the week. In one group the faith is redefined, and in the other it is privatized. While they retain a certain respect for selective moral values of the faith, Protestants tend to find things like angels, demons, miracles and even the Resurrection ever more embarrassing.

No wonder most American churches cannot respond to the human hunger for a mystical encounter with God! The leaders and thinkers of our American denominations have been teaching for decades that the ethics of our faith can be supported without a supernatural component, that modern science has made belief in a supernatural world irrelevant to intelligent people. These leaders do not understand that people do not come to church primarily for information, but rather to experience the presence of God. Christian ethics without God's presence is simply one more human ideology to be accepted or rejected as a matter of personal taste.

POST-MODERN LIBERALISM

A new generation of liberal Christians know that something is wrong. As Elton Trueblood said, they at least know that they "will not win the respect of a pagan society by accepting its ideas, even while covering them with a veneer of Christian language."[22] Unfortunately, they have been away

from home so long they no longer know what it is that is
wrong. So the children and grandchildren of the demythologizers are now actively engaged in the *re*mythologyzing of
their truncated faith. (Remember, their forebears took away
the old myths saying, "modern man doesn't need them.")

• • • • • • • • • • • • • • • •

WHAT CAN HERESY POSSIBLY MEAN TO PEOPLE WHO BELIEVE THERE IS NO SUCH THING AS TRUTH?

• • • • • • • • • • • • • • • •

Amazing. This generation of
post-modern, demythologized,
politically correct, decon-
structed Christians is starving
for myth. That's almost all
they talk about.

However, the new myths
do not speak the language of
Zion, but of Jung, feminism,
Shamanism, Neomarxism and
post-modern deconstruction-
alism. So Bishop John Spong
rages on about how the Bible
must be "rescued" from the
people who really believe in it,[23] Hindus are asked to offer
prayers for the Eucharist at meetings of the World Council of
Churches (as they were in Vancouver) and renegade Methodists urge us to pray to Sophia, the goddess of wisdom.

Stay tuned! All this and more will continue to be the
inevitable provisions of the desert island on which the mainline captains and navigators have shipwrecked their passengers. What can heresy possibly mean to people who believe
there is no such thing as truth? When people are hungry they
will eat anything. When they are naked they will wear anything. When they have lost the key to knowledge they will
believe anything, even a lie which leads to damnation.

The faithful remnant within the great denominations
have been paralyzed by a belief that it is reasonable that
theological pluralism should include the kinds of apostasy we
have been discussing. They tend to be gracious and kind
people who have become accustomed to the vicious treatment
they constantly receive at the hands of fellow ministers and

denominational leaders whose belief in theological pluralism evidently does not cover biblical orthodoxy. For the sake of harmony even the orthodox Christians who make it into leadership are often silent.

One thinks of the many opportunities the Methodist bishops have had to set their house straight, and how many times they have appealed for the spineless kind of unity which has become the trademark of that once-great church.

Unfortunately we must say of most of the once-great American churches what C. S. Lewis said of his own:

> Once the layman was anxious to hide the fact that he believed so much less than the Vicar; he now tends to hide the fact that he believes so much more. Missionaries to the priests of one's own church is an embarrassing role; though I have a horrid feeling that if such mission work is not soon undertaken, the future of the church of England is likely to be short.[24]

Were the mainline churches still at home port, safely anchored at Abraham's harbor, they would not be "making do," grabbing first this and then that modern myth. But they are not in Abraham's harbor. Like the Swiss Family Robinson, they are in a far country, far from the heritage in which they were born.

They should read another story about one who went to a far country and wasted his father's wealth on whores and wine. He ended up in ooze, smelling of pigs and eating husks. That wanderer, however, came to himself. He remembered his father's house. His father was waiting and saw him from afar off. That story had a happy ending (see Luke 15:11-24). By God's grace, this story may have a happy ending, too.

In the meantime, the passion for an emerging church is not likely to come from our mainline denominations. The believers among them are struggling just to survive. Instead, the thousands of independent congregations of various orientations, the parachurches of every description and the small mobile and mutating fellowships of churches and parachurch ministries are likely to lead the way. Perhaps then the great American churches, all brothers and sisters in the American Family Robinson, will follow their younger brothers and sisters home.

CHAPTER 9
• • • • • • • • • • • • • • • • • •

PILGRIMS AND STRANGERS

I am a Pilgrim and a Stranger
travelin' through this wer'sum land.
I've a better home a waitin', Good Lord, an' it's not,
not made with hands.[25]

I was dedicated to the Lord in a building that is, by the grace of God, still standing on MacCorkle Avenue in the tiny village of Chesapeake, West Virginia. In those days, Chesapeake was a town of coal miners and riverboat people. These folks were not yet enjoying the postwar economic boom that was sweeping most of the nation.

My Dad ran tow boats, pulling barges of coal down river, to where or for what I never knew. I suppose he took the coal to the great Ohio River, where it could be transported north to Pittsburgh and other steel cities, or south to Louisville, Memphis and New Orleans.

The coal came from mines which our fathers dug deep into the heart of the mountains on behalf of rich people in New York. At the foot of one of those mountains, winding around its base like an inebriated serpent, was the railroad. The trains that traveled on it loaded coal at the Virginia border two counties over, stopping several times until they loaded up again just above Chesapeake. Then they would come tearing down the mountainside with a roar and a piercing whistle, shaking body and soul and sounding like the call to the Last Judgment.

Our tiny church was about 100 feet away from the railroad. The train often rolled through our town during church services. The preacher would be preaching, grandmother would be testifying or we would be singing the forty-first verse of "Have a Little Talk with Jesus." It didn't matter. Whatever we were doing, the floor would shake and the windows would rattle.

Brother Durst, our pastor, would go on preaching, or grandmother would go on testifying or we would go on singing. You couldn't hear anyone, even yourself. All you could hear was the thundering train, clacking its way down the old track. You watched the peoples' mouths keep moving. Nothing stopped. The piano played on. Everything kept right on going.

I laughed many times about this, but I just now understand what was happening. No one stopped for the train because we were not singing, preaching or testifying for one another. The real audience was the one who knew how to separate the words of praise and glory, however deficient they may have seemed to others, from the roaring racket outside.

Just up the river a bit was a place called Elk Two Mile Holler. We often visited a Pentecostal church there that was built right under the runway of Kanawaha airport.

The airport has a story of its own, and I just have to tell you about it. Back when airplanes were first flying, no one knew where to build an airport. There was no flat land around Charleston. Someone came up with the bright idea of chopping off the tops of two mountains and filling in the valley between. So that's what they did. The result was Kanawaha airport, a pilot's nightmare and not all that reassuring for passengers, either.

When you leave the runway, you are already several hundred feet in the air, which is nice. Flying up in the air is the object of a runway. But if you don't get airborne, you drop into the lap of downtown Charleston. Our mountain airport is like our mountain religion—you don't get a second chance. You get it right the first time or pay the consequences!

Anyway, Elk Two Mile Pentecostal Church stood right under the runway. When the planes took off, it sounded like the wrath of God was right over the roof. The old timers loved to tell about the time Dad preached his first sermon there. Dad announced his text just as Piedmont Airlines took off. His lips kept moving, but no one knew what he was saying. When the noise subsided, Dad was finished. Everyone congratulated him on a good sermon anyway.

• • • • • • • • • • • • • • • •
THE RESULT WAS KANAWAHA AIRPORT, A PILOT'S NIGHTMARE AND NOT ALL THAT REASSURING FOR PASSENGERS, EITHER.
• • • • • • • • • • • • • • • •

As a young person sitting in churches like those, how could I have believed what was about to happen? Had I been told then that Pentecostalism (what our neighbors called Holy Roller religion) would make it to St. Peter's in Rome and into the heart of the Archbishop of Canterbury, I would have laughed out loud.

I wouldn't have been alone. Neither academia, Hollywood nor the barons of the printed page saw it coming. The bishops of the great churches missed it, too. While all the political, religious and social thinkers were deciding how to lead the world's destitute peoples to the Land of Oz, the masses acted on their own. Millions of people around the world were swept up into Pentecostalism, the fastest growing social phenomenon in history.

It's amazing! It's as though a wild elephant is running through town. Everyone is watching the elephant except six-

teen pipe smoking gentlemen in tweed coats who are sitting at
town hall discussing how to entertain the townspeople, too
busy to go outdoors to see what is happening.

In the Christian world, our version of the sequestered
gentlemen are still secluded. Neither the Christian nor pagan
pipe smokers in tweed coats have noticed that Korea is becoming a Christian nation, and that the chosen expression of
Korean Christianity in all its denominational forms is overwhelmingly charismatic and Pentecostal. They haven't noticed
either that while they were inventing liberation theology for
Latin America, Latin Americans were becoming Pentecostals.
Most of the Latin American believers in liberation theology
could fit inside the vestibule of the Jacobeche street Pentecostal Methodist church in downtown Santiago, Chile. The story
is the same in Sub-Saharan Africa, the Philippines and the
islands of the Pacific.

The breadth of the movement is another thing. The
Pentecostal parade has moved not only from country to country, but from denomination to denomination. Why? What do
high church Anglicans and Catholics have in common with
Black Pentecostals? What does either of them have in common with Latin American barrio meetings? They are all Christians, of course, but that in itself has not brought these people
together in the past. Yet this movement of relatively recent
origins, born only in the first part of this century among poor
Americans, has brought them together.

THE PENTECOSTAL CHALLENGE

In almost every way, the charismatic/Pentecostal movement defies traditional analysis. Relationships between Christians of different communions have traditionally begun by
trying to overcome doctrinal barriers. Not this one. Here is a
movement that involves every type of Christian expression on
the face of the earth, from Serbian Orthodox to Southern
Baptist, from Arminians to Adventists. It unites the very
wealthy with the very poor. Yet, even in their newfound unity,
the members of the movement remain as theologically diverse
as before.

My great grandparents were among the first few hundred people to join the movement. I was raised partially in southern West Virginia and partially in the Andes Mountains of Ecuador. I have pastored Pentecostal churches in Managua, Nicaragua, an African-American assembly in Houston, Texas, and Haitian immigrants and French Canadians in Montreal, Quebec. In the last few years I have help pastor one of America's largest independent Pentecostal churches in Nashville, Tennessee. So I have experienced the movement firsthand, from many different perspectives. I have also read most of the major studies conducted on the movement.

But one crucial element seems to be missing in all the analyses, namely that *Pentecostalism challenges the theological, cultural and institutional dominance of the Church by European culture.* In other words, Pentecostalism belongs, in many ways, to the new America much more than to the old; and since the new America belongs more to a world culture than did the old, Pentecostalism has become this country's most successful religious export.

Whatever the spiritual reasons for Pentecostal growth, I believe that to be the sociological explanation. It is the central reason why some sort of Pentecostal unity survives in spite of enormous social and doctrinal differences between those who embrace Pentecostal phenomena. The movement's common denominator is a world view that defines the boundaries between the spiritual and the material quite differently from the way Western Christians have traditionally defined it.

The Pentecostal/charismatics have not yet considered the implications of this world view. Indeed, most of the time they find it difficult to articulate. In the past few decades they have borrowed the theological language of the Western, particularly fundamentalist, churches to explain themselves. It doesn't work. Language limits as well as expresses, and the theological language born in the European enlightenment simply cannot adequately express a world view that so completely challenges the way Protestants have looked at Christian faith since that time. From the standpoint of traditional Western theology, Pentecostals simply do not articulate what they believe.

Articulated or not, Pentecostalism is becoming the Christianity of choice for the Third World precisely because it successfully communicates the gospel in the language and mood of the emerging world culture. The importance of this cannot be overstated.

> **THEY HAVE SEEN THE CHURCH AS A "EUROPEAN THING," JUST AS WE TEND TO VIEW ISLAM AS AN "ARAB THING," EVEN THOUGH MOST MUSLIMS ARE NOT ARABS!**

The fact is, European cultural values are being challenged everywhere. Even its great literary heritage is under attack. In our own country, the great universities are divided over how much of Western culture should be discarded to make room for African and Far Eastern studies. The European heritage is in retreat.

The wealth of European culture, in my opinion, ensures that it will re-emerge. Eradicating it is somewhat akin to performing a cultural lobotomy on ourselves. We just can't completely destroy our European heritage without destroying with it our sense of national identity. Nonetheless, European culture is not likely to regain the absolute cultural preeminence it has traditionally enjoyed, even among the very educated.

This puts the Christian faith in a difficult position. To the peoples of the world, "Christian" has been synonymous with "European" for 1,500 years. They have seen the church as a "European thing," just as we tend to view Islam as an "Arab thing," even though most Muslims are not Arabs! Even though non-European churches, such as Copts and Nestorians, have maintained a vigorous life since the apostles, for a thousand years the overwhelming majority of Christians have been Europeans—until the last few decades.

Those Christians who have not been ethnically European have accepted versions of the faith that were theologically and culturally guided by Europe. This has certainly been true in our country. Our ancestors brought the faith with them from their European homes and transplanted a hundred varieties of it in this new soil.

Now what this has to do with the success of Pentecostalism, both here and around the world, becomes clear when we take a quick look at the history of Western Christianity from a *sociological* perspective.

We are not used to reading Christian history from a social standpoint. We usually study it from the standpoint of doctrinal disputes, or perhaps by the light of great biographies of men and women of faith. However, we gain another perspective by watching the teachings of Christ move from ethnic group to ethnic group, reshaping the culture of those who receive it and, in turn, being itself reinterpreted by culture. Denominationalism owes as much of its existence to ethnicity and class as it does to doctrine.

I first discovered this approach to Christian history in the wonderful work of Kenneth Scott Latourette, in his seven-volume *History of the Spread of the Christian Faith*. Later I discovered H. Richard Niebuher, who also dealt with Christian history in this way, in *The Social Sources of Denominationalism*. I can't hope to reproduce what they have done, especially in these few pages, but we can take a whirlwind ride through the social history of Western Christianity.

It will become clear, I think, that American Pentecostalism is Christian faith *as seen through the eyes of the American Appalachian and Black subcultures*. Since those cultures are philosophically akin to the emerging culture in our nation and the Third World, their Pentecostal faith is taking the nations by storm.

THE PENTECOSTAL MOVEMENT'S SOCIAL ANCESTRY

The cultural womb of the Christian Church was Palestine, a province of the Roman empire. For a considerable time the Church centered its activities around the congregation in Jerusalem. There the members were ethnic Hebrews who loyally held the beliefs and customs of their fathers. Christianity was simply one of the many expressions of first century Judaism.

Almost from the beginning, however, Jewish Christianity had a twin. This twin church consisted of non-Palestinian, Hellenistic Jews. These Jews spoke Greek as their first language and lived their lives in a subculture that existed within the great cities of the Roman empire.

The tension between the Hebrews and the Hellenistic Jews is already evident in the Book of Acts. Very early in the history of our faith, Antioch arose as a rival center of Christianity. There Hellenistic Jews and even Gentiles developed together a version of Christian culture that differed considerably from that held to by conservative Jewish believers.

The church at Antioch developed into what we now call Orthodoxy. The Hebrew church continued as a sect within Judaism. Its followers were first called Nazarenes, and later, Ebionites. Soon there were other cultural variations of the faith, formed by the ever increasing influx of Gentile believers. They were led by churches in large urban centers known as "sees" in the language of historical Christianity.

Christianity was an urban movement. To illustrate how urban, consider that the word "pagan" derives from a word that means "county person," much like our word "hillbilly." Later in history, believers in the old Roman gods and goddesses were almost always rural people.

By the end of the second century, several major schools of the Christian faith existed, each with its own flagship church and its own patriarch. Many of these Christians still exist today, called names like Copts, Jacobites, Armenians, Byzantine Orthodox and others. For an amazingly long time, these groups maintained a strong pretense of doctrinal and spiritual unity. History has demonstrated, however, that a common theology alone will not keep believers united. Just like families, only those Christians who pray together, stay together.

Christianity actually became divided along ethnic and geographic lines, rather than along theological ones. In other words, theological differences have grown, to a great degree, from cultural gaps between Christians. These cultural gaps widened as leaders struggled for power and cultural dominance.

Through centuries of isolation and separation from other believers, churches have drifted from one another. Theological differences have often been the result, rather than the cause, of schism.

THE ROMAN CHURCH AND HER CHILDREN

The Christian culture which became the most significant for our part of the world, was, of course, the one which grew from the aggressive missionary church at Rome. The Roman church gradually accepted a definition of the Church that would decide the stormy course of the Western churches: "*The Universal (or catholic) Church is contained within this branch of Christianity.*" In that context, the famous saying, "outside the church, no salvation" meant very clearly "outside *our* church, no salvation."

The Western church became truly a *Roman* church. The values held by imperial Rome—law, bureaucracy, efficiency, order, hegemony and obedience—were all passed into the new religious Rome through the dying breath of the empire. The charismatic offices, once prized so highly, became standardized and all but eliminated. Mystical experience became largely replaced by regimentation. Individual salvation required obedience to the hierarchy of the church and faithfulness to its official dogmas. Thus the Church stood between Man and God, as heaven's vehicle for Man's salvation. Orthodoxy came to mean faithfulness to the past as the Roman church defined it, in culture as well as doctrine.

That is how things stood until the Reformation. But the Latin south and the Germanic north were again defining Christianity within their own changing cultural context. As civilization developed in northern Europe, Roman Christianity became ever more culturally alien to the Christians in the north. While I do not wish to dismiss in the least the extremely important *theological* differences that gave birth to the

Reformation, the cultural differences played their part also, and are most important to our subject here.

In the last chapter we reviewed some of the development of Protestantism in Europe. We won't discuss that again here. Instead, we will leapfrog to the colonies of North America, where the European powers were dumping their cultural misfits, mystics, explorers and entrepreneurs.

THE PROTESTANT CHURCHES IN NORTH AMERICA

Protestantism developed *national* churches: Anglicans were the Protestant church in England; Lutherans were German Protestants; Presbyterians were Protestants from Scotland. In England, all the "nonconformist" Protestants were persecuted to varying degrees until last century. The Lutheran church dealt with dissent in Germany in much the same way. The national Protestant churches continued to apply Roman ideas of order and uniformity within their own borders. So, the variety of Christian faith one practiced was determined by nationality and geography much more than by doctrinal or liturgical preference.

Then all these folks from their various churches began to immigrate to North America. The situation radically changed. Here the churches were no longer defined by geography or nation; a hundred sects might exist in the same hundred mile square. There was no American Church, there were American churches—denominations based on *ethnicity and class*. Each form of European Christianity found its place in the American class structure, so that Rome, Canterbury, Geneva and Edinburgh continued to maintain great influence over their grandchildren across the sea. For the upper classes particularly, scholarship, hymns and hierarchy were imported directly from Europe.

The Atlantic coast, where the upper classes tended to settle and remain, became Europe's surrogate in America, a tried and true disciple of the traditional and respectable ways of the old continent. The great institutions of learning were built there, schools such as Harvard, Yale and William and

Mary. These continued to import the latest theological trends of the distant European fathers. The churches, tied to these institutions by their educated clergy, continued to reflect their European roots.

Two types of Christianity drifted away from this influence, however: Methodism, an imported sect from England, and the Black Church, the Christianity of converted slaves. Both of these would play an important part in the formation of Pentecostalism, as we will see.

CELTIC AMERICANS

The European immigration to this continent was mainly to the Atlantic coast. That was the place where immigrants landed, and where they often found jobs and put down roots. Some did not feel comfortable there, however. One group in particular had "bad blood" between them and the ruling culture of the East, the so called "Scotch-Irish." These people kept moving west, into the wild Appalachian mountains.

The Scotch-Irish descended from people displaced from their ancestral homes when the British crown rounded up inhabitants of Scotland and settled them in Northern Ireland (1550-1605). The crown wanted to replace the native Irish with a group more loyal to the monarchy, and also because the aristocracy wanted Scottish land for their sheep. As we know from our daily newspapers, the newcomers were not welcomed to the Emerald Isle. Soon after the move to Northern Ireland, many of the displaced Scots began to migrate to America.

They quickly discovered that though they were English-speaking, they did not fit into the culture of their fellow colonists. In America, as in the old country, they did not mix well with their English cousins. The natural animosities between the Anglo-Saxon and Celtic peoples in America became obvious in the Civil War. When Virginia seceded from the Union, her western, Appalachian counties seized their opportunity to declare statehood, breaking the difficult union between the mountain and the coastal peoples. The Virginian house was just too small for two quarreling families.

APPALACHIA

The Appalachian peoples have never quite blended into the national fabric. There is a reason for this: *The Scotch-Irish moved to North America before they were affected by the Enlightenment.* Since they were isolated from circles of educated Americans on the coast, that is to say from people who continued to be influenced by events and trends in Europe, the Appalachian peoples were untouched by the Enlightenment, a movement which transformed the mental landscape of Western civilization.

The music, folklore and clan-consciousness of Appalachia reach back to an earlier period of Europe, before the scientific and political upheavals of the seventeenth and eighteenth centuries. The peoples of Appalachia, as opposed to the peoples of the Atlantic coast, held a world view similar to that of Europeans before the Enlightenment.

After the passions of the American revolution were passed, British-Americans tended to stress *continuity* with Europe. The Scotch-Irish rejected it; their memories of Europe were bitter. They were intent on creating a new world.

The friction was evident in religion, too. The old English families in their Episcopal church, or the old Dutch families in their Reformed Church, or even Germans in Lutheran churches, emphasized order, tradition, lecture and enlightenment. The mountain people, however, emphasized camaraderie, folk music, individualism and emotion. Appalachian religion was personal, experiential and spontaneous: the combustibles which often exploded into "revivals."

There were revivals in New England—the first Great Awakening, for example—but they were extraordinary events, thought to be periods of unusual grace sent by God to call his people back to faith. (The emotional revivals that did erupt in that region almost always had a strong Scotch-Irish contingency.)

The Appalachian people considered the revivals as the *normal* state of religion. The famous Cane Ridge Revival in Kentucky, to remember only one of them, brought as many as 20,000 souls together early in the nineteenth century. When we compare the sparse population of that wilderness area to the size of the camp meetings, we see how big an event they really were.

The periodic camp meetings provided frontier Christians a place to gather. They would build a "brush arbor," summon a gifted preacher, sing, play their banjo and fiddle, and pray for "the power." During the camp meetings, people were seized by great agony over their sin, and then swept by ecstasy as they were convinced that their sins were forgiven. The revivals assured the frontier people that they were God's children, and that they were greatly esteemed by the Lord himself.

Today, it is still important to understand Appalachian religion, because the Appalachian people were a part of the great American migration westward. Wherever these Celtic Americans settled, they carried with them their taste for revivalism, and their ancient ways of looking at life. The camp meeting journeyed with them as they traveled west, a continuing feature of their religious life. The culture of the Appalachian people deeply influenced the religious complexion of the United States, especially the regions away from the Atlantic coast. It is still influencing popular American religion today.

AMERICAN METHODISM

On the frontier, all the denominations were influenced by Appalachian religion, but no denomination adapted to revivalism like the Methodists. Perhaps John Wesley never would have stretched as far as his American followers, but his theology best accommodated Appalachian folk religion. The great American apostle of Methodism, Francis Asbury, gave himself to the Appalachian people. He set in motion the reaping of the frontier. The Methodists grasped as few others did the religious needs of the Appalachian people, the importance of folk hymns, emotional pietism, clans and lay preachers. Most of the other denominations thought changing their ecclesiastical culture was too great a price to pay to extend the Church of Jesus to the half-savage people of the mountains.

The westward migration of the American people proved to be a great advancement for Methodism. The Methodist circuit riders and lay ministers trained for the ministry by self-study and apprenticeship. A circuit rider could service dozens of communities by visiting them once a month. In the meantime, Farmer Brown "filled in" by leading prayer meetings and giving simple testimonial messages in the language of the people with whom he lived. This allowed the mountain people to carry their church with them into the American frontier, without buildings, priests or even sacraments.

The Methodists met the religious needs of Appalachia and the West, and reaped the frontier. But as the settlements grew into towns, and towns into cities, there was a greater call for order. The accumulated sacrifices of the past created new wealth, enabling many to send their sons East for a "proper education." The new churches in the new cities began seeking educated clergymen to fill their pulpits. Methodists leaders, now intent on solidifying the fruit of the frontier phase of their church, began to hush the "mourners' bench" and to close the camp meetings. The Methodist toleration of indigenous frontier religion was coming to an end. Methodists were ready for respectability.

Some were not happy. They wanted the "old-time religion" of their parents and grandparents. By the late nineteenth century Methodism was rent by the struggle between the newly educated, respectable churchmen and the "holiness" faction. The latter group insisted on continuing the frontier version of Methodism. They preached radical separation from frivolity and luxury, and pressed for emotional worship services. The struggle resulted in a proliferation of new holiness denominations. The Nazarenes, the Pilgrim Holiness Church and dozens of other groups were born as Methodism—which seemed to the holiness people to have capitulated to "worldly" values—went on its civilized way.

AFRICAN-AMERICAN CHRISTIANITY

The very existence of African-American Christianity is a miracle equal to any found in Scripture. Enslaved and humiliated beyond endurance by those who professed Christ, Black people looked past those who claimed to be Christians and cast themselves at the feet of Christ himself as their source of human dignity and eternal salvation. The slaves came to see themselves as new "children of Israel in Egypt," longing for deliverance. They began to dream of a day when, in the words of the spiritual, they would be "free at last, thank God Almighty, free at last."

Quaker, Baptist and Methodist Christians, often working clandestinely, found new followers for the humble carpenter from Nazereth among the African slaves. Although there were some wonderful exceptions, once introduced to Christ, most of the slaves were on their own. Several denominations were formed for free and slave Black Americans, a few of them beginning only a decade or two after the Revolution. For the most part, though, they were orphaned at spiritual birth by the American churches. Their leaders were given no theological instruction, no training in formal church music and no instruction in homiletics. All the Black Christians had was their suffering, their intense devotion to the person of Christ, their hymns written in blood and sweat, and a worship service that grew from their own passion about "a land that is fairer than day."

> **ONCE INTRODUCED TO CHRIST, MOST OF THE SLAVES WERE ON THEIR OWN.**

The Church became the only place where Blacks could rise to leadership, so they gave it their most talented sons and daughters. As the Black Church culture developed, it had few links to Europe or to European culture, the first such entity in a thousand years. By the end of the Civil War, poor whites were traveling far to hear Black preachers and to participate in Black worship services.

Then the two streams of disinherited religion—poor Appalachian Whites and African-Americans—met. The two groups, both outsiders to respectable society, began to turn to one another. The social and religious environment that developed from this cultural marriage would give birth to Pentecostalism not long afterward.

The unruly offspring of Methodism, the Holiness movement, represented by both ethnic groups, was truly Protestant, but it did begin to diverge from the mainstream denominations in at least one important way. It came to believe that after conversion one should experience a second spiritual crisis. They called this experience "sanctification," "second blessing," "baptism of fire" or "baptism of the Holy Spirit."

These disinherited Protestants were anxious for the security that they were truly children of God. They did not receive that security from the mainstream churches, so they sought it in emotional experience, particularly in what they called "the second blessing." Unknowingly, they were returning to practices of ancient Christianity, with its rites of confirmation and chrismation—rites which are also post-conversion encounters with the Holy Spirit.

The "second blessing" validated the legitimacy of their Christianity. They had a problem, however: what could serve as an objective witness for such a subjective experience? The holiness movement spent many years trying to establish this "evidence."

THE BIRTH OF PENTECOSTALISM

In 1900 a group claimed to have found the elusive evidence for the second blessing. Charles Parham, a Holiness minister, established a Bible School in Topeka, Kansas. There a small group of students, aspiring to leadership within the Holiness movement, searched the Book of Acts for the missing evidence of the baptism of the Holy Spirit. At last they concluded that the first century practice of glossolalia, or speaking in tongues, was their scriptural evidence. They began to encourage one another to seek this experience.

One evening Agnus Ozman, a Black woman, asked for the "laying on of hands." As the students laid their hands on her, she began "speaking with other tongues." Soon her fel-

low students began receiving the same experience. From Topeka, the "Pentecostal" experience spread throughout the Holiness movement.

For the first few years the progress of Pentecostalism was
slow and painful. The future of the movement was not prom-
ising. The great majority of Holiness leaders, with some no-
table exceptions, rejected "tongues." But in 1906, W. J. Seymor,
a Black follower of Parham, began services in an abandoned
stable in Los Angeles. For three years pilgrims came from
around the globe to witness the strange sight of a Black pastor
leading a racially mixed congregation to speak with tongues
and to witness miracles and wonders. Los Angeles became a
Pentecostal mecca. Most Pentecostal groups in the world can
trace their roots to that Azuza Street mission.

Without doubt the Azuza Street revival would have ended
as a passing fad had it not affected the two ethic groups we
have been discussing. Two men in particlar are important to
the history of American-Pentecostalism for that reason: Charles
Mason, the Black bishop of the Churches of God in Christ;
and A. J. Tomlinson, the White leader of the Churches of
God (Cleveland, Tennessee). After a struggle the two men
were able to persuade the majority of their respective churches
to join with them, giving birth to the first Pentecostal denominations. They were not the only leaders or denominations to join the Pentecostal movement. One thinks of the
Pentecostal Holiness Church and the United Holy Church of
America for example, which have very similar stories. The
point is that these early denominations all represented the two
ethnic communities out of which the movement sprang.

The interracial character of early Pentecostalism is truly
amazing. For many adults living in the early 1900s, the Civil
War was still a vivid memory. Even more amazing is the fact
that more *White* Pentecostals in America have evolved from
Mason and his leadership than from Tomlinson and his. Mason ordained almost all of the early leaders of the Assemblies
of God, the United Pentecostal Church, the Pentecostal Assemblies of the World and, of course, the Church of God in
Christ.

In its beginning, the movement had no central hierarchy, no official theology and no uniform liturgy. Pentecostalism was not the result of a long intellectual struggle over biblical doctrine, as was Lutheranism, for example. Nor did it result from one man's spiritual crisis, as did Methodism. It was born rather from the collective spiritual treasury of two socially deprived groups of Americans, people who recognized their common misery, and who determined to assert together their common human dignity as children of God. That is why "movement" is the best word to describe Pentecostalism. It is not an army, or a company, but more like a force of nature, like a river flowing wherever the natural lay of the land allows it to flow.

> **THE PENTECOSTAL MOVEMENT FLOWED FIRST THROUGH THE VARIOUS STRATA OF AMERICA'S LOWER CLASSES.**

The Pentecostal movement flowed first through the various strata of America's lower classes: among the African-Americans, the Appalachians, the urban poor and the various Hispanic groups. The mainline churches barely noticed that hundreds of thousands and then millions of Americans were adopting Pentecostalism as their chosen expression of Christian faith in a rising flood of lower class religion. When they did notice, they drew caricatures of the movement, after the model of Elmer Gantry. Of course Pentecostalism had (and still has) its Gantriesque leaders and wild-eyed, mindless followers, but they were hardly the norm. Most Pentecostals were just common American workers who wanted to experience God. Whatever Pentecostalism was or was not, mainline dismay couldn't slow down the explosive movement.

Several denominations quickly grew up around the Pentecostal teaching and experience. The Church of God in Christ became the largest Pentecostal denomination in the United States. The Assemblies of God, due to its aggressive missionary work around the world, is the movement's largest international body. The Church of God, Cleveland, is the chief standard bearer for the Holiness tradition within the Pentecostal movement. The Pentecostal Assemblies of the World formed around the movement's early split over Christology, the Trinity and the importance of the sacrament of baptism. The United Pentecostals split from the latter, and became the leading denomination for those of the "Oneness" persuasion.

Pentecostals who are members of these and other denominations are usually called *classical Pentecostals*. These groups are large and growing. Today, however, the majority of Christians who identify in some way with Pentecostal experience are members of historical churches. The largest group of all is Roman Catholic! One out of four Episcopal priests in this nation have been in some way influenced by the Pentecostal movement.

Almost no Christian group in the world has not developed some Pentecostal expression of itself. In fact, as the years have gone by the movement has so mutated outside the ranks of classical Pentecostalism that the newer Pentecostals, usually called charismatics, actually constitute a force in American Christendom that differs in several important ways from classical Pentecostalism. For that reason we will consider them in a separate chapter.[26]

Today Pentecostalism has been transformed into a transdenominational, crosscultural and international religious stream affecting all of Christianity. In an age when time-honored forms of the Christian faith are fighting for their very existence, this new form of the faith is becoming well established in nations long resistant to Christian missionary effort. The movement has tapped into the language, mood and religious needs of an emerging world culture. It has greatly affected the music, language and expectations of American Christians. The reasons for this are many and debatable, but what is not debatable is the Pentecostal contribution to the changing face of American Christianity. Its effects will be with us for a long time to come.

CHAPTER 10

FIRE FOR THE FIREPLACE

In 1959, John and Joan Baker shared startling news with the rector of their Episcopal Church. The Reverend Frank Maguire listened in amazement as they revealed that they had spoken with tongues while visiting Pentecostal friends. That was not all: the Bakers fully intended to remain in their own church and to be faithful to their own tradition.

Maguire kindly and calmly waited for the strange phase to pass. Good sense, he thought, would soon prevail, and his excited members would return to normal.

The rector shared the story with a friend, Dennis Bennett, rector of St. Mark's Episcopal Church in Van Nuys, California. After Bennett listened to the Bakers, he, too, experienced the Holy Spirit baptism and spoke with tongues.

There was considerable controversy over the matter and soon Bennett was relocated to Seattle, Washington. He left behind over one hundred Episcopalians in the Van Nuys area who claimed to have participated in the Pentecostal experience. The charismatic renewal had begun.

Now if you are unfamiliar with the Pentecostal/charismatic world, these terms may seem interchangeable. But the labels are not interchangeable to those who wear them! Usually the word Pentecostal describes an individual or a denomination with roots in one of the various groups that formed in the early part of the century to accommodate the movement's emphasis. Charismatic either refers to individuals or groups with roots in the historical Christian churches, or to members of independent churches formed in the last 20 years.

For the charismatics within the traditional churches, the supernatural phenomena are an addition to their Christian faith. For the Pentecostals it is woven into the very core of their faith. (Indeed for some Pentecostals and independent charismatics, it is almost the entirety of their faith.)

Independent charismatics are rather unpredictable and are not easily categorized. They range from evangelicals who use charismatic worship choruses to hyper-faith healing cults. Classical Pentecostal groups are large and growing rapidly, but the charismatic portion of the movement has clearly taken the lead.

Today probably no Christian denomination in the United States, and very few in the world, have not been affected in some way by the charismatic renewal. In the Roman Catholic Church alone, millions have warmly embraced the experience, including at least one cardinal and most of the church in Africa.

PENTECOSTAL ROOTS

We have already examined the Pentecostal movement. I will not go over it again, except to show how trends within classical Pentecostalism crossed the fence into the fold of the major denominations and into the world of independent churches.

From the beginning, Pentecostals hungered to be accepted by other Christians. In spite of their ridicule of "dead churches," "cemetery" trained ministers, and "preachers with dog collars," they were aching for approval.

Pentecostals regarded themselves as a movement for restoration, a renewal sent from God to lead the whole Christian

Church back to primitive purity. Unfortunately, a number of obstacles kept Pentecostals from contact with, much less renewal of, the mainline churches.

One problem was language. Pentecostals did not understand theological jargon, or even the language of the historical creeds. An important reason for this was that early Pentecostals did not *know* the creeds, the church fathers or the major theologians. They did not know how to explain to their more respected brethren what had happened to them by citing historical examples or quoting great figures of the past, as believers from older traditions might have done.

People tended to become "holiness" or Pentecostal because that was the type of Christianity available to socially alienated Americans. Conversion did not by itself bridge the socioeconomic gap between them and those higher on the scale. The same people who had been socially unacceptable now became theologically unacceptable as well.

THE LATTER RAIN MOVEMENT

By the late 1940s, a large group of Pentecostals begin to feel that Pentecostalism had lost sight of its original mandate. A new type of Pentecostalism, called the Latter Rain movement, evolved from this discontent.

This movement began to move Pentecostal phenomena from the culture which gave it birth. Some ritualized the laying on of hands to receive the Holy Spirit and instituted formal catechism classes for new converts, making a decided turn toward liturgical Christianity. They also began to join Protestant gatherings of different kinds, making contacts that would become valuable in the spread of Pentecostalism to other Christian traditions.

The Latter Rain movement was a mixed bag. On one hand, it produced some of the most reflective and innovative leaders of the Pentecostal movement. On the other, some Latter Rain prophets brought untold misery into peoples' lives. Both extremes are prevalent features of the charismatic movement of today, which contains the best and the worst features of Latter Rain Pentecostalism.

Despite how it may look to outsiders, classical Pentecostals have always guarded the borders of ecstatic experience. Early Pentecostals were really just loud Methodists, and the leaders were always careful of what they called "wildfire," or uncontrollable irrationality.

> DESPITE HOW IT MAY LOOK TO OUTSIDERS, CLASSICAL PENTECOSTALS HAVE ALWAYS GUARDED THE BORDERS OF ECSTATIC EXPERIENCE.

The Latter Rain movement broke over the border. Direct, personal prophesy was one of the most prominent features of the movement. At its best, prophetic word gave courage to some to attempt great dreams, some of which were realized. At its worst, some of the prophets matched marriages and otherwise involved themselves in the most intimate and personal parts of peoples' lives. This movement was not the first to have this experience. Leaders claiming to speak directly for God Almighty is a recurring problem of movements which center on the Holy Spirit.

Many Pentecostals and independent charismatics continue to have a difficult time understanding where authority begins and ends. For Pentecostals and independent charismatics, the Reformation only limited the authority of the Bishop of Rome; it had no bearing on the principle of authority itself. For many of these people, every local pastor is a pope whose utterances are the veritable words of God upon the earth. Every prophet, healer and giver of words of knowledge speaks with an authority that, for many, rivals Scripture itself.

I once dealt with a group of churches in the Canadian plains in which the pastors ruled on the frequency of sexual intercourse permitted for married couples. That was only one example among many of the kind of dangerously tyrannical rule they exercised over the personal lives of their members. When I submitted a resolution in my district asking for an official investigation of the churches in western Canada, even moderate and godly leaders were reluctant to back it because of the issue of "pastoral authority."

Understand that this sort of thing involves a small percentage of the Pentecostal/charismatic movement. Most of its churches and leaders are kindly servants of the Lord. Nonetheless, it must be said that authority is easily abused in a movement where the leader can say "thus saith the Lord" about every issue.

Poor John Henry and his wife Sally, sitting on the pew of Maranatha Overcoming Church of Glory and Praise, are no match for that. They know that they are not perfect, so they figure, "Who are we to second guess the man of God?" Untold numbers of people have suffered under this kind of abuse, and those who suffer most are often the most gentle and trustworthy, people who are ready to lay down their own ambition to serve what they believe to be God's kingdom.

Most of the early Pentecostal leaders were humble people. They were zealous to spread the Word of God throughout the world. They lived simple, godly lives and kept themselves above reproach. The next two generations, however, inherited their fathers' churches (which in Pentecostal circles are often passed down through orderly succession like a kind of monarchy), learned the powerful Pentecostal style of public speaking and settled down to become a hereditary priestly class.

By mid-century, some Pentecostal churches were quite large. Even though the people were poor, there were many of them. Since they tithe, if only a hundred people gave ten percent of their income, and if, as was usual, the pastor collected all the tithe, after he paid the bills of the church he was able to pocket the rest. The pastors often paid staff members—if they had any—pitiful sums, urging these employees to sacrifice for God's work while they drove the finest automobiles, ate at the finest restaurants and played golf most of the week. I wish I could say this is a thing of the past, but unfortunately the practice is widespread. Neither the people nor the staff can say anything about it, however. One must not "touch the Lord's anointed" (see 1 Chronicles 16:22).

I strongly affirm that this sort of abuse does not represent the majority of churches or pastors in the movement. Nonetheless, there is a single underlying cause of the abuse which makes it difficult for even the many honest and hardworking Pentecostal and charismatic leaders to deal with extreme authoritarianism. That cause is the belief that if a leader speaks in God's name, there is no way for the hearer to get a second opinion, to respectfully disagree, or do anything other than accept or reject the veritable Word of God in the mouth of the prophet. This was not a major problem in early Pentecostalism, but became one during the Latter Rain movement, and it continues to trouble the movement today.

This issue is important to understanding what happened when the charismatic movement entered the major denominations, where it encountered groups with longstanding philosophies of ethics and authority. In the denominations one could appeal to a bishop or a presbytery. You may get abused by authority in the denominations, indeed you are likely to, but usually there is at least a process of appeal. So abuse of authority at the local level has not been a major problem of the charismatic movement within the denominations, but remains a major problem for independent charismatic churches. This uncertain definition of authority is one of the unfortunate legacies of the Latter Rain movement.

Nonetheless, with all its downside, the Latter Rain movement contained many sincere and dedicated Christians who were trying to open themselves to the Lord of the Church. Through the many attempts of Latter Rain folk to reach non-Pentecostals, one began to hear of a mainline pastor here and one over there who had accepted the Pentecostal experience.

It is my personal observation that the charismatic movement has been the most productive and healthy where it has found a home within a historical tradition. Many charismatic pastors within the mainline denominations tell how they are the target of constant jokes, prejudice and even harassment from their noncharismatic counterparts. But this has, in more cases than not, provoked study, reflection, humility and courage in those who have endured.

In many groups, charismatics form a major part of the conservative defense within their denomination against heresy and apostasy. For this reason, they are beginning to win wider acceptance among their peers. In such situations, the charismatic movement is beginning to truly appear as a wind of the Holy Spirit, preparing the way for a major recovery of faith and spiritual power in the historical denominations.

Besides the charismatics within the old denominations, there are hundreds of independent charismatic congregations as well. These churches usually have been disenfranchised from one group or another but remain committed to integrity and doctrinal fidelity. Among these churches there is a widespread feeling that this accountability needs expanding.

Those who wear the label "charismatic" represent as wide a spectrum as the Church itself. It is possible, however, to somewhat characterize the movement in a few broad strokes. We'll start with the independents and new denominations.

POST-PENTECOSTALS

The classical Pentecostal denominations have been spinning off large churches for a generation or so. As the denominations evolved from loose fellowships into governing bodies, tension developed between the denominational leaders, usually bureaucratic, managerial types, and the visionary, entrepreneurial leaders of the great churches. The issues leading to separation can be almost anything.

It is a rule of thumb that visionary leaders rarely master the mechanics of denominational organization. They tend not to participate in the long hours of consensus building, diplomatic moves and schmoozing needed to rise to the top. They tend to go directly to the people in large groups, where they exercise their charismatic speaking skills and vision-stirring abilities.

This style of leadership works to their advantage in the local church but is a disadvantage in the denomination. The people in the denomination only come together once a year or so, but the publications, rules, payroll, forms and all the other tools of the bureaucrats can keep endlessly wearing away the vision with the practical, earthbound machinations of officialdom. When the Lenin of a movement dies, a Stalin is always waiting, some stable worshipper who has labored tirelessly behind the scenes, not for the dream but for order and regimentation, defined and controlled by themselves.

Often the tired troops welcome the change, which works to the advantage of the bureaucrat. But one thing is certain: Visionaries will surround themselves with bureaucrats, people who know how to work the machine that carries out their dreams, but bureaucrats will rarely tolerate visionaries, whom they neither understand nor respect. They will either destroy a visionary's spirit or push him or her into exile.

Pentecostalism is visionary and charismatic by definition, but the Pentecostal denominations are no different from any of the others in this regard, except that instead of saying, "Do this because it is orderly and reasonable" they are more prone to say, "Do it because GOD says do it." Often, then, persons with bureaucratic, controlling personalities can ease their way to the top of denominational leadership, and then arms themselves with "thus saith the Lord." Most of the troops respond.

The visionary leader of a strong local church which belongs to a denomination usually goes about his or her business with a casual nod now and then at the company headquarters. This is rarely enough for the bureaucrat, who becomes determined to make the visionary bow. This finally erupts in a showdown, and the visionary loses the struggle or doesn't care enough to fight it out.

On the other hand, when a Pentecostal denomination attempts to discipline strong local leaders, even for serious moral or doctrinal error, they can arm themselves with "thus saith the Lord" and lead their flocks out of the denomination. When the Assemblies of God disciplined Jimmy Swaggart, he was able to tell them to go fly a kite. His ministry had lifted him so high that he was above the rules that regulated everyone else.

The American landscape is filled with large post-Pentecostal congregations that have, for one reason or another, been hurled out of the orbit of their parent denomination. These are the flagships of the independent charismatic movement. Some have continued to evolve in one direction or another; some faithfully preserve the era of their departure.

The world's most influential church of this type is Full Gospel Church in Seoul, South Korea. It is possibly the world's largest assembly of any denomination. A few years ago, the local Korean church leadership got into a squabble with the denominational officials and missionaries. The local church was larger than all the rest of the denomination in the country. The tail was twice the size of the dog, and the dog could not move it very easily.

The issue that caused the separation finally came down to the practice of honoring ancestors. The Koreans put food on their ancestors' graves. One missionary is reported to have asked Pastor Cho, "Do you really think that your ancestors can eat that food?" To which Cho is supposed to have replied, "Do you believe your ancestors can smell the flowers?" Full Gospel Church became essentially its own denomination and a powerful evangelistic force in the Orient.

Some of the more influential American churches in this category are Bethesda Christian Church in Detroit, Word of Faith in New Orleans, and my own Christ Church in Nashville. Each of these congregations have circles of influence around which smaller congregations, sometimes numbering into the several hundreds, revolve. They have extensive contacts as well throughout the charismatic world, because people from all denominations can meet there on neutral ground. Their influence can vastly outweigh their size, because they have an impact on believers in many different circles.

THE FAITH MOVEMENT

When I was a young Pentecostal preacher, there was sort of a underground network of healing evangelists and their followers within my denomination. The people who moved in those circles interested me, and I tried to be a part of them. They were always passing around pamphlets and small books by evangelists, mostly of the Latter Rain variety, which were not well thought of in our classical Pentecostal denomination. One of the most popular of these authors was a shadowy character named E. W. Kenyon, evidently a brilliant and powerful communicator.

Kenyon was an evangelical of sorts who was greatly alarmed by the rise of Christian Science and other metaphysical movements. He thought this was the future of religion in America, and worried about the Christian response. So he entered a college which was run by one of the new cults. He hoped to learn the language and concerns of the movement. In the process, he came to believe in spiritual healing and became convinced of its biblical foundation.[27]

As an interesting aside, much of the Christian Science approach to divine healing came indirectly from Suffism, the mystical side of Islam. The most influential Suffi movement in the United States is led by one Pir Vilayat, whose mother was Ona Ray Baker, sister of Mary Baker Eddy, founder of Christian Science.[28]

Unfortunately, Kenyon communicated his belief in spiritual healing in the language of the cults rather than in the language of traditional Christianity. Kenyon was not a Pentecostal, but it was they, possibly because they did not understand the theological problems involved, who drank deeply from his well. By mid-century, influential evangelists like T. L. Osborn—a delightful Christian man—began to quote extensively from Kenyon's books.

By the time the charismatic movement was hitting its stride, another post-Pentecostal, Kenneth Hagan, was rising to prominence within the movement. A congenial and interesting speaker, he won a place for himself in the hearts of the new charismatics.

Where Osborn had quoted Kenyon, Hagan plagiarized him, reissuing pamphlets under his own name that I had read from the shelves of old Pentecostal pastors 20 years before. Hagan said God gave him those books. It was a case of "thus saith the Lord" again. His followers believed him, and memorized the dozens of Kenyon's books which had been reissued under Hagan's name.

Churches began to spring up all over the nation which taught and preached Kenyon's words in a Texas drawl: "God always wants you well, symptoms of sickness are illusions and Satanic phenomena, and believers have power to create and destroy matter by speaking and believing spiritual words."

Oral Roberts and his university are somewhat fellow travelers of this movement, but not quite in full agreement. Roberts has always believed in medical practice as a divine calling—hence his famous hospital. But even Roberts has had to be careful because the faith movement has enormous influence in the independent charismatic world.

Most of the people in the faith movement have no idea of the origin of their ideology. Since they will not expose themselves to "negative, faith-destroying" words, some of them will never know. Most of them are sincere Christians, attempting to follow Christ. There is no doubt, however, of the heretical nature of some of their key doctrines.

> WHEN YOU LIVE OUTSIDE OF INFLUENCE AND AFFLUENCE, IT IS WELCOME NEWS WHEN THE MAN OF GOD TELLS YOU THAT IT'S TIME TO MOVE UP.

The central issue of this movement is, above all, the so-called "prosperity gospel": "God wants all his children to enjoy the material abundance of the earth. God doesn't want you to be poor. Praise God, he owns the cattle on a thousand hills, and he is your Father. You are his child. Now get out there and enjoy your inheritance."

This sort of talk is uplifting to those who have come from the bottom of the economic heap. I know. When you live outside of influence and affluence, it is welcome news when the man of God tells you that it's time to move up.

Saying that the movement has heretical ideas is not to say that all its beliefs have no merit, or that its believers are

not really Christians. They do believe some dangerous doctrines which will, in time, lead away from Christianity if they
are not dealt with. Nonetheless, as Robert Schuller says, we
need a theology that deals with man's search for glory. Humankind was not created in a fallen condition, and we hunger
for our lost estate.

This "faith theology" attempts to deal with the human
hunger for glory, as does Eastern Orthodox theology, but it is,
unfortunately, inadequate and deceiving. These folk would be
blessed by a study of highly readable and delightful Orthodox
theologians like Schmemen, Myendorff and Losski, who have
similar interests in the human need for glory, but who develop their ideas from the Orthodox doctrine of *theosis,* as it
arises in turn from the writings of the church Fathers.

RESTORATIONISTS

One of the most fascinating figures of American
Pentecostalism was William Branham. My wife's parents used
to travel to his meetings, and we have had many interesting
talks about them. I also have met many others who were in
one way or another connected with his ministry, and have
read much of his written material.

Evidently Branham's meetings were filled with the most
startling sorts of miracles. People whom I trust tell me of the
opening of blind eyes and other amazing works of healing. I
have seen enough of that sort of thing to believe them.

Nonetheless, William Branham fell into the same error
as many other founders of American religion: the poverty-
stricken idea that the centuries of Christian history between
the apostles and ourselves were mostly a wasteland of corruption, and that God was going to start the church all over
again. Once he began to teach this, it was only a small step to
accept the role of restorer for himself.

Pentecostals had always thought of themselves as a restoration movement. Branham was only taking an original Pentecostal idea one step further.

The difference, and this is a fatal difference, was that
early Pentecostals expected the historical churches to respond

to this new wave of the spirit; they did not intend to replace the churches.

Branham represented a new way of looking at restoration. His view was that Roman Catholics were hell's counterfeit church, and that Protestants were going to be swallowed up by them. Only the restored New Testament church led by new apostles and prophets would survive. This notion swept through much of classical Pentecostalism, particularly the Oneness part of the movement, came to full flower in the Latter Rain days and is an accepted truth for most independent charismatics.

Restoration of apostles and prophets means different things to different people. In the group to which I belong, *Global Christian Ministries*, our doctrinal confession includes a statement about the ongoing ministries of apostles and prophets. What we mean by that statement is that those ministries have never ceased, that though they have been called by different names, they have continued through all the branches of Christian faith.

Apostolic ministry, which means to us foundational and cross-cultural ministry, certainly continues. If Francis Asbury were not an apostle to our country, then I don't know what an apostle means. St. Columba and St. Patrick are two other examples of apostolic ministry. The restoration folk, however, believe that the apostles God is raising up today have the same authority as the original twelve. They do not have a clear belief that the writings of the twelve apostles of the Lord should be regarded differently from the pronouncements of the restored apostles. This notion smacks of Mormonism, and should be soundly rejected by the people of God.

One major center for this type of thinking is the Kansas City Fellowship. Several prophets operate from that center and have had quite an influence on the charismatic movement. I have met the Senior Pastor, Mike Bickle and found him to be a likable and sincere person. I was moved by his appeal to a simple lifestyle, and his contention that charismatics should forsake the monarchical style of leadership many have assumed. I do not doubt that work for the Lord is being done in this fellowship and others like it. Nonetheless, when we follow this group's thoughts to their logical conclusion, we see that Christianity is being redefined.

To return to an earlier theme in the book, a loss of history is tragic to any institution. To begin all over is to become someone else. We can't return to any era. For example, what if we were wanting to return to the days of the American Revolution? That was before the Civil War and Abraham Lincoln. There was no Gettysburg Address, no gold rush, no cowboys, no Alamo and no Thomas Edison then. So we can't get back into the frame of mind they had in the American Revolution because the Gettysburg Address, the Civil War, the Alamo, the gold rush and cowboys have changed the way we see the world. To pretend none of it happened, or that if it did, it does not affect us, is foolish. It is like a man claiming that the legs of the chair in which he is sitting do not really exist.

There were church Fathers who defined our faith, there were crusades, there was a great schism, there were monks who copied the Bible for future generations, there was a Reformation, there was the translation of Scripture into modern tongues, there was a Methodist revival and there are hundreds of denominations with roots and traditions. The claim that a guy in Nebraska can hop over the events of the last 2,000 years and start the Church of Jesus Christ over again from scratch, just as the apostles left it, could only be made in an age when the *National Inquirer* is the nation's best-selling newspaper!

KINGDOM NOW

The Kingdom Now portion of the Pentecostal movement is postmillennial, interracial and quasi-reformed in its theology. It is as though John Calvin, Oral Roberts and Martin Luther King, Jr. merged all their ideas into one theological package and started a church. The main center for the Kingdom Now movement is Chapel Hill Harvester in Atlanta, Georgia. Bishop Earl Pulk leads the local church and the ministries that revolve around it.

The most visible sign that a charismatic assembly is related to the Kingdom Now folk is their use of the clerical collar. This is rather traumatic for White Pentecostals of any kind. In Pentecostal mythology, the early church had no liturgical elements and certainly no hierarchy. So any special clothing for a clergyman runs against the grain, unless of course the pastor wears a white shirt and tie to "look like a minister." (Older White Pentecostals thought preachers should wear a suit of some sort wherever they went, but never a robe, which only Black Pentecostals permitted.)

The Jesus movement and the churches which sprang from it had an impact on the charismatic movement the other way, toward extreme informality. They feel a preacher should wear a short sleeved, flowered shirt and be called Sam. The Kingdom Now teaching takes one in the opposite direction.

This group makes a major contribution by its emphasis on the arts. They understand that the arts are the central source for cultural definition in the country, so they are attempting to pick up the pieces of Christian art. They are also aware of the history of the Church and encourage the use of historical symbols and sacraments.

There is a strand of strong authoritarianism among the Kingdom Now believers, however, that from the outside seems to have little accountability. The American Church needs to reestablish its authority, in my opinion, but it must be accountable. Particularly troubling are the continuing rumors of immorality in the ranks, and their leaders' lack of sensitivity to this charge.

OTHER GROUPS

These are a few of the influential movements that guide the constantly changing face of independent American charismatics. I use the word independent loosely, because numerous small groups are, despite themselves, proto-denominations, and these are interrelated to such an extent that a nondenominational denomination exists in the huge network that holds them all in loose confederation. *Charisma* magazine gives an unofficial voice to the movement as a whole, and attempts to accommodate all the various branches of American charismatics.

In hindsight, the failure of *Logos* magazine, the predecessor to *Charisma*, symbolized the passing of an era. *Logos* tended to slant toward charismatics who remained in their denominations. It was, in my opinion, a magazine with much more substance. *Charisma* caters to a very different crowd. The passing of *Logos* and the rise of *Charisma* announced a general shift of attention in this country from the charismatic renewal of the churches to a restoration attitude in which the more flamboyant healing/evangelistic ministries took the lead. For many years, any sort of doctrinal analysis or historical scholarship has been put on hold for most of the independent charismatic world. In the meantime, the charismatic movement within the historical churches has continued to broaden and deepen, silently and consistently.

WITHIN THE CHURCHES

The relationship between the Pentecostals, the independent charismatics, and the old denominations is much like an old estate with a magnificent, ivy-covered mansion on the hill. The mansion has many wings in which elderly folk rock away their hours, remembering old times and muttering about the freezing cold. Meanwhile, down on the edge of the estate are dozens of rundown shacks filled with distant cousins of the folk on the hill. The shack dwellers are young, loud, often rude and warm. They have fire. They are sometimes careless with the fire, because there are no rules in the shack. Anyone can play with fire any way they choose, anytime they wish. The shacks are forever burning down, and when they do the rowdy folk inside rush out clutching this and that to quickly build a new shack.

The shack people tell jokes about their cousins on the hill and laugh at them because they have no fire and do not know how to conceive children. The folks in the mansion watch all the goings on down below through the mansion windows and shake their heads, laughing at the crazy antics of the shack dwellers. As they sit in their rocking chairs, they reflect on weighty issues and enjoy the culture surrounding them. They only wish they were warm, and that they had some children to take over the place when they die.

Neither seems to see the obvious solution: Invite the shack people, who are kin after all, to bring their fire up to the old fireplace. They could learn about their inheritance and take their place as future guardians. They can learn from the wisdom of their elderly kinfolk, and in return, their fire can help warm up the freezing place. Seems like a solution to me!

In fact, that is what is happening across the world. In the old Armenian church, the Pentecostals have brought in praise and power, and the old liturgies are sparkling with life once more. In the Coptic Church in Egypt, the charismatic movement has brought about an evangelical surge of scriptural preaching, and thousands are returning to the church. In the Mar Toma church of India, a church many believe to have been started by the apostle Thomas, the priests are praying for the sick, calling for their people to make public professions of faith, and exercising the gifts of the Holy Spirit. What is left of the old Persian Nestorian Church has become almost entirely charismatic and evangelical. The Roman Catholic renewal movement continues, despite some setbacks, and claims many millions of followers. In Romania, the charismatic Army of God continues to influence Orthodoxy in that country. In every one of the old communities of faith, the fire is returning to the fireplace.

Much work remains to be done, especially in our own country. But the work will be done, because it is not our work, but the work of him who anointed the prophet to write, " 'Not by might nor by power, but by my Spirit,' says the Lord Almighty" (Zechariah 4:6).

CHAPTER 11

DON'T EAT THAT WORM

Before I would build a wall, I would check to see if that which I wished to enclose is valuable enough to keep out all the rest of the world that will be excluded by my wall.—Winston Churchill

The little terror always got her way. She would pout and push until her parents were putty in her hands. She used her blood-curdling scream to enforce her authority over the house, and her two subjects would do almost anything to avoid it.

One day she came running into the house, her little face all aglow, holding between her fingers a long, fat worm.

"Mama, Mama, look what I have!" she yelled.

Her Mother, not impressed, told the girl to take the worm outside, "right now."

At this, the precious little thing began to scream, "I want my worm, I want my worm. You're mean. I'm gonna scream." The Mother wasn't up to hearing the scream, so she told the girl to go play with it somewhere else.

So the girl rolled it around, held it up, tossed it in the air, and in general had a wonderful time with her worm. When she got tired of it, she had a new idea.

"Mama, Mama, cut the worm in half."

"Absolutely not!" replied the mother.

The girl began to scream. So the mother got a knife and cut the worm.

"Fry it for me," the little girl said. "Fry both pieces."

"I won't, I won't," said the mother.

But of course she did.

She fried both pieces, then showed the culinary concoction to her sweet child. Surely the girl would be happy now.

She wasn't happy.

"Eat your half," the girl demanded.

This is where I will draw the line, the mother thought.

But it wasn't where she drew the line. Eating a worm, after all, however terrible, could never be as terrible as facing the wrath of the child. The mother picked up the worm. She got it down in one gulp. She was so nauseated from eating the worm she hardly noticed what was happening to the child.

The child went into the worst fit of her life. She wailed. She wept. She whirled about. She bit and she kicked. She rolled and roared, and she threw herself against the wall. It was forever before the mother could get the child quieted down.

"What more could I do, precious?" the mother asked. "I fried and ate a worm, for Pete's sake."

Between her sobs, the child whined an answer that would have driven anyone with less fortitude instantly insane: "You ate *my* half."

Some people are never satisfied, even when you eat the worm.

I first heard that story on a hunting trip 25 years ago. I guarded it in my heart until the week the Sunday lectionary reading was Acts 15, the passage describing the Jerusalem council on circumcision. I was aghast! What did that have to do with a church filled with baby boomers in Nashville, Tennessee? I thought, *this will be a good day to do away with tradition, and just follow the Holy Ghost.* But the Holy Ghost didn't say anything that he hadn't already said in the lectionary. I get so frustrated when God doesn't cooperate.

Anyway, I fretted and worried. I researched and doodled. I wrote and scratched out what I had written. Then it began to dawn on me what had really happened at the council. The lectionary reading *was* relevant to modern people in a modern church, and besides, I could finally use my worm story.

The passage says there was "a sharp dispute." *That can't be right,* I thought. *A dispute? The early church was pure and holy. That church was the great example for the ages! A dispute?*

> ●●●●●●●●●●●●●●●●●●
> # THE PASSAGE SAYS THERE WAS "A SHARP DISPUTE." THAT CAN'T BE RIGHT, I THOUGHT.
> ●●●●●●●●●●●●●●●●●●

A *dispute*, or a *dissension* as the King James Version reads, means a difference of opinion. So there was a dissension in the early church! So God's people have always had differences! I reflected on how the apostles and elders of the church called a council to deal with the dissension, the very first of several councils of the church. Other councils, in the second and third centuries, would determine the position of Christ and identify the official Christian Scriptures. This council in Acts 15 was called to settle the church's first doctrinal division.

The controversy centered on how new converts ought to live. The church had been growing because Paul and Barnbas were reaching thousands of Gentiles with the good news of Jesus Christ. There were signs, miracles and great growth. There was new blood! But some of the new Christians were also Pharisees.

Pharisees were, as their modern counterparts often are today, good people. They always emphasized doing the right thing, and doing the right thing the right way, and doing the right thing the right way with the right people. They had, and have, right doctrine, right opinions and right methods. But they were, and are, a royal pain. They specialize in getting other people to eat worms.

In this case, they wanted all the new male Christians to be circumcised. They had no objection to letting new people in, they just wanted them to bleed a little first! Also, no bacon. Also, intricate rules about the Sabbath. Also, proper reverence toward the good people at First Church Jerusalem. The Pharisees' message was simple: Jesus saves, but then he turns you over to us.

The council's decision is recorded in Acts 15. The new converts were not to eat the meat of animals that had been strangled and they were not to fornicate. In almost everything else, there was to be liberty. In essence the council was saying, "Dear Greek-speaking brothers, you don't have to eat the worm."

Unfortunately, that was not the end of the dissension. The Pharisees kept screaming, kept throwing their tantrums and kept insisting on their own way. At times even the mother church in Jerusalem caved in to their demands.

The Pharisees followed Paul everywhere he went. They couldn't raise up churches of their own, so they went after his converts. Their message was, "Paul is good, and Jesus has saved you, but there are a few little matters we need to discuss." (A matter involving a worm.)

Pharisees, who have not changed in 2,000 years, believe their doctrine is so self-evident that only a fool or a wicked person could overlook it. It can be humorous to watch what happens when they meet people who just don't get the point.

I once served as translator for a group of Pentecostal young people traveling through Colombia. One stop was the beautiful Caribbean city of Santa Marta. There were beaches there, and people were out having a good time, except for us, because swimming in public is a sin to American Pentecostals.

The missionary, an old Irishman named Bill Thompson, had met us there. He had some advice. Not knowing that it was unthinkable for the American young people to swim, I heard him say to the American adult in charge, "When you go to the beach, make sure the young people swim within the shark net!"

I was watching the leader, because I knew he came from a particularly conservative region of our movement. His voice trembled a little when he asked, "Brother Thompson, what will the brethren in America say?"

Thompson had a classic answer. With a look of innocent confusion he replied, "I don't know. Do they have sharks in the United States?"

Pharisees come in various packages. But they all emphasize what we do to please God. (This often means what we must do in order to please the Pharisees.) However, if I understand the decision of the first council of the church, the gospel emphasizes what *God* in Christ Jesus has done to come near to *us*.

Legalists want justice. They always talk about doing right. Jesus offers justification. He talks about our surrender and acceptance. God is not willing that any person should perish, but that all would come to repentance. His message is: "The war between God and Man is over. Surrender without delay!"

The gospel of grace involves putting to death in ourselves the evil urge that seeks to dominate others. If we understand grace, we will not always be so sure that we are right. We come to a heightened understanding of the exceeding sinfulness of sin, and the extent of our involvement with it. We stop exalting ourselves over our brothers, knowing that we have enough troubles of our own to deal with. We stop trying to make our brothers eat the worm.

CONSEQUENCES OF THE FALL

One of the consequences of the Fall is an inner hostility toward others, God and even ourselves. Fallen human nature is always fighting. It is never at rest. It is never happy with others as they are, but seeks to bend them into conformity with selfish desires. It delights in dominating and stripping others of dignity. Little children have this fallen nature. So do you. So do I. Sometimes it manifests itself openly, in dictatorial-minded people. Sometimes it manipulates in subtle ways, like when we become living martyrs—"Go ahead," we say, "don't mind me. I'll just get by the best I can." The strategy may change, but the object of the game is the same: controlling others.

Sometimes this enmity gets really religious. We try to push some different twist on other believers or to introduce some system in which only we are fully proficient. We become messiahs, helping lead the rest of God's ignorant and confused flock out of darkness and spiritual infancy. But the name of the game is really power and control. We want to put others down. Sometimes we even want to destroy people, strip them, ridicule them, question their sincerity. We want them to eat the worm.

Satan deceives us sometimes by making us chase nonexistent rainbows. We look for the *perfect* marriage, the *perfect* church, the *perfect* friendship. We forget that it is always a mistake to cast away the concrete good in an attempt to gain some abstract perfect. Nowhere is this more true than in churches. No perfect church exists, except that spiritual body already perfected in glory. It will never be perfect down here until the true Pastor comes down from heaven to make it perfect.

I get so tired of being pushed. Every year there is some new fad, some new teaching, some new revelation. People seem to be forever saying "it's my way or no way," or "this issue concerns a decision between heaven and hell." Every personal opinion in many of our conservative churches seems to be prefaced with "thus saith the Lord." I tell you in the love of Christ that this stuff is nothing more than that old spirit of the Pharisees.

It is sin. We are born with enmity toward others. We are born not liking other races. That is why we like to humiliate the foreigner, and why we laugh at the ways of other groups. When all else fails, we like to think we have something from the Father that the Baptists didn't get, or the Catholics, or the unenlightened ones within our own circle. We know we have an inside track with God, and if other Christians get in our way, we'll make them eat the worm.

We have worms galore:

"How do you baptize?"

"How do you dress?"

"How often do you take communion?"

"How does your church govern itself?"

"Do you have the latest revelation?"

"Is Jesus coming before or after the Tribulation?"

"Do you use the common cup or the shot glasses for communion?"

"Is the bread leavened or unleavened?"

"Do you use musical instruments or just your own vocal cords?"

"Why do you have a stage curtain in the church?"

"When are we going to have spiritual warfare?"

"Why all the emphasis on tongues?"

"Why don't you speak in tongues more often?"

"I forbid you to speak in tongues!"

We feel pushed. We feel pressured. We feel coerced. We are troubled. We hate to hear people scream. Nevertheless, I for one do not intend to eat the worm.

If you want to worship with a bongo drum, I'll go along with it. If you want to wear a beard down to the floor and shave your head, that's fine. If you want to take out all the pews and stand for the entire service, I can handle it. If you want me to wear a robe, a T-shirt or a jogging suit, it's all the same to me.

But the moment you tell me that God demands any of that to be saved, or that people who do any of these things are more important than those who don't, then I am going to read you some of Brother Paul's writing. I don't intend to eat the worm. The stakes are just too high.

FUNDAMENTALISM

I hate to add to the deplorable caricatures of God's people that have been created by Hollywood and the nation's print media. The word fundamentalism is not a bad word. I trust that I believe in the fundamentals of the faith! In that sense I, too, am a fundamentalist.

Yet we have to admit that like all unfair caricatures, this perception is based on something. The spiteful spirit among many of those who are "defending the faith" is more fierce and fearsome than the disease which they claim to cure.

BANISTER POLISHING AND WALL PAINTING

The truth is, many fundamentalists haven't a clue about what the church is truly up against. They believe our current crisis consists of issues of flag, rock music, girlie magazines, beards, women wearing pants, drums, speaking or not speaking with tongues, dances and so forth. They are like passengers on the Titanic furiously raging about the mess the panicking people are making of their deck as they flee the disaster below. They haven't yet seen for themselves what's happening below. They are angry at the people running through, but they haven't asked why everyone is so upset. They don't know that the culture has a huge leak, and that we're taking on water fast. They think we should paint the walls and shine the banisters.

Strictly speaking, I suppose that fundamentalists are independent Baptists and Reconstructionist Presbyterians. They wouldn't include in their own ranks the really rigid Adventists, Pentecostals and charismatics, but they are not writing this book and I think they are all fellow travelers. They all share a tendency toward Pharisaism. In some ways, we are back to the age of Jesus and St. Paul; the mainline denominations are becoming Sadducees and conservative groups are becoming Pharisees.

I can't believe that I am really including this chapter. I am much more closely aligned with fundamentalists than I am with the liberal side of the church. Yet I must say that I fear the Pharisee as much as I do the Sadducee. One says there is no resurrection. The other says if I don't keep the Sabbath as he prescribes or follow his dress code or share his musical taste, the resurrection will be my only comfort. He'll join me to those now waiting for the resurrection. The Sadducees think there are no angels in heaven; the Pharisees think there are none on earth. The Sadducees tell me there will be no hell in the hereafter, and the Pharisees compensate by giving it to me now.

If these are the only choices then it is plain that all believers in Christ must choose whether they prefer to become a fatality of freezing or to burn in a furious flash. Some of us are asking, "Isn't there a box for 'none of the above'?"

Every Christian expression has its own brand of Pharisaism. The Adventist version deals with what I eat for breakfast and what day I worship God. The Pentecostal version deals with how often I speak with tongues and whether or not I jump and shout when they turn on the Leslie speaker of their Hammond organ. The Baptist version deals with my haircut, my voting record and whether or not I have walked the aisle. The Churches of Christ version deals with whether or not I play a piano in the church, have a hot dog sale or support orphanages. The Roman Catholic version deals with preachers not having wives; the Orthodox about whether I quote the creed with or without the *filioque*. This is all banister polishing, wall painting and furniture rearranging—legitimate concerns when the ship is afloat but rather irrelevant when it is sinking.

Every church has both a doctrine and a culture. To some extent, culture grows out of doctrine, but only to some extent. As orthodox Christians, our doctrines are not very far apart. What Christians usually argue about with each other is their respective cultures: music, dress, architecture and other serious issues. Discussions over dance and drums in worship have divided churches.

How foolish! Is it not equally obvious to everyone that a man can bang a drum in praise to God? It's incredible! Is the drum somehow more likely to become demon-possessed than the pipe organ? Is making the sign of the cross somehow more idolatrous than raising one's hands? Is raising one's hands more disruptive than bending one's knee? Isn't dancing nothing more than bending the knee, raising one's hands and signing the cross in rhythm? Isn't getting up out of the pew for the responsive reading and sitting down again a sort of two-step dance? Doesn't a drum do nothing more than repeat the same basic rhythm long enough to build a foundation for a more involved sort of dance?

Are we really concerned with defending the truth? Not when the issues are things like these. These are cultural issues. They involve personal taste. I can't understand why we fuss about all these things.

> IN THE DENOMI-NATION IN WHICH I WAS RAISED, THE NEW CHARISMATIC CHORUSES OF THE 1970s WERE REALLY SUSPECT.

The Pharisee confuses personal taste with eternal truth. In the denomination in which I was raised, the new charismatic choruses of the 1970s were really suspect. That they were nothing more than Scripture sung to folk music wasn't the point. Those people were strange, raising their hands with palms turned inward, arms slightly bent, rather than palms turned outward with arms straight up in the air, as God had ordained. They were bizarre, with those silly grins on their faces, all sweet and syrupy-like. ("We don't need their stuff! HAH! We were here long before they got here, with the real Holy Ghost! HAH! We'll be here long after they're gone! HAH! Praise God, give me the old-time religion! HAH! Give me songs that have kept us clean and holy! HAH! Songs like 'Camping in Canaan's Land' and 'I'll Fly Away in the Morning'! HAH!")

Are Pentecostals, like these, the children of the Lord? Of course they are. Are the charismatics? No question. Then what is the problem? The problem comes from confusing personal taste and comfort with the "faith once delivered to the saints." The liberals do not believe there is such a thing as a faith delivered to the saints for which we ought to contend; the fundamentalists are ready to contend not only for the faith, but for every jot and tittle as well. They believe the Bible from cover to cover, from Genesis to the maps and concordance and Scofield's notes at the bottom of the page. But what really gets fundamentalists going are not issues about lost men and women and how to reach them—the real issues for them involve worms and who should eat them.

One thing is for sure, the members of our secular society are not going to eat worms. They are as adverse to worms as were the ancient Greeks, Romans and barbarians Saint Paul converted. They might, however, be enticed to taste the bread of heaven, if it were served to them with joy and grace.

In a generation where thousands pay good money to hear the likes of Shirley MacLaine and a lady who claims to "channel" for a 6,000-year-old warrior, we may be sure that there is no lack of spiritual hunger. There is hunger all right. My old Bishop, Brother Poling, used to sing, "Jesus has a table spread, where the saints of God are fed, and he invites his chosen people come and dine." Jesus has prepared the table, and the heathen have the hunger; they will come if the Lord's good disciples don't pelt them with rocks.

If we really want them to come we must understand the differences between culture and faith. I once attended a retreat with a concerned pastor from a fine Baptist congregation somewhere in Appalachia, in a college town. The members of the church were mostly faculty and students of the college, and they came from out of town, except for the board members and deacons, who were all members of important local families. When he found out that I was from the region, he wanted some advice. It took him a while to get to the point, because he was very kind and didn't want to offend.

"How can I open the church to the natives of the area?" he asked. "I don't want to pastor a church that the people of the area perceive as snooty."

I thought about it, and then offered a solution.

"Next time you have a board vacancy," I said, "fill the position with someone whose favorite singer is Dolly Parton, and who sometimes watches wrestling on TV."

He chuckled that strange sort of gurgling sound one makes when one is not sure whether or not you are kidding. I wasn't.

"Well, I doubt if that would fly in our congregation," he said. Actually, I thought it probably would fly, right toward the fan.

His church was organized as a refuge for immigrants to the area, people who have no intention of accommodating mountain culture. I don't have any problem with that, I just wanted him to be honest about it. He needed to realize that by rejecting our mountain culture his church was rejecting our people. Our people weren't about to go to a church filled with professors who talk over coffee about the roots of the Romantic movement or the results of Cartesian philosophy on nineteenth-century theology. Not during squirrel season.

BECOMING ALL THINGS TO ALL PEOPLE

The struggle to maintain the purity of the faith is an important one. The struggle to maintain cultural comfort is also important, at least to our personal comfort. What we must not do is freeze-frame an era of history and say, "things must be maintained to the standard of this holy historical era." Whether it is fifteenth-century Europe, the nineteenth-century American frontier or the sixth-century Byzantine empire, no century and its ways should be enshrined. They all have their place, as do the contributions of modern Christianity, in this cultural mosaic through which God glorifies himself.

As sunlight takes the form of the stained glass windows through which it passes, our joy and delight is due to our appreciation for the uniqueness of each piece of glass and how it colors the glory that passes through it to us. In the same way, we should learn to appreciate—even if we never come to prefer—the way Christian faith is proclaimed through the various cultures through which it passes, even when it passes through the lips of a Dolly Parton.

This is what St. Paul means when he says, "I have become all things to all men so that by all possible means I might save some" (1 Corinthians 9:22). Does that mean he would approve our opening a St. Basil's Bordello or a St. Paul's Bar and Grill to entice sinners? Wouldn't such things be included in *all possible means?* Of course not, and we know it. He meant that he was willing to give up any preference of his own, or to employ any style or technique which did not contradict the gospel he preached, in order to win people to Christ. He would not be bound to the culture of the Jerusalem church. He would not make the saints of God eat the worm. There is a church in America and the Western world today because he took that stand. It took courage then, and it takes courage now. But it is the right thing to do.

COMMUNICATING WITH A NEW GENERATION

Strategy demands we examine how we communicate with heathen people around us. The so-called New Age movement demonstrates that the boundaries of the debate have changed. A generation ago, we used things like *Evidence That Demands a Verdict* to combat raging secularism. A new generation of American nonbelievers are not interested in evidence of that sort; they are incurably spiritual. They have been rejecting the rationalism of their parents all their lives. Their deepest concerns have become more closely connected with our Christian faith than previous generations. And yet they are turning inward and to the Far East for solace, because they simply cannot connect with a Christian rationalism that offers answers to questions they are not asking. American Christianity must come to grips with this fundamental cultural change.

Only the most entrenched Pharisees would refuse to see that we are struggling for the attention of our nation. A new American generation has risen that has very little in common with the Church. Sometimes that generation includes our own Christian children. If they cannot hear and understand what we are saying, does it matter how wonderful our exegesis is? I for one will not sacrifice my children to please some homiletics professor. The pews of my church are not filled with homiletic professors. They are filled, thank God, with people raised on Sesame Street, the citizens of the New America. I intend to serve them as God gives me the strength. I don't like worms any more than they do.

CHAPTER 12

BLESSED ASSURANCE

I can, I will, I do believe, I can, I will, I do believe
I can, I will, I do believe, That Jesus saves me now.
—Appalachian folk hymn

It was a hot day in the Amazon rain forest. (Every day in the Amazon rain forest is hot.) I was in the middle of the river, sitting on the deck of a houseboat owned by my good friend, missionary Paul Molton.

We had journeyed several days upriver to minister to some tribal people. We had walked the jungle paths, listening to the sounds of exotic birds and God knows whatever else participates in the ongoing symphony of the jungle. We had conducted worship services by the light of kerosene lanterns. We had paddled on streams which would have been sizable rivers anywhere but near the Amazon, the mighty giant that shames its rivals and collects tribute from its neighbors like an ancient despot.

We were returning to Iquitos, a jungle city that sits solitary, surrounded by nothing but green, the result of last century's rubber industry and this century's love of oil. Paul was piloting his boat. I was studying, fishing and loafing. I had been reading Ephesians, and William Barclays' commentary on that book. Suddenly, something clicked in my mind. A deep joy in my heart pushed me to my feet. Tears were running down my face as I said to no one in particular, "I'm saved! I'm saved." A dolphin jumped in the middle of a sun-kissed streak of water, and it seemed to me that Nature herself joined my joy.

I was a missionary, and I had been preaching for several years. I was raised in a good Christian home. I was sent by my denomination to preach the gospel, having met the Lord many years before. But it was that day on the Amazon river, reading the book of Ephesians, when I first realized that I was saved by nothing less than the grace of Jesus Christ.

All the Baptists, Campus Crusaders and assorted born again evangelicals in the world know about justification by faith. They learn about it as infants. I knew about worship, faith for healing and godly living as a child. What I did not know was that one could be sure that one was born again, because the new birth was a gracious act of God through the sacrifice of Jesus Christ. Nonetheless, since the Baptists and the rest of the "born again" crowd didn't worship God as we did, and did not "press on into deeper waters in God," they obviously did not have anything to say to me! At least that is what I thought until St. Paul got through to me.

When I was a child, we used to sing a chorus in our church, (and would sing it a good forty times, or however long it took before "the glory came down") that tells the story, *"Running, running, trying to make a hundred, ninety nine and a half won't do."* In the Pentecostal world of my youth, hell was hot, the devil was real, and one had to run at a hundred percent to keep away from them. The problem was, I didn't often reach even eighty-five. In fact, sixty-five was my normal running speed, with bursts of eighty-seven or so during revivals and camp meetings!

Grandma sang another song, with her knowing, piercing eyes that looked into one's soul, *"Watching you, watching you, there's an all-seeing eye, watching you."* We were all in trouble. A periodic trip to the altar for "reconsecration" helped, but it was definitely a touch-and-go situation.

To tell you the truth, I wish people in our country had more of a healthy sense of the fear of God these days, which is, after all, the beginning of wisdom (see Proverbs 9:10). Fear of God was not something I had any lack of as a child. I should add that I also heard about the love of God. My parents and grandparents were loving and kind, but "holiness" people were not very big on assurance. *Better safe than sorry,* they thought. In many ways I think it is good to feel the bite of the law before feeling the relief of grace. Perhaps no one really grasps the message of grace without first understanding the seriousness

> MY PENTE-
> COSTAL NEW
> TESTAMENT HAD
> CONSISTED OF
> THE FOUR
> GOSPELS, ACTS,
> 1 CORINTHIANS
> AND THE BOOK
> OF REVELATION.

of sin. At any rate, the seriousness of sin I already knew. Now I became intoxicated with that wine of Pauline theology which had turned the heads of the Reformers.

In the months after my "Amazon revelation," I read the Epistles of St. Paul in earnest. My Pentecostal New Testament had consisted of the four gospels, Acts, 1 Corinthians and the book of Revelation. Now I found out that there were books in between, and that they were very interesting. As a matter of fact, I discovered the Epistles at the same time many Baptists were discovering the book of Acts.

I reflected on things I had seen and heard as a missionary child in the lives and teachings of evangelical missionaries in Ecuador. Suddenly, sermons I had heard as a high school student in the Alliance Academy in Quito, on the campus of the famous HCJB radio complex, made sense. I started reading Spurgeon, Moody, Luther and Calvin. I was anxious to become a full-fledged evangelical.

My Pentecostal friends were uneasy about my new obsession. They were certain that "salvation by faith alone" would undermine the dress codes and rules of conduct which separated our group from everyone else. They also were certain that we should not put ourselves on a level playing field with the likes of Baptists. I was admonished to back away from the direction in which I was heading. I tried, but it was impossible. Once the brain is stretched with a new thought, it is impossible to shrink it back to its original shape. I was convinced that we are saved by grace alone.

So I walked on. In the process, my speaking engagements begin to drop rather dramatically, and old friends were nervous when I came around. Gradually, I found myself in unfamiliar territory. Like my wandering ancestors, I lost sight of a familiar shore, moving toward a new world about which I knew very little. I discovered books, tapes, conferences and churches that I did not know even existed.

During this time, I accepted the call to become the assistant pastor at Christ Church in Nashville, Tennessee. The senior pastor, L. H. Hardwick, had made a journey similar to mine many years before. He introduced me to pastors and writers of the broader evangelical community. I joined the National Association of Evangelicals, paid due respects to Wheaton, Illinois, and subscribed to *Christianity Today*. I entered with earnest into the world of American evangelicalism.

WHAT IS AN EVANGELICAL ANYWAY?

Millions of American Christians call themselves evangelicals, but what does that mean? Most people reading this book will probably know that the heart of American evangelicalism is in Wheaton, Illinois. They will also know that its unofficial voice is *Christianity Today*, called *CT* by the initiated.

So we agree that evangelicalism exists; we're just not completely sure what it is! So if I can define "evangelical" to everyone's satisfaction I will achieve two things: (1) clarify an important term used in this book, and (2) achieve an automatic elevation to the Theological Hall Of Fame.

It will not be easy. "Evangelical" means a hundred different things. Pentecostals claim to be evangelical; independent Baptists say "no way!" Lutherans say they are evangelical; the Missouri Synod says most of them are not. The evangelicals say that the Southern Baptists are evangelical, the Southern Baptists say, "what's that?" Billy Graham includes some Catholics and Eastern Orthodox in the term; Bob Jones excludes Graham. There is considerable confusion about what "evangelical" means. Nonetheless, millions of American Christians use the term as a word that in some way describes them. We should try to define it.

The word evangelical, as it is used in the United States, expresses a certain unity between rather divergent groups who act more like cobelligerents than allies. Those who call themselves "evangelical" tend to be descendants of American frontier Christians of the last century. Those believers jettisoned their respective traditions, stripping down to their most common spiritual and cultural denominators. They passed the resulting spiritual culture of the frontier to their offspring.

By the end of last century and the beginning of this one, the major denominations were insisting on regularity while underground currents of resentful "old-time religion" begin reacting beneath the denominational surface. Outside the denominations, the converts of Moody, Sunday and a hundred lesser-known figures organized thousands of independent churches. The twentieth century saw the explosive growth of Pentecostalism—more "evangelicals." The same century also saw the bitter struggle between liberal and fundamentalist ideologies. This created yet more evangelicals. Today, the term "evangelical" may apply to conservative Presbyterians, independent Baptists, Pentecostals, fundamentalists and the conservative wing of Anglicanism. These all move together rather uneasily. They distrust one another; but they distrust others even more.

Even in their distrust, evangelicals have been working ever more closely together. The masses of evangelicals began growing weary of the distinctions between themselves. By mid-century they started forcing their leaders toward unity.

228 THE EMERGING AMERICAN CHURCH

Billy Graham dedicated Oral Roberts University and Pat Robertson introduced Francis Schaeffer to his television audience as a veritable Father of the Church. Jerry Falwell stopped publicly despising the charismatic movement (which was prudent since thousands of them were supporting his ministry). Then American politics gave evangelicalism a boost by identifying them as a voting block.

So I suppose we could say that American evangelicals are people who hold to the theology of the Protestant Reformation, especially to the doctrine of "salvation by grace alone," who usually have a "low" doctrine of the visible church, and who, as a rule, live in a subculture which has descended from frontier camp meetings and from the likes of Moody, Sanky and Sunday. In this sense, the Baptists, who are certainly fellow travelers, are evangelicals too, though they do not often use the term, simply because they have a longer tradition of their own. The Anglican evangelicals and conservative believers from the Reformed tradition agree with the centrality of salvation by grace alone, but are not part of evangelicalism's American subculture.

Properly speaking, all Christians who proclaim the gospel—the *evangelion*—are evangelicals. In practice, however, the word evangelical, like the words catholic and orthodox, takes on a more restricted meaning in popular speech than the dictionary calls for.

EVANGELICALISM'S HISTORICAL BACKGROUND

Evangelicalism, as we popularly speak of it in the United States, has its roots in the English Reformation. It is difficult for historians to say at what point English Catholics began to be Protestant. Well after Henry VIII broke with Rome, religious life continued with very little change.

After the publication of *The Book of Common Prayer,* one of the most far-reaching innovations in Christian history, the interest in renewal and reformation began in earnest. The Church of England moved slowly toward doctrinal change. A growing group of clergymen, called the Puritans, felt the change was simply not coming quickly enough. Some, called Separatists, were even more radical. They felt that the entire structure of English Christendom should be discarded. By the early 1600s there were separate congregations which are the recognizable ancestors of Baptists, Congregationalists and other dissenting groups.

In England and on the European continent, Protestantism took two different paths. One pointed toward the reasonable reformation of an existing church. The other path led to coming out of "corrupt Christianity" in order to form churches with no formal links with the past. The two movements are known as *magisterial Protestantism*, mostly national churches, and *radical Protestantism*. It was the more radical groups which began to move in large numbers to the North American continent, where they laid the foundations for our embryonic nation.

The colonies in New England were almost entirely founded by these new groups. The colonists were motivated by a "kingdom mentality." Here, in a new land, they planned to demonstrate what English society would be like if it were governed by reformed principles. Each generation put more distance between its understanding of Christianity and the medieval understanding of the faith. In time new groups of Christians were no longer baptizing infants, church buildings were built without altars (later the very word altar would come to mean "mourners' bench" to many evangelicals), and "Christian" could only signify one who had experienced a crisis conversion.

With the passing of time, American churches formed denominations, organized around the ideas of European theologians. The Westminster confession, Calvin's *Institutes*, and the experience of the Church in Scotland were particularly influential for the American Presbyterians. The Methodists came, too. They represented an entirely different strand of English Christianity, one that in many ways diverged less from Anglicanism than the other American Protestants. Methodists particularly made an impact on the western colonial frontier, as we have seen.

The Protestants of continental Europe brought other influences to the Americas. Lutherans from Scandinavia and Germany immigrated in increasing numbers. Mennonites, Quakers and Huguenots came in different waves, and at different times. As Americans moved from the coast, as generations arose with weaker ties to Europe, and as the various kinds of Christians met, read each other's writings and married one another, a common essence began to emerge. Revivals began to stress that one should be concerned with conversion, the experience common to all radical Protestants, and little or not at all with ecclesiastical tradition.

By last century there were community churches, Christian meeting houses not easily categorized under traditional denominational labels. "Evangelical" is a convenient way to describe them. This century, too, has seen enormous growth of "nondenominational" churches.

As Americans have become mobile, migrating from city to city and from coast to coast, they have abandoned all pretense of loyalty to particular Christian denominations. They have forced each group to incorporate elements from other traditions that are to their liking. The nonaligned churches have been able to accommodate this demand with less turmoil than those under extra-local authority, and this adds to the number of those who label themselves as evangelicals.

A PERSONAL ENCOUNTER WITH EVANGELICALS

A few years ago, some of our church leaders decided to attend a conference of the National Association of Evangelicals in Buffalo, New York. The trip would do us good, we thought. We were an isolated independent congregation, and we needed fellowship and accountability. Where better to go than to a convention of people whose doctrinal and ethical reputation we respected?

We were delighted to be among people who believed the Gospel. And they did. They proclaimed it night after night. Had it not been for the excellent preaching (excellent con-

tent-wise that is; we were already convinced so they did not have to fight for our attention as they would have to do if they were preaching to unchurched people or even their own children) we would have been hard-pressed to justify the price of our tickets to the conference. The "preliminaries" (a hateful word) were boring and pointless. The music was neither inspiring nor fun. People mumbled their way through a few songs, heard a few announcements about this and that, and then settled down to hear the preaching. After that we hit the lobbies.

I have never returned to an NAE convention. I like the people. I believe in what they preach. I respect the issues for which they stand. Why won't I go back? Because I am a baby boomer, and they bored me, and because I do not believe such goings on will win my country to Christ.

> **EVANGELICALISM AS A *CULTURE* IS DEAD, AND TRYING TO PRESERVE THAT CULTURE IS HARMING THE PROCLAMATION OF THE GOSPEL . . . .**

Don't misunderstand me. I'm not asking them to become Pentecostal. They are already overrun with Pentecostals, and that hasn't helped them. I am not asking them to adopt the liturgy either. I am just saying that evangelicalism *as a culture* is dead, and trying to preserve that culture is harming the proclamation of the gospel which they probably understand better than anyone else.

Fortunately, other things are going on in the evangelical world besides preachers' conventions. There are the parachurches, one of the most innovative structures ever devised to serve the Church. These agencies do a vast amount of gospel work, from Bible translation and food distribution to church growth agencies and publishing firms. These non-aligned agencies are powerful tools. They are like a fleet of speed boats that rush around the globe doing this and that, running messages and supplies between the troops of the army of God.

They are run by independent-minded captains who sometimes take orders from no one. They are feisty and fierce. But they are on our side, and when the chips are down, we can depend on them. The parachurches represent one of the greatest offerings the evangelical world brings to the emerging American church.

THE PARACHURCHES

Kenneth Scott Latourette, late dean of Yale University, Donald McGavern and Ralph Winter have all contributed ideas which together became the pillars of the American church growth movement. One thing they have all addressed is the amazing synergy through history between two types of church structure. Winter calls them the modality and sodality. Evangelicals usually call them "church" and "parachurch."

Winter defines *modality* as the parish church. The parish church is primarily concerned with pastoring its people. Its leaders help the people through the various stages of life: dedicating them, marrying them and burying them. It attempts to teach them the ways of the Lord. The *sodality* he defines as a tight-knit group organized around a single purpose.

In *The Two Structures of God's Redemptive Mission*, Winter says that the parish church was responsible for almost none of the growth of the church in Europe during its expansive stage. He says that it contributed almost nothing to Bible translation, nor to other academic pursuits, and founded almost no hospitals or orphanages. All these things were carried out by what he calls the sodalities, which in Europe were usually monastic orders.

On the other hand, wherever the parish church did not cooperate with the sodalities, the progress was rarely consolidated. Any gains made were quickly lost. Monastic orders carried on Bible translation and copying, but the churches had to provide the recruits to keep the job going. Monasteries won new groups to Christ, but local churches had to organize the people into communities.

In the ongoing synergy between church and parachurch, the sodality has the option of keeping highly qualified and motivated people, but the churches must deal with the whole flock (or in the language of the Lord's parable, those who produce 30, 60 and 100 percent.) The sodality has the luxury of remaining trim, quick and efficient, so by contrast it often seems more exciting and innovative than the local church. But the long-term security and stability depends on the local church.

In short, history teaches us that without sodalities there is little advance, and without local churches there is no consolidation. Parachurches are the harvesters, and local churches are the granaries.

After the Reformation, Protestantism did not continue monastic life. So for 200 years, Protestants remained a phenomenon of Northern Europe. Roman Catholics used Protestant lack of interest in the Great Commission as proof that they were not the true Church.

Finally, of course, Protestants did began to take seriously the great commission. However, it was not the churches which undertook the work of missions, but parachurches, groups led by fiery young dreamers who were almost always opposed by the leaders of the churches. Looking back on what has been accomplished, only God knows what the world would look like now in terms of the Great Commission without Wycliffe Bible translators, the Billy Graham Association, China Inland Mission, the Navigators, Youth With a Mission and the World Bible Society. Even the YMCA is a product of parachurch work!

Protestants have had a difficult time, as Winter points out, with the spiritual legitimacy of the sodality, or parachurch. We can't decide if they are a help or a hindrance to the local church. On a whole, the Roman Catholics have done much better than we at managing the synergistic relationship between the sodality and modality. They have at least allowed a structure to evolve that puts creative tension, as opposed to destructive tension, between parish church structure and the various monastic orders.

At any rate, we have a job to do in our nation that involves no less than the reevangelization of our people. As we have been discussing in this book, while a vast majority of Americans claim Christian faith, the faith they actually live often has little content. In many ways it is reasonable to fear that viable Christian faith in the United States is a generation removed from total extinction. We can't be about business as usual.

But a local church simply is not flexible enough in its structure to do the work at hand. The need demands vision; the strong suit of the local church is stability and teaching. The local church must spend an enormous amount of energy on its own facilities and the maintenance of its own internal life. It rarely has enough energy left to dream, much less to launch out and do what must be done. We must have vigorous and ethical parachurch structures to mobilize our forces.

Among Protestants, the evangelicals have developed the parachurch into an art form. The free enterprising atmosphere in American evangelicalism has set free an amazingly productive network of interrelated agencies dedicated to spreading the gospel.

There is a down side to this religious free enterprise, though. Unfortunately, the parachurches have often been successful at the expense of the local church. Thousands of evangelicals live out their spiritual lives outside of a regular relationship with a community of faith. Because of this, American evangelicalism demonstrates a lack of inner coherence and authority that is leaving many evangelicals disillusioned and empty, as we will see in our next chapter.

CHAPTER 13

FROM ILLINOIS TO ISTANBUL IS A LONG, LONG WAY

Gordon Walker, an Orthodox priest, used to be a Baptist pastor. He is a good example of just how disillusioned many people feel about the state of American evangelicalism, and what they are willing to do about it.

In 1963, Walker was the young pastor of a growing Baptist church in Xenia, Ohio. He was also Chairman of Evangelism for the Greater Dayton Association of Baptist Churches. That same year, Walker left both his pastorate and the association to join Bill Bright's Campus Crusade For Christ. Walker had a global vision and he was ready to expand his world. He had no idea just how much he would be stretched before his quest ended.

He worked hard for that organization, traveling from campus to campus, converting students to Christ. But Walker was troubled. He and others on Bright's staff began to feel that evangelicalism was adrift, that the parachurches were more part of the problem than the solution. They began to feel that they were without roots. In 1968 this resulted in several leaders leaving Campus Crusade. Walker was one of them.

THE EVANGELICAL ORTHODOX

After leaving Campus Crusade, Walker moved to a farm near Mansfield, Ohio, which he called "Grace Haven." Young people came from all around to be converted and instructed in the Christian faith. Walker was thrilled with the zeal of his converts, but continued to be troubled over what he represented. He began to contact ex-Campus Crusade staff members with whom he could share his feelings. In 1973, in Dallas, Texas, he met with about seventy of them. They expressed similar concerns.

In 1974, a number of these old friends met at the farm of Peter Gillquist, the former Big 10 Regional Director for Campus Crusade and well-known evangelical writer. There at Grand Junction, Tennessee, a consensus began to develop. For the next several years, seven leaders of the group met quarterly for a week at a time to discuss theology and church history. By 1979, they were ready to form a very new kind of denomination in American religion, one dedicated to the establishment of an America branch of Eastern Orthodoxy.

Of course, other Orthodox Churches had existed in the United States for a long time. But this denomination was not Greek, Russian or some other ethnically defined church. It was an "American" church—with evangelical roots. They organized under the name The Evangelical Orthodox Church, and chose Peter Gillquist as their presiding Bishop. Gordon Walker became the Bishop of the Nashville Diocese.

I attended their Holy Trinity Church, now St. Ignatius, on August 17, 1986, which is located on a farm on the outskirts of Nashville, called the St. Athanasius Christian Community. The group had built a lovely place of worship, a building that architecturally expressed their theology. Throughout the building were hints of Byzantium, but also the undeniable influence of the common evangelical church one may see anywhere in rural America. The icons were few and tasteful; an admirable painting of Christ and his Apostles was just behind, and above, the altar. The church used St. John Chrysostom's liturgy, but interspersed it with hymns from both evangelical and Orthodox origins. As the liturgy began, musicians skillfully played on guitars the African-American spiritual, "Let Us Break Bread Together." Both Baptists and Orthodox would certainly have found common ground in the service.

Bishop Walker's homily was an exegesis of Scripture, like a sermon one would hear in any evangelical church. The worshippers, a yuppie constituency of about fifty adults, followed his message in their Bibles. Some raised their hands in charismatic fashion. The influence of Russian Orthodoxy, too, was obvious in the choir's polished musical responses. Convergence was evident in everything: convergence of East and West, of Orthodoxy and evangelicalism, and of the old and new American culture.

In 1985 the EOC suffered two set backs. In June of that year, the Bishops traveled to Istanbul to meet with the Ecumenical Patriarch, Dimitrios. He had little interest in receiving the American Church into his fold. They were told to continue their dialogue with the various ethnic branches of Orthodoxy in America, but were given no definitive hope. Later that year the National Association of Evangelicals denied the EOC membership in that body as well. Both the evangelicals and the Eastern Church seemed to be saying that the EOC was neither evangelical nor Orthodox. Just as a bridge belongs to neither shore, it appeared that the EOC could belong to neither East or West if it attempted to belong to both.

In 1987, however, the EOC was received into the Antiochian Orthodox Archdiocese. The American prelate, Metropolitan Philip Saliba, with full support of the Patriarch of Antioch, Ignatius IV, scandalized many Eastern Christians in the United States by joining hands with the Evangelical Orthodox. Metropolitan Philip justified his actions with an appeal to the decision of the apostle Peter to baptize the Roman Cornelius and his household (see Acts 10). It was a move that seems designed to have a great impact on both Orthodox and evangelical Christians in this country. The Orthodox are extraordinarily conservative, so this must be seen as a major move toward the establishment of an American Orthodoxy, with roots in American spirituality.

All the EOC churches did not go into the Antiochian community. Some felt that the move to "canonical" Orthodoxy destroyed their ties to the evangelical world, and thus seriously hindered their vision for liturgical renewal among American Christians. One pastor said it was as though one side of the bridge they had been trying to build had been blown up. One of the EOC churches holding this opinion was the assembly in Illiopolis, Illinois, pastored by Bishop Jensen. That assembly, along with the other dissenting EOC congregations, has since reached out to a broad section of evangelicals and Pentecostals now on a similar path.

As the Orthodox Churches in Eastern Europe continue to grow in number and influence due to their regained freedom from communism, and as growing numbers of American evangelicals reach for their roots, Eastern Orthodoxy will likely influence more and more American Protestants, particularly those of independent evangelical churches.

A growing number of young evangelical leaders believe that the Eastern churches have developed a theology in their long history which will be helpful in dealing with the emerging new culture of our country. Orthodox theology presupposes the mystical longing of a generation like ours. So while it is unlikely that most evangelicals will convert outright to the Eastern Church as the EOC has done, it is probable nonetheless that the new road between Illinois and Istanbul will see a growing amount of traffic as the years go by.

ON THE ROAD TO CANTERBURY

Walker's story and that of his EOC colleagues is hardly unique. In 1989, an Assembly of God congregation in Valdosta, Georgia, joined the Episcopal Church. The 400-member congregation retained its Pentecostal music and preaching style while embracing the liturgy of *The Book of Common Prayer*. Church of the King represents a very strong movement among American baby boomer Pentecostals toward liturgical worship in general, and toward the Episcopal church in particular. Had it not been for the extreme theological liberalism which has overtaken many quarters of that denomination, it is likely that thousands would have already joined the charismatic wing of the Episcopal Church.

The Anglican tradition contains elements that appeal to many American Christians at this time. It offers apostolic roots within the Anglo-Saxon culture. It is both Protestant and "catholic." It has a strong charismatic wing. It has a strong evangelical tradition. It has a Celtic strain, a mystical side, which stretches from antiquity. It is perhaps the closest thing we have to a national church.

Many of those watching on the sidelines believe that the liberal leadership of the Episcopal Church in this country is about to pass from the scene, and that the younger priests who replace them will likely be more orthodox and evangelical.

Meanwhile, in June of 1992, a group of charismatic leaders organized *The Charismatic Episcopal Church*. In their opening declaration, they proclaimed themselves to be "sacramental, reformed, evangelical and charismatic." That seems to cover all the bases! They are currently in dialogue with the continuing Episcopal churches, groups that are conservative breakaways from the American Episcopal Church. So they seem serious in their stated intention of leading charismatic and evangelical congregations into some sort of unity with the ancient Celtic and Anglo-Saxon roots of the Anglican tradition.

What is going on?

There seems to be a growing feeling of historical bankruptcy among noncharismatic evangelicals, as well as a hunger for a worship service that is more than "preliminaries." Among Pentecostals, there is a growing desire to understand the faith and to come to grips with Christian heritage. An encounter has begun between churches born on the American frontier and ancient forms of the faith. It will change them both.

A HISTORICAL BACKDROP

Many Christians around the world would find it incredible that I think it necessary to introduce the history of the liturgical churches to American Christians! After all, the vast majority of Christians around the world are liturgical. Nonetheless, many parts of the United States do not have large numbers of these ancient types of Christians. So let's take a moment to look at some of them, and how they came to this country. We will examine in more detail those who are less known to most American Christians. (The space devoted to discussing each group is not based on my idea of their importance, but on how remote and unknown I think they are among American evangelicals and Pentecostals.)

First we should recognize that liturgical Christians have several shared concerns. They all organize their worship services around ancient patterns derived from Judaism. The sacraments form an essential part of their religious experience. They hold to some version of the doctrine of *apostolic succession*—the belief that legitimate Christian ministry is handed down by ordination at the hands of a bishop or presbytery, and has been since the time of the apostles. They govern themselves above the local level, usually under the authority of a bishop. They give great respect to the writings of the Church Fathers, the creeds, and Christian tradition in general. They believe that the visible Church consists of all who are baptized into faith, regardless of their spiritual "experience."

ROMAN CATHOLICISM

With over 900 million members, the Roman Catholic Church is by far the world's largest group of Christians. There are many historical reasons for this which we simply cannot go into here. Rome was one of the earliest centers for the Christian Church—St. Paul wrote a masterpiece to be read by Christians there—and it was the most important and powerful city in the empire. The Roman Church was the only one in the western part of the Mediterranean to have been founded by apostles. More than anything, though, the Roman Church has always been the most missionary-minded of all the ancient seats of Christianity. In every generation since its founding, Christians have gone out under Roman authority to evangelize the world.

After the Eastern and Western churches broke fellow-ship, all of Western Christendom looked to Rome as the undisputed center of authority. The Bishop of the Roman Church became to them the voice of God upon the earth. After the fall of the Caesars, the Roman Bishop and his clergy also assumed secular power and came to rule, directly or indirectly, much of Europe.

After the Reformation, the missionary energies of the Roman Church were directed toward the ends of the earth. Roman Catholicism was first established in what would later become the United States through Spanish and French missionaries. Missions were planted among native people and colonists throughout the vast holdings of New Spain and New France, 150 years before any sizable work by Protestants in New England.

> **TODAY THE ROMAN CATHOLIC CHURCH IS THE LARGEST CHRISTIAN DENOMINATION IN THE UNITED STATES.**

The first English-speaking Roman Catholic work of any size was located in Maryland, a colony founded as a refuge for Roman Catholics who were ill at ease in their native England. Substantial mission work also began in western Kentucky before the Revolution. After the Revolution, wave after wave of European immigration brought millions of Roman Catholics into the country. These people were members of numerous ethnic groups. However, unlike the Eastern Orthodox Church in America, the Roman Catholics established an American episcopacy, organizing their church by parishes and dioceses rather than by ethnic groups. This was a far-sighted decision. Today the Roman Catholic Church is the largest Christian denomination in the United States.

That fact would have amazed the English Fathers of our nation. The English colonies were mostly organized by radical Protestants who were trying to escape the Protestant Church of England because they felt it retained too much of its Roman heritage. They also feared the Catholic French and Spanish who had beat them to North America a century and a half before. So American Protestants have a long history of fear and irrational antagonism toward Roman Catholics.

Having said that, the differences between Catholics and Protestants are real, despite the drastic changes made by Rome during Vatican II. Dealing with the foolish fear does not mean ignoring all the real differences.

THE EASTERN ORTHODOX CHURCH

There was a time when Eastern Christianity was nearly on par with the West. Many of the great Church Fathers were there. Christendom's greatest building was the Hagia Sofia in Constantinople. The birthplace of the Savior was within its jurisdiction. A moment's reflection on words like disoriented and orientation demonstrates how our ancestors regarded the East. We still pay linguistic tribute to the birthplace of our faith. All Christian liturgies retain the Greek words *Kyrie Eleison*, *Amen* and *Alleluia*. Many a local charismatic church in many an American town carries the name *Maranatha*. Pentecostals read magazines called *Logos* and *Pneuma*, and go to seminaries called *Rhema*. The Greek influence on the Christian faith is branded into the Christian consciousness.

Christian East and Christian West chose different paths from the earliest centuries. The old battle between Roman Law and Greek Philosophy continued after the Christian Era began. The West emphasized doctrinal definitions; the East discussed metaphysical experience. The West pushed for uniformity and monarchy; the East developed plurality and decentralization. The West worried about church government; the East discussed proper worship. The West theologized about salvation; the East theorized about becoming divine. Western theologians were lawyers; Eastern theologians were artists. As in the Empire before it, the Christian Church saw its Latin West and its Greek East drift steadily apart.

Constantine's flight to Byzantium helped widen the gap. After he built Constantinople, the cities of Rome and

Constantinople divided the soul of the empire between them. In time, Constantinople became a center for the Christian East. A great civilization flourished around the Eastern empire for centuries. After numerous invasions and occupations, the Christian East became a shadow of its former glory.

Today, Eastern Orthodox Christianity, the spiritual descendant of the Eastern empire, is still a force to deal with, with its 350 million adherents. The two largest communities of Orthodox believers are the Greek and the Russian churches, the ones which form the backbone of Eastern Orthodoxy in America.

ORTHODOXY IN AMERICA

One of the greatest Orthodox achievements was the conversion of the Slavs. The roots of that victory go back to Cyril (826-69) and Methodius (815-85), two brothers from Thessalonika. The two were excellent linguists, fluent in Hebrew, Arabic, Greek and Slavonic. They translated the Scriptures and liturgical works. For that purpose they developed what we call the Cyrillic alphabet, the basis of modern Russian script. Their work soon spread throughout most of the Slavic peoples. Slavic culture so merged with Orthodoxy that it is difficult to determine where one ends and the other begins.

After the revolution of 1917, the state attempted to obliterate the religious soul of the nation. Thousands of priests disappeared and hundreds of churches were closed. Seminaries ceased to exist and every effort was made to stop any type of religious instruction. In the Second World War, Stalin found a need for the Old Church, that of rallying the nation. He allowed a limited revival of religious life and, since then, the church has steadily grown in power. In 1980 there were 70,120,000 communicants in the Russian Orthodox Church. After the fall of communism, the church continues to revive and rebuild.

The Russian Church became the first Eastern Christians to evangelize what was to become the United States. John Venianoff, a native of Siberia, began a mission in Unalaska, an

Aleutian Island, in 1824. He translated a catechism, a book on Bible history, and portions of the New Testament into the Aleut language. Between 1841 and 1860, he moved to the capital of Alaska under the Russian government, Sitka, and baptized several thousand people. He built his work on earlier efforts which began in the mid-1700s but had remained struggling outposts. However, Eastern Orthodoxy in the United States grew for the most part by Eastern European migration to North America.

To describe the Eastern Church in America is no easy thing. The American scene is so confusing because all its branches are represented here by an ethnic community. There are rival claims to authority even within these. The three million Orthodox in this country are divided into the Antiochian Orthodox Churches, the Byelorussia Autocephalic Orthodox, Greek Orthodox of North and South America, The Orthodox Church in America, Romanian Orthodox Episcopate of America, Russian Orthodox Church in the Americas, Russian Orthodox Church outside of Russia, Serbian Orthodox Church, Ukrainian Orthodox Church of the USA, and twenty more small Orthodox bodies totaling no more than 4,000.[29]

Many younger American Orthodox hope for an American Patriarchate, where the tenants of Orthodoxy will be their main mark of identification rather than ethnic subcultures.

THE UNIATE CHURCHES

The Uniate Churches have roots in the various Eastern traditions and maintain the heritage, liturgy and apostolic succession of the Eastern bodies, but who recognize the Bishop of Rome as the head of the church. Uniate Churches were born from schisms in the Eastern bodies at the time of the Crusades. Now there is a Uniate Church that corresponds to almost every Eastern body, the largest of them being the Ukrainian Catholic Church.

For the most part, they maintain their patriarchs, who, despite having sworn loyalty to the Pope, function independently of normal Roman structure. The most outstanding divergence from their Roman brethren is that Uniate priests, like Orthodox priests, may marry. All the Uniate bodies are represented in the United States.

ORIENTAL CHRISTIANS

A number of Eastern Christian churches resulted from doctrinal strife in the early centuries of the Church. They do not recognize the Patriarch of Constantinople nor the decisions of certain church councils. Five major churches comprise this family: Armenian, Coptic, Ethiopian, Syrian and Syro-Malabarese (sometimes called the Church of St. Thomas, or Mar Thoma). The global membership of the Oriental Orthodox in 1985 stood at approximately 30,531,500.

All branches of Oriental Orthodoxy may be found in the United States, mostly in large metropolitan areas.

ANGLICANISM

The history of Christianity in the British Isles is a matter of much dispute. There have been Christians there since at least the third century, though there are legends of a first-century Christian community at Glastonberry, in southwest England.

The first Christians were no doubt Roman soldiers who practiced their faith in London and other Roman centers. The native Celts became Christians early on, and established a church which stood long enough to resist the church structure brought by Roman missionaries a few centuries later. The Roman structure at last won the day, though elements of the earlier Celtic spirituality remained within the English Church.

In 1534, King Henry VIII and the English parliament officially separated themselves from the authority of the Roman Church. Little by little, the Church of England forged its famous *middle way*, a church that believes itself to be both Catholic and Protestant.

Today one finds Anglican Churches wherever the British Empire has held sway. It retains the doctrine of apostolic succession and is governed by an ancient episcopate. It has four major streams, the *Anglo-Catholic*, which emphasizes the catholicity of Anglicanism; the *Evangelical*, which emphasizes its Protestant side; the *Broad Church*, which is theologically liberal, and the *Charismatic*. Some people refer to Anglo-Catholic Anglican worship services as "high church" and Evangelical Anglican services as "low church," terms which indicate the amount of religious symbolism used by each. It is not unusual for an Anglican (who is called an Episcopalian in the United States) to borrow from more than one stream, or for a single congregation to have members of each. At present, the Archbishop of Canterbury, the head of the English Church, is evangelical and charismatic.

> ● ● ● ● ● ● ● ● ● ● ● ● ● ● ● ● ●
>
> ## AT PRESENT, THE ARCH- BISHOP OF CANTERBURY... IS EVANGELICAL AND CHARISMATIC.
>
> ● ● ● ● ● ● ● ● ● ● ● ● ● ● ● ● ●

The Church of England came to North America with the English people who came to establish their colonies. In the part of the continent which became the United States, the English Church was greatly shaken by the Revolution. Many of the priests and church members fled to Canada. But as tension subsided, Anglicanism, known in this country as the Protestant Episcopal Church, took its place among the great denominations of the nation.

It has been the church most often represented among upper classes of Americans. Many prominent American leaders have been Episcopalians.

THE REFORMED CHURCHES

We should mention the Reformed tradition here, even though it is not usually listed with the churches we have been discussing. However, the Reformed tradition, like the Anglican church, is an attempt to retain catholicity while, as the name implies, *reforming* the visible church.

This tradition has its roots in the magisterial Protestant churches of Europe and in the Puritan movement which was so influential in the founding of this nation. Reformed churches replaced the bishop with a presbytery, essentially creating a collective episcopate, rather than putting the power in the hands of one individual.

Reformed churches depart in many ways from the older churches, but they retain to some degree the high importance of the sacraments, the creeds and liturgical worship. Churches that are part of this tradition include the various Presbyterian bodies (from English and Scottish roots), the Reformed Church of America (Dutch in origin), and, in the case of Swedish Lutherans, even the historical episcopate.

LUTHERANS

The Lutheran Churches are the various spiritual off-spring of the Protestant Reformation in Germany, Holland and Scandinavia. Lutheranism comes to our country through immigration from those countries. It retains the liturgy, the centrality of the sacraments, and in some cases, even the historical episcopate.

CONVERGENCE

Many people from a high church background are amazed at the new evangelical and Pentecostal interest in liturgy. Believers from liturgical backgrounds often leave their churches because they find them to be detached from life and emotionally cold. We should listen to them. Liturgy and ritual doesn't have to be dead, but it often is. There is no need to convert to church systems which have become geriatric societies. What has meant death to them may well mean death to us. What *will* work is convergence, the blending of our strengths.

As we have seen, many Americans from the independent charismatic and evangelical churches are looking at these traditions now. It remains to be seen whether they will join one or more of these bodies, or whether they will be content to simply borrow certain elements from them. Likely, most will incorporate those elements of the liturgical tradition which seem helpful into their own worship, and will perhaps move as well toward a church government modeled after what they learn from the liturgical churches.

A growing body of resources is emerging to help those Christians in the various traditions who wish to learn from their neighbors. *Touchstone* magazine[30] is a delightful scholarly journal that ministers to both conservative believers within the liturgical expression of the Church and to interested evangelicals and Pentecostals. *First Things*[31] is a magazine with a more political and social slant that also caters to the growing conservative American ecumenism. Robert Webber, well known Wheaton College scholar and writer, has released two works that speak to the growing convergence. His book *Signs of Wonder* addresses the charismatic/liturgical encounter, and his seven-volume *Encyclopedia of Christian Worship* catalogs the movement in all its phases, inside and outside the historical denominations. Even the gospel music industry has begun to respond to the expanding musical tastes of the converging churches.

Thousands of independent American congregations of both the noncharismatic and charismatic variety are experiencing a revival of interest in the Church Fathers, church history and liturgy. We are likely to see a growing sacramental understanding of spirituality that will sacrifice neither Protestant beliefs such as justification by faith nor cultural accoutrements such as American baby boomer music!

The African-American church, Pentecostals and evangelicals have encountered ancient Christian tradition. The stage is set for an amazing movement, a *conservative* Christian ecumenism! This growing convergence will be a powerful influence upon the emerging American church well into the next century.

PART 4
······················

THE EMERGING
CHURCH

CHAPTER 14

• • • • • • • • • • • • • • • • • • •

THE TRIUNE
CHURCH

*When all is said about the divisions of Christendom,
there remains, by God's mercy, an enormous common
ground.* — *C.S. Lewis* [22]

In June of 1988, I was invited to travel to the Soviet Union with a group of young people from a Presbyterian church in Atlanta, Georgia. The group was to sing at various communist gatherings, including the famed Artec camp outside Yalta. I and three friends from Christ Church took advantage of the invitation to deliver Bibles and study materials to Christians in each city the group was to visit. Two occasions on that trip stand out in my memory.

Before we left Frankfort, Germany, for Moscow, someone gave me a large ceremonial Bible with the Russian cross imprinted on the cover. I put it with the rest of the Bibles in the massive speaker case we had filled with literature. When we arrived in Moscow, the customs officials waved us through. They did not check the sound equipment. The Bibles were safe. In my pocket were addresses of believers in each city I would visit, given to me by Peter Dayneka, president of the Slavic Bible Association. I was determined to take literature to evangelical and Pentecostal Christians. I did not have a clue what I would do with the large Orthodox Bible.

After prayer, I felt the Lord impressing me that the Bible was meant for a group in Tashkent, Uzbekestan, our second stop. Uzbekestan is a fascinating place that borders China, Pakistan and Afghanistan. Its inhabitants are overwhelmingly Muslim.

I had never before been in a Muslim nation. I didn't know much about what one should or should not do there, but I knew that we had a divine appointment.

We were not free to look for a church until the last day we were in the city of Tashkent. In our broken Russian we asked several taxi drivers where one was. All of them said that there was no church in Tashkent.

We prayed. The Holy Spirit impressed upon us that the next driver would take us to the church. He did. He dropped us off on a back street and told us to go through the gate he pointed out to us. We tried to pay him, but he just smiled. "Go in peace!" he said in English.

We had hardly gotten over the shock of the taxi driver when we went through the gate. There, hidden from view on the other side of the wall, was a church. The courtyard around it was filled with old men and women. A man who watched the gate came and asked our business there. I said "*U meye Biblia* (I have a Bible)." I showed it to him. He took the Bible and lifted it up in the air. "*Bratye, eta Biblia* (Brothers, this is a Bible)," he said. They all crowded around and passed it over their heads, touching it as it passed. I was moved beyond words.

They took me to the back of the church where an old stooped priest with a long white beard was preparing for Divine Liturgy. They told him what had happened. He hugged me, kissed me on both cheeks, and then asked me to leave. Too many years of trouble would not allow him to believe that he could be safe around foreigners. I understood. I left with a sense of a mission fulfilled.

After we left the Orthodox, we walked until we found the Baptist church. We were received there with great kindness and left literature there as well.

Our next stop was Tbalisi, Soviet Georgia. Few places I have visited in the world have left such an impression on me. Georgians are a most gracious and hospitable people.

One evening in Tbilisi, we decided to look for a place to worship. We walked to an Orthodox church we had seen earlier, but to our disappointment, they were just concluding their service.

However, a young man overheard us and asked us to walk with him. He took us a few blocks to a church which had been built in the sixth

> **THE SENSE OF AWE AND HOLINESS IN THAT PLACE CONTRASTED RATHER STARKLY WITH OUR "AUDITORIUMS."**

century on the ruins of one built in the fourth. We entered the ancient place and were struck with the contrast between that small, dark, place and our spacious, modern buildings back home. Yet, the sense of awe and holiness in that place contrasted rather starkly with our "auditoriums."

We knelt, not on carpet but on stone, and began to pray. We were alone, I thought, so we began to sing a worship chorus from home, "The steadfast love of the Lord never ceases / His mercy never comes to an end." We were thanking God for the reopening just two weeks before of a church that had heard the voices of God's people in prayer for 1,400 years and was now hearing them again.

Then, suddenly, several women began to talk to us. They had come from nowhere. I could understand neither their Georgian nor their Russian. One of them spoke fairly good French.

"Saint Esprit," she said, "Je vois le Saint Esprit (The Holy Spirit, I see the Holy Spirit)."

"Yes, I replied. "We are Christians."

"Suivez-moi (follow me)," she demanded.

We followed, finally ending up at the residence of the Patriarch of Georgia. I thought that it would be nice to see the place, so I was delighted when we were invited in. They motioned for us to wait. In a while, I was shocked to see Patriarch Illia himself walk through the doors in a long flowing robe. We were stunned, but managed to rise to our feet.

"Please," he said in broken English, "sing." So we began to sing the choruses we had sung in the church. As we sang the charismatic chorus which consists of the one word Hallelujah, he pulled a handkerchief from his robe, buried his face, and wept like a child. Then he came to each of us, laid his hands on our heads, and prayed. The Holy Spirit was in the place.

As we walked back to the hotel, one of the young Presbyterian girls said to me, "What was that all about? I can't stop crying." I astonished my Pentecostal self by replying, "It is the Holy Spirit; we have been in the presence of God."

And so we had. In spite of all the strong feelings I had against ecumenism, what I had experienced there was the same presence of God I had known all my life. From that evening, several of the young people with whom we were traveling began receiving what Pentecostals call the baptism in the Holy Spirit, even though I had told them nothing about this experience. What was I going to do with that? It began to dawn on me that Orthodox, evangelicals and Pentecostals could find a common ground in the presence of the Holy Spirit.

American Christians have been forced to deal with religious diversity. Certainly in the past, a Swede knew only Lutherans and the occasional atheist. A Russian knew about unbelievers and Orthodox. The Spaniard knew about Catholics and Jews. But it has always been possible for an American to be a Methodist who is married to a Baptist, who has a Roman Catholic brother-in-law, and a sister who has recently converted to Adventism who will not eat bacon at the family reunion! Our plurality forces us constantly to deal with Christian division. It is no surprise that ecumenism has had its strongest base in the United States. We are forced to deal with the issue to maintain family harmony, if for no other reason.

Ecumenism is not new. Christians have yearned for unity for a long time. However, for most conservative Christians, including myself, modern ecumenism has been decidedly negative. Ecumenism means to us an attitude that sees doctrine as nothing, that believes absolute religious truth cannot be found and one man's religion is as good as another. It means apostasy, kissing up to the communists who terrorized God's people in the East and embracing every novel attack on the integrity of Holy Scripture and the tradition of the Church of Jesus.

Nonetheless, a new move is on among conservative Christians. We are beginning to believe that though our differences are real and must be faced, we can do so only after we recognize the common faith in Christ we share. Still, it is difficult for people who truly believe in truth to conscientiously find the sort of unity they can live with. I would like to offer a paradigm which I believes puts the issues in a new perspective.

SOME PERSONAL BACKGROUND

I, together with L. H. Hardwick, the founder and senior pastor, lead an assembly called Christ Church in Nashville, Tennessee. Every week I preach to the thousands of people who call our assembly their church home, and I teach classes relating to doctrine, worship and personal spiritual growth. I also am responsible for the pastoral ministries division, which includes the departments of missions, evangelism and benevolence. (I have excellent colleagues who do most of the real work. That is how I can write books!)

The responsibility of leading a major congregation has weighed heavily upon my spirit these past few years. Many smaller churches are influenced by what we do. I, and my colleagues in ministry, have taken this very seriously.

Our church was established 43 years ago as a Pentecostal congregation. Under the capable leadership of the founding pastor, the church moved from a rather sectarian posture, finally evolving into an assembly of people from every con-

ceivable Christian denomination. Together, we have had many
years to reflect on what each of us have brought to the church
from our own roots. If the Lord wills, and I am still responsible for leading Christ Church in the twenty-first century,
what sort of church will she be? How should she be accountable to her sister churches? Where is she going? Is her direction connected in any way with that of churches across this
country? These are the questions I and the other leaders of
the congregation will face. They are the questions all Christian churches and denominations should face.

The first question, the question every honest Christian
must ask, is: "Why are there so many churches and denominations?" The answer used to be obvious to me: all other
Christians, except my own kind (and sometimes some of them,
depending on my mood), were impostors and frauds. True
Christians were those who belonged to my denomination,
plus the few sincere souls in other groups who were ignorant
of the true path.

Things became more complicated as I began to believe
that all believers in Jesus Christ were members of his Church.
I had to face the fact that Christians act and believe in very
different ways, and they are attached to the ways they believe
and worship, yet continue in some sense to be united in
Christ.

The question of Christian unity became very important
to me and Christ Church, because we were almost entirely
disinherited from our own Christian tribe. While I continue
to value many things from my own parent denomination, it
denies fellowship to those who leave it. I and the other leaders
of Christ Church were forced to define ourselves apart from
our own roots. We searched for a spiritual resting place and a
new circle of friends, and in that search, we examined a wide
spectrum of theological and cultural expressions of Christian
faith. The journey has been rewarding and enriching.

Since the personality of our local assembly centers around
music and worship, that's where we were most impacted. We
expanded our understanding of worship. We started planning
our preaching and public reading of Scripture around the

common lectionary. We placed a greater importance on the celebration of the sacraments. We borrowed charismatic praise choruses. Now we are learning that how one worships sooner or later impacts one's theology.

While one may classify the various kinds of Christianity in several ways, we have come to see that in terms of *how we worship* Christians fall into three broad categories: liturgical, evangelical, and Pentecostal. Looking briefly at each will help us see how their convergence effects us all.

THE LITURGICAL TRADITION

The liturgical style of worship grows out of the ceremonies of the Jewish Temple. If you read certain passages in Exodus, Leviticus, Numbers and Deuteronomy, you will see many parallels with what one finds in a modern Catholic, Orthodox or Episcopal church. Water at the entrance for washing, special clothing for the ministers, bells, incense, set times and places for the public reading of Scripture—all those things are carry-overs from our Jewish heritage.

Of course, Christians disagree among themselves about how much of the Jewish style of worship *should* be carried over into the Christian era. We will not resolve that issue here, but we can see that there must have been some carry-over in the form of worship from the old to the new covenant. To use just one example, Hebrews 9:1 says, "the first covenant had also ordinances of divine service . . ." (KJV). The word "also" hints that early Christians followed a definite pattern of worship rather than a free and formless approach.

In a liturgical setting, God is primarily worshiped as Father. He is a king, seated upon the high throne of heaven. The church is his court and reflects his royalty and majesty. The model of biblical ministry for this part of the church is, of course, the priest. Liturgical Christians want us to revere God, and they use symbols, ritual and sacraments toward this end.

The liturgical side of the church has much to offer post-modern America. We are a people in great need of dignity and lift, and that happens as we properly approach majesty and awe. Worshipping God as a high and holy king tends to raise our sights to a higher plane.

A sacramental understanding of life is a transforming dogma. It pushes us to redeem things, events and people into consecrated instruments for God's use. The rites of the church underline the seriousness of vows and commitments. Understanding marriage as a sacrament, and surrounding the ceremony with the dignity due the occasion, changes a photo opportunity into a covenant rite. The importance of this is not that we wish to draw attention to the ritual, but that through the ritual we may underscore, in a way deeper than language, the reality which lies behind it. Marriage becomes something done by God in heaven rather than just by two humans upon the earth. As C. S. Lewis explains,

> When our participation in a rite becomes perfect we think no more of ritual, but are engrossed by that about which the rite is performed; but afterward we recognize that ritual was the sole method by which this concentration could be achieved.[33]

It is the responsibility of the church to respond to this human need because our call is to place "human experience in the bright light of the ultimate."[34] That means taking people to a point beyond good preaching and fine music, into the timeless space of eternity, where life is transformed by peering into the face of God. Only then will they truly "have tasted the good word of God, and the powers of the world to come" (Hebrews 6:5, KJV).

IS IT BIBLICAL?

From an evangelical standpoint, the issue of liturgy must be settled on biblical grounds. Does the New Testament allow us to worship this way, and even if it does, is it the way New Testament Christians worshiped? After studying this for some years, I have to answer yes to both questions.

I'm sure you will agree that worship in the Old Testament was liturgical. Exodus, Leviticus, Numbers and

Deuteronomy describe a very detailed procedure for sacrifice, architecture and vestments. Incense, water, blood, oil and even plants are frequently mentioned as being used in ceremonial ways. The question is, "Was this all done away with in the New Testament?"

That is an interesting question. We evangelicals assume that all the ceremonial aspects of the Old Testament were done away with in the New. But think about it for a moment. The book of Hebrews claims that Moses constructed the tabernacle according to a plan he saw in the heavenlies (see Hebrews 8:3-6). All that he instituted on the earth was merely a copy of the pattern he had seen in heaven. We get only a few more glimpses of heaven after that: Ezekiel and Isaiah claimed to have seen into heaven. Wasn't what they saw there still the same pattern of worship?

Only three New Testament people claimed to see heaven: Steven at his martyrdom saw Christ standing to receive him into glory (Acts 7:55-56), Paul was caught up into heaven in a vision, but tells us nothing of what he saw, and John the revelator. What did John see and describe for us in the book of Revelation? He saw the same eternal pattern of worship going on, with incense, bowing, prostration and altars. It can be argued that the apostle John was using metaphors. However, would an apostle, particularly one who lashes out against heresy in his epistles and whose whole life was devoted to establishing a New Covenant community, have drawn his metaphors and illustrations from a type of worship that was no longer legitimate? The stronger argument seems to be that since John was writing to Gentile congregations and assumed they would be familiar with the liturgical nature of what he saw in heaven, at least some of what he describes must have been compatible with the early Christians' own experience of worship.

If the liturgical model is an eternal, heavenly form, our next question then must be, "Should we attempt to worship on the earth the way they do in heaven?" That question begs for another: "Why not?" If that is the way worship is conducted in heaven, then it must be the way God wants to be

worshiped. It must be consistent with his nature. Why would
he be worshiped one way in heaven, instruct Moses that he is
to be worshiped that same way on the earth while the Old
Covenant is in force, but then decide that not only is it not
necessary but that it is even repugnant to be worshiped that
way during the next epoch of human history?

GNOSTICISM VS. THE CHRISTIAN VIEW OF MATTER

The evangelical reluctance to face the issue of liturgy has
many causes, one of which is a legitimate fear of idolatry.
Another, less noble, reason is a hateful view of matter. A
Christian view of the material world is that God created matter and that he delights in it. It was a heresy, called Gnosti-
cism, which made a spiritual goal of repudiating matter. The
Christian view is that matter should be redeemed.

Man lives in a three-dimensional world; spirit alone cannot sustain him. For example, we don't want platonic relationships in our marriages—we want flesh to touch. While it
is true that we are spiritual beings, and that matter by itself
cannot satisfy us, we usually prefer spirit with some matter on
it. We don't like ghosts, which is a spirit without matter. We
don't like a corpse, which is matter without spirit. We like
matter and spirit to be united. God made us that way. That is
why God became a man, after all. The incarnation is God
saying yet once more of the material universe he created, "It
is good."

So to say that spiritual worship does not require an element of the material is to reject reality, to reject the way we
are made. The sacraments are God's chosen vehicles for moving toward us as we move toward him in faith, because we are
material beings as well as spiritual.

When my wife kisses me, my inner, spiritual self responds! Just talking and reflecting on love together doesn't do
nearly as much for me. My spirit is united with my wife *by
means of physical contact.* Is it possible to have physical contact
without love? Yes, of course. Is it possible to have marital love
without physical contact? Yes, in unusual, usually tragic cir-

cumstances. But in a normal marriage the deepest sharing of love takes place when both elements—physical and spiritual—come together. The same thing happens in our worship of God.

Roger Grainger writes that:

> Any refusal, rejection, or mitigation of the incarnational, in which flesh and spirit are one in mutuality and wholeness, is a distortion of that very humanity which was assumed by the godhead in Christ's' incarnation.[35]

St. Augustine wrote in his *Confessions*, "Oh Christ, when you were in your mother's womb, you married the world to yourself, so that we who were mortal would not remain mortal forever." The incarnation changed forever the radical gulf between flesh and spirit, time and eternity, this world and the next. Eternity has invaded time, and is conquering it.

Rite, ritual and ceremony can be very dead affairs. So is a corpse. Grainger writes:

> A relationship must be held to proceed its outward signs and symbols. The prophets castigate emptiness and vanity, and quite rightly. The rite is an expression of spiritual fact, not any kind of substitute for that fact.[36]

The reason ritual has been dead in many Christian churches is not because ritual is evil, but because too often the participants have not had new life in Christ. They have had a "form of godliness but denying its power" (2 Timothy 3:5).

Ritual cannot satisfy our spiritual longing any more than a glass can satisfy our physical thirst. A glass is nice, however, when it has water in it. Otherwise I have to use my hands, which will work, but it is not nearly as satisfying. My physical being is constructed in such a way that a glass brings together my thirst with that which satisfies it.

Ritual can neither be praised nor blamed for spiritual power or the lack of it. It is one of the ingredients of spiritual life that, in its place, can be useful to us, and which at its best demonstrates something of the eternal nature of God. We need to stop being afraid of ritual; as Grainger observes, "the

prophets did not attack the use of ritual, but its misuse."[37]
The following quotes provide other helpful insights from
Grainger's book, *The Language of Rite.*

> . . . Ritual makes the most sense if it is regarded as a
> language, a code of communication. But it is a special-
> ized kind of language. This knowledge is experiential,
> and it is knowledge about three things: time, space, and
> relationships.[38]

> Rite is the language of the unthinkable.[39]

In a nonliterary age like ours, an age which processes
information through visual symbolism, the rites and ceremonies of the church are powerful tools, signposts if you will,
which can lead a generation into the presence of God.

THE EVANGELICAL TRADITION

The evangelical mode of worship also comes from Judaism. But evangelicalism draws its character from the synagogue instead of the temple. Evangelicals worship God
primarily as the Son, the Redeemer. Their primary goal in a
worship service is to explain what the Scripture means. Their
primary model of ministry is the rabbi. They want us to
understand God and his Word, and to realize that God is
close to us in the person of Christ.

The evangelical gifts are essential for our times. The
people of God need to understand the Scriptures and to have
a personal encounter with the Lord Jesus. When we confront
the Scriptures, our intellect is forced to explain the gap that
exists between modern life and thought on one hand and the
teachings of the Word of God on the other.

Not long ago a pastor of a Presbyterian church was talking to some of us who are exploring our heritage in the
historical church. He approved, but he had a warning.

"You cannot ignore the Reformation," he said. "You
can reject its teaching, after you have heard what it has to say,
or you can accept it. You cannot ignore it. The Roman Catholics were changed by it, and, of course, it gave Protestants

their birth. Both Roman Catholics and Protestants were greatly affected by the Reformation. One has to confront it to understand the church in history."

He is right. However, contrary to what many Protestants believe in this country, the reformers did not question the legitimacy of ritual and sacrament. All the reformers remained rather "high church" from the standpoint of, say, a Baptist. The liturgy was altered, but it was still the way Christians worshiped. As an example of this, the first church we know of where the altar (or communion table) was replaced by the pulpit at the center of the church was built in New England. It amazed even the Protestants who came from England. So if we are to hear the Presbyterian pastor's warning as he intended it to be heard, we have to put it in proper context. We have to know what the central issues of the Reformation were really about.

SOLA SCRIPTURA

The first issue of the Reformation was the centrality of the Holy Scripture as the bedrock of Christian faith. All major doctrines of the church had to be defensible by Scripture.

The Protestants found out very quickly that this could mean two different things. It could mean that Christians were free to believe anything and do anything not expressly forbidden by Scripture. Or, on the other hand, it could mean that Christians were forbidden to believe anything or do anything not expressly permitted by Scripture. Those positions don't sound terribly far apart, but when you follow the thoughts of each position, you can end up in very different places. The Churches of Christ believe you cannot play a musical instrument in worship because the New Testament doesn't say that you can. Anglo-Catholic Episcopalians, on the other hand, use incense in worship because it was an Old Testament practice which the New Testament does not forbid.

There is another difficulty with the doctrine that major church doctrines and practices must be based on Scripture. The church decided which writings belonged to the New Testament in the fourth century. How did the church for four centuries stand under the authority of the New Testament when its contents were not yet fully decided?

So the doctrine is not without its problems. Yet, for all of that, it is an important doctrine. Those early councils of the church were not writing the Bible; they merely decided which writings were genuine. The ones they decided belonged in the New Testament had already been honored as Scripture for centuries. So it is wrong to contrast the authority of the Church with that of Scripture. The Bible has judged the people of God from the beginning. The Church Fathers were submitting to the Scriptures, and merely separated from them what they felt did not belong.

> **IT IS IMPORTANT TO REALIZE THAT WE DO NOT REINVENT THE FAITH EVERY GENERATION.**

It is important to realize that we do not reinvent the faith every generation. We are called to preserve and defend the faith. The foundation on which we do this is the Holy Scripture.

Evangelicals take seriously the preaching and teaching of the Scriptures. Many Roman Catholic and Episcopal priests show next to no familiarity with the Bible. Their homilies (sermons) are delivered with no conviction, and are obviously a chore and even an afterthought, not the proclamation of the Word that the apostles took so seriously. This is the evangelical strong suit, their particular gift to the body of Christ. Pentecostals on one side and liturgical Christians on the other have much to learn from them.

The Pentecostals also preach the Scripture, of course, and often do it extremely well. The evangelicals, however, unfold the text. They labor with the Scripture and attempt to make it live in today's context. The Pentecostals have another gift, the power to motivate and inspire to action. (As a lifelong Pentecostal, I know why Walter Hollenwegger dedicated his book *The Pentecostals* to "the Pentecostals who moved me to love the Bible, and to the Presbyterians who taught me to understand it.") Evangelical instruction in the Word of God is an essential ingredient in the emerging church.

SOLA FIDE

Faith alone. This doctrine states that sacraments cannot save, priests cannot save and the Church cannot save. You are saved by grace through your faith in Jesus Christ and his sacrifice on the cross. This does not eliminate the importance of the sacraments; it defines it.

God has established water baptism as the place he chooses to meet a new believer in his or her first act of discipleship. To accept Christ and refuse the water is unthinkable. The two are so linked that Jesus is quoted as saying, "Whoever believes and is baptized will be saved" (Mark 16:16). Early Christians called people to Christ and then baptized them. Still, it is wrong to say that baptism saves.

We say in the wedding ceremony, "With this ring I thee wed." What do those words mean? Does it mean one is not married without a ring? Does it mean that the ring contains something which bonds the couple together? We know the words have meaning, and that the exchange of rings is important, but the meaning breaks down when we attempt to put it into words. In the same way, I acknowledge "one baptism for the forgiveness of sins" (The Nicene Creed), but I do not believe I can take a person's sins away by ritualistically putting them in water.

Our problem is rooted in our distrust of mystery. Everything cannot be explained by words. There is a time to simply trust.

We do need protection against idolatry, which is the sin of substituting symbol for that for which the symbol stands. If I see an arrow with the word Chicago written on it, I don't camp under the sign, thinking I am in Chicago. Rite, ceremony and sacrament will take us to Christ only if we approach them with the understanding that they are not the source of our salvation but only the signposts that point us there. We look *through* the minister, the sacrament and even the Scripture with faith in Christ alone to save us.

THE PRIESTHOOD OF ALL BELIEVERS

Again, the reformers did not mean by this doctrine that the priesthood was of no account. The priests, or ministers, stand between people and God in the sense that they speak to God on behalf of the people, and to the people on behalf of God. However, the reformers did object to the belief that the priests stood between people and God in the sense that people cannot get to God except through them. Ordained priests and ministers only do by vocation and special calling what all of God's people may do as the need arises. The New Testament did not abolish, but rather expanded the priesthood.

The reformers did not object to ordination, or to a set apart clergy. There are people with gifts and callings who, in the normal flow of church life, will administer the sacraments, pray for the sick, preach the Word and pastor the churches. We set them apart through the rite of ordination. This does not mean that any believer is prohibited from doing any of these things. For example, if a believer is in a Muslim country, and a Muslim comes to Christ, the believer can and should baptize the convert, serve communion or perform whatever rites are called for. A belief in the priesthood of the believer protects this right.

The ordained clergy should model what the entire body of Christ is called to do: serve, pray and proclaim the gospel to lost humanity. Christianity is not a spectator sport. All of the people of God are called to the work.

THE PENTECOSTAL TRADITION

Pentecostals descend from the prophetic tradition of ancient Judaism. They worship God primarily as the Spirit who moves among us right now to assist, convict and empower us. Their model of ministry is the prophet. The Pentecostal preacher does not primarily attempt to explain, but to proclaim. As in ancient Israel, this tradition needs no particular setting. In fact, there is a real ambivalence among them about having buildings at all. Pentecostals want us to *experience* God.

The Pentecostals force us to take seriously the promise of the Lord to be with us until the end of the age, and to confirm our words with "signs [that] will accompany those who believe" (Mark 16:17). However much abuse we have witnessed in all the miracle workers and healers, only the most opinionated person would be blind to the effectiveness of power evangelism. Their willingness to perform exorcism, for example, often opens doors for Pentecostals, particularly in the Third World. (Evangelicals, who also believe in a real devil, rarely do this; they believe in a disease without a cure.)

Pentecostals are warriors, and at their best they open the nations to hear the Word of God. The Holy Spirit is often truly present in their powerful celebration services. The people of God in all traditions are hungry for this sort of divine visitation.

Pentecostalism is an experience and a world view. It has no liturgy of its own. The gifts it treasures are available to all God's people in whatever tradition they find themselves. Roman Catholic priests can, and do, speak with tongues, pray for the sick and shout praises to God in a loud voice. Adventists, too, may pray in tongues, pray for the sick and shout praises to God in a loud voice. The tongues, healing and shouting do nothing to affirm or deny the doctrines of Roman Catholicism or Seventh Day Adventism. Doctrinal inquiry, as important as it is (and it *is* important) belongs to another arena all together.

I will not add an iota to the already prevailing disastrous notion that doctrine is not important. I will say, though, that if we are ever to find unity in the faith, we must first find unity in the Spirit.

I will say, too, that the Pentecostal revival, with all its faults, offers the Church the best opportunity for spiritual unity and renewal that she has had in the last thousand years. Pentecostalism brings life. It turns the dispassionate scholar into a proclaimer of truth, the meek and apologetic Sunday school teacher into a mentor for the next generation of Christians. It encourages the church member who has fallen in love with Christ and the gospel to say so without embarrassment.

Pentecostalism sometimes gives an excuse for the ignorant to remain ignorant, and that is a shame. It sometimes gives charlatans and frauds an opportunity to make mockery and merchandise of our holy faith. Pentecostalism is guilty of all that its detractors say of it, but it is responsible at the same time for much of the current growth of the kingdom of God around the world. It is difficult to see how any tradition of the church will survive without coming to grips in some way with the offerings Pentecostalism brings.

Pentecostals have come from the bottom of the social heap. They have often done things which embarrass and distress the older churches. But let us be careful: the Savior of the world was born in a haystack, and God's Church was placed on the broad shoulders of men who smelled of fish and seaweed. It is a pattern that God has used before, to bring some important thing to his people through the back door of the world.

Pentecostalism, like its Methodist parent, is a spiritual reawakening among the poor of the world, people who often feel they have no place among the established churches. It is a collection of spiritual orphans who have decided to claim their inheritance, and are just learning how. Their Father God did not abandon them, even when their mother church did. He is insisting that they have their place at the table, and to ensure that their brothers and sisters receive them there, he has given them gifts that his other children must have in order to survive. At the same time, he is insisting that the orphans get the chips off their shoulders and stop glorying in their ignorance, and that they learn the rules of his house and stop trying to burn it down.

WHAT DOES THIS MEAN?

All three of these traditions—liturgical, evangelical and Pentecostal—have something to give to the emerging American church, because they each represent an essential element of its divine nature. We serve a triune God, and this triune God reflects something of his own being through his triune Church upon the earth. Our God—Father, Son and Holy Spirit—is reflected through the different ways that his people praise him and carry out their unique calling.

If we put this in table form it looks something like this:

	Liturgical	Evangelical	Pentecostal
Worship tradition:	liturgical	evangelical	Pentecostal
Biblical source:	temple	synagogue	prophetic
Central activities:	sacrament ceremony	study exposition	celebration spontaneity
Worship focus:	Father	Son	Holy Spirit
Ministry model:	priest	rabbi	prophet
Central concern:	reverence	understanding	experience

Each stream has its own strengths and weaknesses.

The strengths of the liturgical tradition include things like roots, a sense of connectedness with the past and deep understanding of the incarnation and how the gospel impacts culture as well as individuals. Its weaknesses include a tendency toward enslavement to the past, a reverence of God to the point of alienation from him, a confusion of symbol with substance that can degenerate into idolatry and a focus on social issues to the detriment of individual faith in a living Christ.

Evangelical strengths include scholarship, a serious encounter with Holy Scripture, concern for orthodox doctrine and understanding the need to lead the individual to personal faith. Their weaknesses include a tendency to worship the Bible rather than the living God, a poverty of worship (in this tradition worship is often called the "preliminaries"), individual faith that can degenerate into autonomous individualism, a rather weak doctrine of the Church and a focus on the individual to the neglect of cultural and social issues.

Pentecostal strengths include an acute awareness of the presence of God, the expectation that God will act in contemporary and personal life, and celebrative worship. Their weaknesses include an addiction to orgiastic religious experience sometimes based on little more than experience itself, attraction to magic and a distrust or even hostility toward historical Christianity.

Our local church has been trying to come to grips with all of this. We remain committed to Pentecostal renewal. But Pentecostalism is no longer a complete picture of who we are.

A few years ago, our senior pastor led us through a five-year study of the book of Romans. During that time, we connected with our evangelical brethren. We became committed to evangelical doctrines such as justification by faith and the priesthood of all believers. Later we were influenced as well by the liturgical and sacramental parts of the church, and began to observe the church year: Lent, Advent, Pentecost, etc. We began preaching through the Scriptures every three years, using the common lectionary. We began teaching a higher view of the sacraments, believing that real power from God is released through the sacraments to do a work in us who believe. We began to use a catechism as our primary vehicle to incorporate members into church life. So while we are Pentecostal, we have not been shy about borrowing from other Christian traditions.

We believe that the Pentecostal movement is sent by God for the renewal of the Church, not to replace it. Our local assembly wishes very much to be an agent of renewal within the Church, but we are willing at the same time—no, we are more than willing, we are anxious—to receive the full heritage of the whole Church for ourselves and our children. We believe that our feelings are far from unique in our country.

We believe that the challenges of our nation demand a reassessment of the Church in this nation, and that it will take the gifts of the whole Church to meet these challenges. A triune Church may fit the bill.

CHAPTER 15

THESE BONES CAN LIVE!

One text that any Pentecostal preacher enjoys preaching is Ezekiel's vision of the dry bones (see Exekiel 37:1-14). That probably was my first sermon. The story is very instructive for the American Churches right now.

The liberal churches are dead and rotting. We all know that. Perhaps even they know it by now, if they read statistics. But many types of conservative churches are also dying, churches filled with people who love the gospel and who are dedicated to the Lord's work. Why are they dying? Why is the Independent Baptist movement, for example, which was once growing so quickly, running out of steam?

One group that has been trying to answer that question is the American church growth movement. It is one of the gifts of God to our nation at this time. I believe in it. It has been especially helpful in analyzing these patterns of growth and decline and in helping us understand what lies behind them. It has been used by the Lord to show us all sorts of sociological and cultural shifts, and how the churches should respond. So I will risk the ire of many whom I truly admire by saying that church growth alone is no indication of spiritual vitality. There are many megachurches that are wonderful communities in which to grow and nurture our children which nonetheless have little spiritual power, and which will not endure. They are like Ezekiel's bones after they had been assembled and had grown skin. They look healthy and they have all their parts, but they are not alive.

The first thing that needed to happen was for the emerging church to be reassembled. No movement has helped with that more than the church growth movement. It is American ingenuity at its best, a wonderful example of how the economic understanding of our country can be applied to the church community. I applaud it. I use the statistics and analysis it has gained.

Church growth does not give life, however. God did not ask Ezekiel, "Can these bones be reassembled?" He asked, "Can these bones live?"

Ezekiel was speechless. All he could respond was, "Oh Lord, you alone know."

Then God said to him, "Preach to these bones. Tell them that they are going to come back together. Tell them that flesh is going to come on them once more. Tell them that I will send the wind, and when the wind comes, breath will return to their lifeless forms."

The Lord told Ezekiel that the bones represented the household of faith. He told him that the dead forms were nothing but the remains of the past, all lying in the sun, hearing nothing, seeing nothing and caring about nothing. The man of God was charged to preach to them nonetheless.

Ezekiel reports, "So I preached as I had been told."

As he began to preach, the bones came together. The carpus found the metacarpus, the metacarpus found the phalanges, and the phalanges found the tarsus. The ilium found the pelvis, and the fibula found the tibia, while a humerus floated around looking for the bone of a shoulder. What a racket, clicking and clacking—it must have sounded like six million knuckles cracking at once! Finally, a host of skeletons was assembled.

The preacher kept preaching. As he preached, organs began to reappear in each of the skeletons. Lungs and lymph nodes, thyroid glands and bronchii, trachea and liver, stomach and colon, all found their distinctive place of service in the renewal of the body.

The preacher kept preaching. As he preached, he watched angel hands make the last finishing touches. The various levels of skin began to cover the recreated bodies. Ezekiel watched optic nerves growing from the brain, suddenly blooming like a flower come of age into the eye socket, preparing for vision. He watched it become the globe of an eye, complete with lens, iris, cornea and retina. Finally, he saw hair grow out of the bodies, adorning the creatures made a little lower than the angels.

So the preacher was surrounded by beautiful bodies, complete with all their parts. But they had no life. They just stared into space, seeing everything, understanding nothing.

That is where church growth takes us—it brings in the bodies. It does not mean they are alive.

Then God spoke once more. "Son of Man, preach to the wind. Say to the wind, 'Oh wind, thus saith the Lord Almighty, breathe into these bodies that they may live.' "

When the preacher called to the wind, the renewed bodies suddenly stood up and became a vast army.

WAITING ON THE WIND

Like Ezekiel, we must say to the American Church that there is a time to plan. There is a time to organize. There is a time to rehearse. There is a time to collect offerings. There is a time to prepare. There is a time for ritual and ceremony. But when we've done all we can do, there comes a time to wait until we are anointed from on high. There is a time to wait on the refreshing, to wait for the Spirit to breathe life into what we have done.

Jesus organized his church. He trained his disciples. He taught them the words of life. But when he was finished, he still had a group of fearful and failing men. That was the condition in which he left them: a pitiful crew made up of timid souls with no idea what to do next. It was these men whom he commissioned to evangelize the world, heal the sick, bind up the brokenhearted, set free the captives and proclaim the coming of God's kingdom.

"Before you go about the task," he said "wait in Jerusalem until you are anointed with power." Wait for the Wind. Watch what will happen to you and your mission when the Wind gets involved.

So they went to Jerusalem to wait for the Wind.

Pentecost was the day the disciples kicked into high gear. After that day the word began to spread everywhere. When Christians called on the Wind, their word was given life.

The American Church can preach, plan and organize, but only the Wind can give life. Without the Wind, we are just one institution among many. Without the Wind, we are a memorial society gathered to recall precious memories. Without the Wind, we wander aimlessly and without direction.

Look over the Christian landscape today. The leaders of the Presbyterian Church USA attempt to con their people into accepting wicked teaching. The Episcopalians are still considering ordaining homosexuals, no matter what God says about it. Bishop Spong writes openly about his personal apostasy, but remains a bishop, a man with the responsibility of overseeing the house of God. The Baptists keep fighting about who loves the Bible the most. The Pentecostals are preaching about how to get rich quick. The Methodists are embracing all sides at once and think their main concern ought to be removing from their hymnal any remaining hymns that may actually be singable. The Fundamentalists curse them all from the sidelines.

Someone in America needs to hear the voice of God crying to the prophet: "Do you believe that these bones can live?" Someone needs to call to the Wind.

Scripture says that there is an unseen spiritual world all around us. It tells us that this unseen world affects our everyday life. Either this is true or it is not. Either there is a God or there is no God. Either there are spiritual beings around us or there are not. Either Jesus rose from the dead and lives today, or he does not.

Why do we continue to halt between two opinions? At some point we have to decide whether we are believers or not. We cannot hold on at the same time to both a Christian and a secular world view. American Christians have done this. It has resulted in liberal Christianity on one hand, which accepts the logical consequences of the secular world view. (That is honest: the world view of the Bible is incompatible with secular humanism, and we ought to have the courage to become either honest believers or honest unbelievers.) On the other hand, we conservative Christians have been greatly affected by the secular world view, even though we have not been willing to follow it to its logical conclusion, as have our liberal counterparts.

We cannot continue to confess to believe in Christ and the Bible and at the same time reject the supernatural world that the Bible presupposes. I am saying that our churches need to be reconverted. They need the Wind of Pentecost to move over their tired, dead remains. I tell you, too, with all the conviction of my soul, that I believe that very thing will happen in the next few years. I tell you the Wind is coming, and when he comes, the bones will live.   Ez 37:1-14

Now before that happens, we must become aware of just how foolish we have been in the last generation or two. We have believed lies, and we have nearly been damned by those lies. I have a wonderful story that illustrates how this can happen.

WHY FROGS DON'T JUMP

A scientist had a government grant to study frogs. He had one frog in particular that was doing very well. He had trained the frog to jump at his command. He would say "Jump!" and the frog would jump. Then the scientist would mark down comments on the clipboard that he always carried.

One day the fellows at the Bureaucratic Center for the Control of Scientific Bureaucracy, the agency the government had assigned to oversee the project, sent new forms to the scientist. These forms contained a new category: MOBILITY

EFFICIENCY QUOTIENT, or MEQ for short. He was supposed to put numbers in that little box.

The scientist thought about it. He sure didn't want to be inefficient, so he came up with a new series of experiments. He decided to cut off the frog's legs, one at a time. Then he would have his Mobility Efficiency Quotient. So he cut off the first little front leg. After testing the frog, he determined that the MEQ for that day was –25%. His frog had lost a quarter of its mobility. A few days later, he cut off leg number two. Testing revealed a new MEQ of –50%. The frog was losing ground. The third leg was removed the following week, which reduced the Mobility Efficiency Quotient to –75%.

• • • • • • • • • • • • • • • •

THEY FIRST TOLD US THAT THE CHURCH NEEDED TO STOP BELIEVING IN HELL AND THE COMING JUDGMENT.

• • • • • • • • • • • • • • • •

Finally, the last leg was removed. The scientist then said to the frog, "Jump" but the frog just sat there. "JUMP," he shouted louder. But the little frog was immobilized. The new MEQ was –100%. The scientist had to fill out something under "comments," and so he wrote: "When all four legs are removed, the frog goes deaf."

That is what I call a misdiagnosis. But it is no more foolish than the diagnosis we get from the experts in our denominations. They, too, have been doing studies. They, too, have been experimenting.

Their job was to find out why the churches are shrinking. They were supposed to give us recommendations. They first told us that the church needed to stop believing in hell and the coming judgment. They told us that it didn't matter whether or not Jesus rose *physically* from the dead. They told us to ignore the Ten Commandments as an ancient Hebrew tribal code. They told us that Genesis was written by a committee and then woven together by a clever secretary hundreds of years after Moses died. They told us that the idea of angels and demons came from popular mythologies that have instructive literary value but cannot be taken literally in our scientific age. Now they tell us not to call God Father, not to think he has opinions or passions and not to believe that he ever really wrote a book.

Some people will be upset about my little story of the mutilated frog. Most of those who are upset are not upset at all about the mutilation of our faith. We are supposed to take the ideas of the mutilators seriously, and we are supposed to remold our faith by their findings.

Very well. I thought I would try my hand redoing the Lord's prayer in the light of their agenda. I think it would have to go something like this:

> Our Benevolent Collective Consciousness which lives in the recesses of our hopes and ambitions: Thy names are as many as our pluralistic society in its infinite capacity for variety can conjure. May Thy Force bring peace and pleasure. May we learn not to think any idea better than any other, but to esteem all ideas and opinions to be of equal worth. Watch over us as we learn to bring forth the riches of Mother Earth in such a way as to bring sustenance to our growing human utopia. Help us with our guilt complexes that are the residue of our foolish religious notions of the past. Lead us into fulfillment, and deliver us from all rules and reasonable standards of conduct, for ours is the initiative, the society and the self-actualization forever. Amen.

If the experts ever read that prayer, I'm sure it will make it into some denomination's revised prayer book. For years now we have watched the denominational bureaucrats, the professional theologians, the leaders of the churches and the publishing houses connive to cut off the legs of the American church until it is a quivering mass of agonizing and immobile flesh. Then the experts and the denominational committees on mission and church affairs, the theological studies on human initiative, etc., etc. ad infinitum, look at the carnage and destruction they have caused, and still have the audacity to say that the problem with the church in America is that it is irrelevant to a scientific age!

First of all, someone needs to tell these poor souls that we are not living in a scientific age. We are living in a technological age, and there is a world of difference. "Scientific" refers to the way we prove a theory; "technological" deals with clever toys. An age which makes the *National Enquirer* the nation's best-selling newspaper can hardly be called "scientific."

But the real issue before us is this: human beings are no different than they were in the age of Alexander the Great, the first century A.D. or the age of Napoleon. They are spiritually hungry, looking for God, and in need of a Savior. Christ founded his Church to respond to these needs. If the American Church can't respond to the unbelievable spiritual hunger in our country, it may be because it has been immobilized by its experts.

As I travel, I often talk to ministers of denominations that actively persecute those who really believe in the gospel. These good people are sad about their churches, churches which have wonderful legacies. They often realize that they are immobilized, but do not always realize that, like their Lord, they have been wounded in the house of their friends. They love their heritage too much to understand that their experts have cut off their legs. They don't seem to realize that it is abnormal for the church to be immobilized. They don't seem to realize that frogs will jump in any age if you'll just leave their legs alone, and, in any age, the Church will do the work of God if we do not deny the source of its power.

The Church of Jesus in this nation must recover the source of its power: the resources of the invisible world surrounding us. We need to understand—really understand, not just pay lip service to the idea—that there is a power available to us from another dimension. We need to live in the knowledge that the God of heaven has bound himself to the believing prayer of his Church upon the earth. We cannot hope to compete with the world system, upheld as it is by the dark forces of hell, without the backing of these spiritual resources.

This is not just a theory. Through the ages and in the world today, the Church moves when she relies on power from heaven. During the Korean war, less than 1% of the people were Christians. Today, one of every three South Koreans is a Christian. Africa is becoming Christian so rapidly that statisticians believe that by the year 2000 every Black African will be at least a nominal Christian. Nigeria was 69% Muslim ten years ago; today it is 65% Christian. The story is the same everywhere new Christians take the Bible seriously, call on the Lord's name and rely on the resources of the unseen world.

In the light of this unparalleled growth and revival of the Church of Jesus Christ in our time, why did the Presbyterian Church USA lose a million members this last decade? Why are so many Episcopal churches turning into geriatric societies? Why is the United Methodist Church losing hundreds of thousands of members every few years? This is not a bad time for churches; it is an age of unparalleled, global revival! But no matter how powerfully built nor how well trained, frogs can't move when experts cut off their legs. And churches, no matter how wonderful their heritage or how marvelous their official doctrine, will fail if they deny the power of the gospel. There are just not enough tricks and gimmicks to keep the Church alive if we chase away the Holy Spirit.

Of course, it's not just liberals who are chasing away the Holy Spirit. Cold conservatism can be just as restrictive to the Holy Spirit. My old denomination is conservative enough, but it became mean to people. It browbeats and oppresses the human spirit. Liberals are right to point out this tendency in conservative circles. We need to stop it. The Holy Spirit will not move among mean people.

To get back to Ezekiel's story, it's time for the Wind! These bones, on the right and the left, really can live again!

PRAISE

The first time a Christian from another background visits a Pentecostal, charismatic or African-American church, he or she is struck with the fact that these people are not quiet!

They enjoy clapping their hands, singing loud and fast songs, raising their hands and moving their bodies to music. Older visitors are often aghast, and younger ones want to change churches immediately. They are both wrong to react this way. There is nothing wrong and everything right with people enjoying church, but, as we have seen, worship is not just a matter of goose bumps and high performance, either.

The historical churches at their best lead us into a worship that reflects on the demands of the gospel and teaches us to meditate on the ways of God. Their wonderful gift to us in an age of turmoil and confusion is stability and peace. However, they almost always neglect the human need for rejoicing and celebration.

The human spirit needs emotional variety. In marriage, it is good to sometimes get into deep conversation and serious confession of our love for one another. That is like worship in the historical churches when it is done as it should be. However, there are also times in a marriage when couples need to just have a blast, to laugh and tell jokes, to skip and tease. That is like celebration and praise in Pentecostal, charismatic and African-American churches.

I can admit that Pentecostals and their ilk can be superficial, as I can accuse the historical churches of sometimes being dead. But Pentecostals do not have a monopoly on celebration. All of God's people have reason to praise God. If we object to celebration because it is not dignified, all I can say is that God is not nearly as concerned with his dignity as we are. I have said throughout this book that liturgy, awe of God and reflection upon truth are important, and I have said that Pentecostals and charismatics need these elements in their churches in the worst way. They don't like to hear it any more than other Christians like to hear that they need to celebrate, but both are true.

Praise brings faith for God to demonstrate his power in our lives. Praise releases certain inhibitions that we need to release. A praising church opens people up to the presence of God.

PRAYER

People of all denominations, and even of all religions, talk about prayer. Thousands of books are written about it, and we hear countless sermons concerning it. What we can gather from all of this is that most people find prayer a bit difficult. If it were a natural thing, we would not see so many books about prayer. No one has ever written a book called *How To Breathe*.

No, prayer is not a natural part of life. Ordinarily, we pray only in times of emergency. That is why the most basic prayer of all is simply: "God, help me," or "Lord, have mercy!" You will often find that very prayer in the Psalms and in the most ancient prayers of the Church. Ancient Christians said it so often in the church services that the Germanic pagans called the Christian house of worship a "kirke," from the Greek prayer "Kyrie Elieson" (Lord, have mercy). Our English word church comes from that German word.

Prayer is nothing more than talking to God. Different people pray in different ways, just as people converse in different ways. In my Pentecostal background, people prayed all at once in a thunderous shout. Praying that way is distracting and confusing to many people. To those of us raised in that environment, however, it was a group experience that allowed us to overcome whatever reservations we might otherwise have had in praising God in public. We were people with few refined words, but in this sort of group prayer no one but the Lord was listening anyway. I have often touched heaven in this way, and I thank God for it.

Later, I was introduced to the type of prayer most evangelicals use in a group setting. In this sort of extemporaneous prayer, one prays, and then another, until everyone present who cares to do so has taken a turn. It was unusual to me at first, but in that way, too, I experienced the touch of the Lord. It seemed that at first the prayers were self-conscious and tailored for our partners' ears more than for the Almighty. But as the prayer went on, the Holy Spirit often seemed to mold and guide the prayer.

Then I encountered another tradition, one that I had disdained in years past: the written prayer. My first experience was with what is called *The Great Litany*, which I heard on a recording of an Eastern Orthodox choir. It involves a prayer leader, a priest, who either speaks or sings a sentence while the congregation chants or sings a response. (I was amazed at the similarities between this and prayers in the Black church, where the minister often sings a prayer and the congregation responds.)

> ● ● ● ● ● ● ● ● ● ● ● ● ● ● ● ● ●
>
> # A WRITTEN PRAYER, MUCH LIKE A SONG, DIRECTS OUR THOUGHTS.
>
> ● ● ● ● ● ● ● ● ● ● ● ● ● ● ● ● ●

I first experienced this litany as music. I enjoy classical music, and the piece was well done. However, the more I listened, the more powerfully I was moved toward a *spiritual* experience. I began to use the litany as a model for my own praying. In so doing, I found myself praying about things for which I had never prayed before. Many of God's children through the ages have found it to be useful in their lives.

A written prayer, much like a song, directs our thoughts. When we are in the right mood, a song written by another can become our own personal praise. The same is sometimes true of written prayer.

Many Christian traditions have prayer books, collections of prayers prayed by God's people through the ages. *The Book of Common Prayer,* used by the Episcopal Church, is a collection of written prayers that many non-Episcopalians find very useful in their spiritual lives.

Common prayers are prayers we pray together, or in common. The Lord's Prayer is the most famous example. All Christians everywhere use that prayer, of course. Many other famous prayers are used by Christians of different traditions. Who would not be blessed by the famous prayer of St. Francis, *"Lord make me an instrument of Thy peace . . ."*? The greatest source of written prayers is the Holy Scripture, particularly the Psalms.

For most of us, when our prayer reaches its greatest intensity, we most generally compose the prayer as we are praying; this is a prayer of our own words, our own thoughts, our own concerns. In my all too inadequate prayer life, I usually begin with a written prayer and flow from that into my own, extemporaneous prayer.

I cannot discuss the subject of prayer without mentioning prayer in other tongues, or what Pentecostals and charismatics call "praying in the Spirit." St. Paul said that he sometimes prayed "with the spirit" and sometimes "with the understanding" (see 1 Corinthians 14:14-15, KJV). Most Pentecostals feel that he was referring to praying in tongues. (When we pray in tongues, he said, our understanding is unfruitful; but in the Spirit we speak mysteries.) The idea behind this is that when we have the most fervent desire to pray, we often have no words or even thoughts by which to express ourselves. When we pray in tongues, the Holy Spirit within us carries the matter to God in a way that bypasses language.

In the tradition in which I was raised, a tradition strongly influenced by African-American Christianity, people in prayer often moaned and sighed. These sounds were hardly inexpressive, even if they were nonlinguistic. In a sense, any sound which carries meaning is language. A sigh or a moan satisfies that definition, even though it is not a language in the everyday use of that word.

There may come a time in your spiritual life when there are no words in your own language to express what you need to say to God. Whether the motivation to pray is great joy or great pain, there is a limit beyond which our language cannot go. When this happens, there is tongues. Tongues should not replace praying "with the understanding," and is subject to certain limitations required by the apostle Paul. Nonetheless, it is a permissible form of prayer, and millions of Christians have found it to be highly rewarding.

If you are uncomfortable with tongues, then try humming the tune of a favorite hymn, first without words, and then, if you wish, adding words in your own language and of your own composition which seem appropriate to your current spiritual mood. This, too, is praying in the Spirit, and you will notice a growing aptitude for using this vehicle to express your deepest emotions.

However we do it, we need to pray. Prayer is the common denominator of all religious awakenings. The emerging American church must recover the power of prayer if it is to do God's work.

PROCLAMATION

A glance at the New Testament reveals a church that was not afraid to declare who it was before the watching world. The American church must recover its voice. We are the people of God. We have truth and a message that saves.

We must give the Wind a mighty voice. When we celebrate Easter it should be because a real Jesus died a real death, was laid in a real tomb and on the third day really got up in a real body and rolled away a real stone. When we celebrate Christmas we ought to be remembering a real virgin who saw a real angel, and whom the Holy Spirit overshadowed that she would give birth to a real baby, born on a certain day in a certain city in a certain year, while a certain governor named Quirinius was ruling Syria. We ought to talk about heaven as though it were a real place, like Boston or Burma, and as though we will live there some day. We should talk about hell in hushed tones, as we do AIDS, famine and other unspeakable horrors.

We are dealing in reality. That same real Jesus who was born on a real day in a real country, and who rolled away a real stone, comes into the lives of real men and women who are tired of sin and death, drugs and disease. This real Jesus transforms them as they encounter the real presence of God among his people. Then these real men and women should have a place where they can praise God in a real voice, and where they can feel that when they pray, a real God really hears. We are not talking about wonderful fables, interesting mythology nor instructive narratives, but real flesh and blood events that happen today. We must proclaim it.

MIRACLES

Some of my fondest memories of my years in Latin America are the many times crying mothers brought their babies, burning with fever, for prayer. They had no access to medical help, and we were not medical missionaries. (Thank God for every medical missionary—they are the salt of the earth.)

I would take the child in my arms and pray until the fever came down. I wouldn't give the child back to the mother until I felt its temperature drop to normal. When I would hand the child back, the reaction was always the same: a relieved mother glorifying God. This sort of healing ministry should be a part of all our churches.

Consider the position of the Church at the Lord's ascension. The apostles have just been given the leadership of the church, Jesus is about to lift off into the heavens and the new church is supposed to preach the gospel to every man, woman, boy and girl in the world. They have no money, no buildings, no friends in Caesar's household, no seminaries, no building for their national headquarters, no printing presses, no television studios, no blessing pacts or prosperity plans and no cassette tapes. You talk about a handicapped church!

But then Jesus, ignoring all these impossibilities facing the infant church, said,

> And these signs will accompany those who believe: In my name they will drive out demons; they will speak in new tongues; they will pick up snakes with their hands; and when they drink deadly poison, it will not hurt them at all; they will place their hands on sick people, and they will get well (Mark 16:17-18).

Ancient Israel and the early Church both operated on the understanding that their weapons and abilities were not all material. They believed that they had at their disposal invisible, immaterial, supernatural forces.

A story in 2 Kings 6:15-17 really illustrates this. Elisha and his servant Gehazi lived together in a cottage on the top of a hill. One day they were surrounded by the armies of

Syria. The servant panicked. He compared the resources of the enemy with their own. All he could do was wring his hands in despair and cry, "What shall we do?"

Elisha calmly replied, "The forces with us are greater than the forces with them." Then God opened Gehazi's eyes. He saw then on all the tops of the hills flaming soldiers with flaming chariots, angelic armies ready for battle, their swords, spears, lances and pikes all glistening in the sun. When Gehazi saw the supernatural side of the conflict, he suddenly lost his fear.

THE MODERN WESTERN CHURCH HAS COME TO BELIEVE ITSELF LIMITED TO THE SAME WORLD AS THE UNBELIEVER.

The people of God in Scripture understood that we who do the work of God live in two worlds, the one we can see and the one we cannot. The modern Western church has come to believe itself limited to the same world as the unbeliever. We have become like Gehazi. We need the God of glory to open our eyes so that we can see beyond the limitations of our material world.

A few years ago I did follow-up work after a crusade in Buenos Aires, Argentina. Many times these healing crusades leave behind little of substance. This one was different. I met many wonderful people who had been converted after seeing the hand of God revealed in the crusade.

I talked to one businessman who had become a disciple of Jesus after his shriveled, useless arm, which had hung by his side for years, was instantly healed. He left the crusade with a restored arm. He and all his family and friends were won to Christ because of it. This sort of thing is consistent with the New Testament and the history of our faith. There is no reason to fear praying for the sick. Sometimes they get well!

Miracles have accompanied many of God's people as they spread the good news to new places. It is said that St. Patrick healed blinded eyes and opened deaf ears in the name of the Lord. Ireland was converted because of it. Most missionaries of any denomination have stories to tell of how God manifested his power to confirm the words of the gospel.

Our country now is heathen, too. Our people need a demonstration of the power of God. Not everyone who believes in miracles is a fake or ignorant. For example, I am neither, and I believe. I believe, too, that we all can learn together in the coming days how to appropriate our unseen inheritance in that invisible realm of the Spirit.

All the things we have discussed here are available to all of God's children. There is no expression of Christian faith which cannot avail itself of the Wind. It only takes a bit of preaching to awaken the valley of dry bones. It is time. These bones can live!

CHAPTER 16

A THEOLOGY FOR THE EMERGING CHURCH

Those who believe absurdities, commit atrocities.
— Voltaire [40]

I can hear a roar of concern, especially from my Pentecostal and charismatic readers. "Why theology?" I hear them say. "Doesn't theology divide us and rob us of a personal encounter with the living God?" No, it doesn't. I know that we modern Christians tend to see theology as a needless encumbrance to the faith, but we are wrong.

C. S. Lewis, who was nothing if not a romantic, stresses the need for definition in matters of faith. He tells about an officer of the Royal Air Force who argued against formal theology. He said to Lewis, "I once met God in the desert, and compared to that experience this is nothing."

Lewis agreed. If you were to compare going to a real beach with looking at a map of the Atlantic ocean, you would feel the same way about maps. If you think about it, though, a map is made by comparing the experiences of thousands of pilgrims and explorers. A map helps you to see where you are, and to find out where you are going. If everyone had to discover geography for themselves, we would never get much of a handle on the world.

Certainly theological speculation can be barren and dry, particularly when it consists of word puzzles which have no application to real life. What use is a map of a country which does not exist? But Christian theology, by accumulating the witness of the saints of the ages and the understandings of scholars throughout history, can give us a map that helps us figure out where we are going.

Theology means merely "the study of God." Anslem defined it as "faith seeking understanding." So everyone has at least a primitive personal theology. It consists of all that we believe about God and the spiritual world.

PERSONAL EXPERIENCE—THE REAL THEOLOGY?

Most modern Christians insist that this basic level of personal religious understanding is the most "real" kind of theology. But is that so? Do we want to trust our own map-making ability in this journey of journeys? If we construct our theology without reference to the testimony of others, aren't we saying in effect that the witness of other Christians, past and present, is of no use to us? If we do this, we must be brilliant enough or spiritual enough to have no need of comparing our findings with those held by the body of Christ through the ages.

It is true that there are different opinions among even the greatest saints of the church. But they all deserve a hearing, because they all contribute to making the map. That is what theology in the formal sense is really about.

Theology is the attempt to infer from the basic principles of Scripture and the history of our faith how life should be lived, how God is to be found, and how the church should function. Theology should not consist of dead ends and sterile speculations about nonessential things. When that happens, someone is guilty of abusing theology. Theologians are supposed to be what Jesus called scribes of the kingdom (see Matthew 13:52). They help prepare our spiritual maps.

Unfortunately, there are erroneous maps in circulation. How serious it is for a theologian to prepare an erroneous map! People who attempt to follow it will be lost. Because there are erroneous maps, though, it makes sense to compare our maps among ourselves to check for accuracy. We must do that even when, perhaps especially when, we are sentimentally attached to a particular map we have been using.

Another problem with creating a personal theology out of private experience is that mystical experience is something which happens to people of all religions. It seems to be a universal human phenomenon that takes place when we are in certain religious modes.

Just a few months ago, I was talking to the Bosnian ambassador to the United Nations. He is a Muslim and had been our guest on a Sunday evening. We gave him several minutes to address our people about the conditions in his country. When he finished, we prayed for him and his nation. We even anointed him and laid our hands on him, asking God for peace and a visitation of his presence in that part of the world. The ambassador was moved and wept.

Afterwards, we went to a restaurant. During our conversation over sandwiches, our senior pastor asked our guest if he had ever heard tongue-speaking before, as he had in the service that evening. He replied that he had.

"That's interesting," pastor Hardwick said. "Where?"

"Well, sometimes our Sufis[41] speak with tongues. Also it happened to me twice."

"Tell us about it," the pastor said.

"Well," he replied, "While I was repeating the holy name of God in prayer, I felt ecstatic, and I momentarily lost my language."

"Hummm," we all said together.

I speak in tongues, and it is a wonderful part of my experience with God. I am not worried that a Muslim here and there speaks in tongues, too. We human beings are all wired pretty much the same way, and when we meditate, or make love, or hear nice music, or see a wild lion loose in the forest, we feel certain similar emotions. In their search for God, all human beings likely encounter similar emotional and physiological phenomena. The question is, what does spiritual experience prove?

I have had ecstatic religious experiences. I once heard a little girl speak in English by the Holy Spirit, a language that she did not know. (I knew her and her parents when I lived in South America.) She praised God with beautiful words, and I was filled with joy and wonder. I witnessed another mighty miracle when a dear friend, after suffering with a brain tumor for three years and through three unsuccessful operations, went for his fourth surgery. He was given an uncertain prognosis. The doctors took a biopsy through his nose, performed a CAT scan and scheduled him for surgery in 48 hours. The elders gathered as they had done many times before, laid their hands on his suffering brow, anointed him with oil and submitted him to God. This time, God said, "enough." When the surgeons opened up his head, the tumor had disappeared. It vanished into air. I have seen the hand of God, so far be it from me to make light of religious experience.

The fact remains, mystical experience should not define our faith. If our faith is true, then experience must accommodate itself to the faith. A good analogy may be this: Married people have sex; unmarried people also have sex, both the heterosexual sort and innumerable perversions. Everyone who has sex of any kind, married or unmarried, has an experience. The sexual experience of unmarried people is physiologically similar to that of married people. Normal marriage includes sex, but sex does not necessarily include marriage. That is because marriage is bigger than sex, and encompasses more—things like "in sickness and in health, for richer for poorer," wills to provide for those left behind, mothers-in-law and piano recitals for little girls who were conceived by its warmth.

In the same way, covenant with God should include ecstasy and emotion (an emotionless religion is like a sexless marriage—it exists, but who wants it?) but the covenant must legitimize experience. Experience by itself does not legitimize covenant.

C. S. Lewis puts it like this: "True religion gives value to its own mysticism; mysticism does not validate the religion in which it happens to occur."[42] So we need theology, not to replace experience but to give it definition and to ensure its spiritual health.

A THEOLOGY THAT ANSWERS TODAY'S QUESTIONS

Traditional Western theology seems to be breaking down among all Christians. This is happening for several reasons. Some theology was irrelevant to life from the day it was written. It was a parlor game for the Christian intelligentsia, a way to separate the initiated from the rabble. Some theology was conceived as a defense for the doctrines that separate Christians from one another. A central reason for breakdown in Western theology, however, is that for several hundred years our thinkers have been defining Christian doctrine within a rationalistic environment. They addressed objections to our faith which rose from a materialist view of the world. They assumed that the nonbeliever would reject the idea of life after death or the existence of spiritual beings. That is no longer the case, which explains why so much of our theology answers questions that are no longer being asked. Now we need a theology which addresses an increasingly *pantheistic* environment.

A number of theologians are, I believe, well suited for helping us develop such a theology. My favorite, you may have noticed, is C. S. Lewis. He is suited for the task because he appreciates spiritual experience and because he transcends denominational rancor, and does both without sacrificing the essentials of our faith.

Now some will say that Lewis was no theologian. I disagree. I think what is at fault is our definition of theologian. It is interesting that in the Western Church theologians are almost always lawyers. In the Eastern Church, they have usually been artists. That results in very different approaches to theology. Lewis is more like an artist, and though he does not disdain the sort of careful definitions and analysis that is in the strong suit of Western tradition, he is a refreshing change. While not disparaging the mind, he leads us to God and not into our own heads.

It is time that American Christians of all stripes began to search for a theology which, like the ancient Hebrew one, is based on action, obedience to God and application of revealed truth to everyday life. While we will never agree on everything, I believe we can at least agree on most of the areas of study which should be addressed. Let's look at a few of them.

REVELATION

We must recover the notion that Christianity is a revealed religion. It is rooted in the belief that God spoke out of heaven at Sinai. Our faith proposes to know about things which are beyond human experience. It worships a king whom it believes to have the right to enact and enforce whatever laws he wishes. We did not create this faith. It was not, as some have said, "the product of the religious genius of the Hebrew people." It was God speaking from heaven. It has been elaborated upon and defined by the "genius of the Hebrew people," and by all of God's people since; but the core of our faith does not consist in "cunningly devised fables" (2 Peter 1:16, KJV).

We also believe that the deposit of faith that has remained true from age to age is a binding interpretation on how we should view God's law. If the word adultery means one thing in the first century, and the same thing in the tenth, and still the same thing in the nineteenth, then this revealed understanding remains binding upon us in the twentieth and twenty-first centuries. So we believe that God's Word is revealed through his Church.

We believe, too, that the canon of Holy Scripture is a closed affair, having been decided by the Fathers of the Church and affirmed through the many centuries since, by the widest possible spectrum of Christian faith. While we may come to it in different ways, Scripture remains useful for exhortation, consolation, edification, rebuke and reproof (see 2 Timothy 3:16-17). So we believe that God's Word is revealed to us through Holy Scripture.

Because we believe that Christian faith is a revealed religion, we do not attempt to bend it or to make it compatible with our present circumstances. We come to it in order to submit our present circumstances to its divine authority.

CREATION

I am convinced that one reason the influence of C. S. Lewis will grow is because his writings reflect concerns that are just now becoming viable in the emerging world of the twenty-first century. He saw the coming tide of pantheistic thinking that he knew would engulf Western religion after rationalism had run its course. He understood the post-modern mind while remaining faithful to orthodoxy.

He aimed to reintroduce us to a world view that contains nature, and thus the sciences that deal with nature, but which extends beyond it. He believed that Western movements such as the Enlightenment had already moved each generation, Christian and non-Christian alike, toward a world view that shrinks the borders of reality to those things perceived by the five senses. On the heels of that non-Christian understanding of nature came the new pantheism, which we discussed earlier in this book. This has resulted in a set of beliefs, held by many within and without the Church, that is not only incompatible with Christian faith but is a false understanding of the nature of reality itself.

This is especially important to us in the emerging American Church because a "creation theology" is being proposed by several theologians in the mainline churches, and even the Roman church in the United States. Their line of thinking can only lead to pantheism and (I'll open myself to liberal ridicule here) even witchcraft. Matthew Fox, a Dominican priest (now defrocked), together with many so-called feminist theologians, has advanced a view of creation that must be resisted. It is nothing more than ancient Canaanite religion. It is not Christian at all. Christians already have a "creation theology." They believe that "In the beginning God created the heavens and the earth" (Genesis 1:1).

However, because the emerging American Church exists in an environment of expanding pantheism, we cannot be silent on the nature of creation. We must define the relationship between us and nature and explain the Christian basis for ecological action.

The environmental movement will not go away, because it voices valid concerns which move most people in the New America, including Christians. However, we must face environmental issues on the basis of what nature means to us. Christians should respect and care for nature. God has made us the guardians of the earth. G. K. Chesterton said that we should not call nature "Mother." Nature is our sister. We are children of the same Father. We admire and love nature, but we are her elder brother, and have been given oversight over her. We must not worship nature. That is idolatry.

THE FALL

One pillar of Christian faith that must be reaffirmed in our times is that humankind, indeed all of nature, has fallen from its original state. There can be no retreat from this doctrine, because it is true. The doctrine of the Fall accurately describes life. G. K. Chesterton (another important contributor to our emerging theology) says that we are all victims of a shipwreck. We have a faint memory of a state which we believe to be normal, but which we have never personally experienced. We know what we ought to do and know that we do not do it. Only the doctrine of the Fall can explain that reality.

We must realize that we have a flaw at the most basic level of our being, and that fallen human beings, and the institutions they build, tend to drift downward. We need checks and balances to protect us from ourselves. Modern sociology and psychology will continue to be hopelessly muddled because they refuse to acknowledge this central truth of human nature. Modern theology is in the same situation. When we build a system of thought based on truth, it does seem to make much more sense!

THE COVENANT

We are a people who have been called apart to serve the Lord and the rest of humanity. We have joined the Old Covenant people of Israel in submitting ourselves to the words spoken on the holy mountain. We have acknowledged Christ Jesus as the rightful monarch of the earth. Therefore, we no longer belong to this present age. We are members of a coming kingdom.

Being in covenant brings us certain rights and responsibilities. We belong to a community of faith, and our first loyalty must be to that community.

The charismatics have been teaching about covenant for years, and have made great strides toward a biblical recovery of this important theme. While we may not agree with all that they say, such as in the matter of absolute divine healing for all, they have been seeking to live according to God's divine plan as they understand it, and so should we all.

We would do well to read John Calvin on this theme, and all the great Puritan authors. Their teaching was important in motivating the Puritans to establish the early American colonies. Early American writings are filled with references to the Reformed notion of covenant.

HUMAN DIGNITY

One component of human psychology often ignored is our hunger for glory and dignity. This is not a theme that occurs often in traditional Western theology, but it is a prominent one in the Eastern Church. Robert Schuller, of Crystal Cathedral fame, has also dealt with this theme. That has brought him criticism from evangelicals, but his understanding on at least this issue is very close to that of Eastern Orthodoxy. Glory is almost a preoccupation of Eastern theologians, and their insight is valuable. I have found Alexander Schemann, Vlandimir Lossky and John Meyendorf especially helpful. [43]

In my opinion, C. S. Lewis best articulates his understanding of glory in his preface to the *Introduction to Paradise Lost*. He is, as usual, busy defining words, and the word under consideration there is the difference between the Middle English word *solemne* and the modern English word solemnity, and the two ages' respective understanding of the words pomp and pompous.

> The Solemne is . . . the stately and ceremonial, the proper occasion for pomp—and the very fact that pompous is now used in a bad sense measures the degree to which we have lost the old idea of "solemnity." To recover it you must think of a court ball, a coronation, or a victory march, as these things appear to people who enjoy them; in an age when everyone puts on his oldest clothes to be happy in, you must re-awaken the simpler state of mind in which people put on gold and scarlet to be happy in. Above all, you must be rid of the hideous idea, fruit of a wide-spread inferiority complex, that pomp, on the proper occasion, has any connection with vanity or self-conceit. A celebrant approaching the altar, a princess led out by a king to dance a minuet, a general officer on a ceremonial parade, a major-domo preceding the boar's head at the Christmas feast—all these wear unusual clothes and move with calculated dignity. This does not mean that they are vain, but that they are obedient; they are obeying the hoc age which presides over every solemnity. The modern habit of doing ceremonial things unceremoniously is no proof of humility; rather it proves the offender's inability to forget himself in the rite, and his readiness to spoil for everyone else the proper pleasure of ritual.[44]

For Lewis, ceremony and pomp are a temporary acting out of what unfallen man should look like, of the glory to which he should reach. This idea runs in every way counter to our present age. We believe that pomp is ridiculous, that it is presumptuous to act higher, or even different from our neighbor. We are wrong. There is a time for solemnity. Far from being arrogant, it can be a humble recognition that there are situations which call for a dignity higher than everyday life can hope to convey.

We need to keep before us in this age what it really means to be made in the image and the likeness of God.

Robert Schuller and Viktor Frankl[45] have been most helpful to me in understanding this doctrine, for both of them stress the human need for significance. We must recognize that need as a wholesome human drive. Indeed, without it we will never even seek for an escape from the shame of our fallen state.

THE INCARNATION

I was "catechized" by music. Our little Pentecostal church taught what it believed through its songs. (I will dare say that this is true of most Christians now; our catechists are musicians, not teachers.) I will never forget Bishop G. T. Haywood's words in his gospel song, "Thank God For The Blood":

How wonderful God's mighty plan,
How grace the awful gulf did span,
When he took on the form of Man,
to take my sins away!

There it is in all its grandeur: the doctrine of the Incarnation. It means more than just God visiting us in human form, however. Christians do not believe that God took a human shape, they believe that he actually became a man, that humanity and divinity came together, never to be separated again. St. Augustine puts it this way in his *Confessions*: "O Christ, when you were in the womb of your Mother, you married yourself to our mortality, so that we who were mortal would not remain mortal forever."

If this doctrine is true, then the universe is being transformed by the incarnation of Christ in such a way that the separation between spirit and matter, and time and eternity, are in the process of being healed. That is what Bishop Haywood meant by, "How grace the awful gulf did span, when he took on the form of Man."

Christian art, Christian worship and Christian lives simply cannot be the same when we realize that we are called to reveal God's glory to this darkened planet through sanctified matter. That is what God began through Jesus Christ. That is the work in which we are still involved. The doctrine of the Incarnation is a transforming doctrine. It casts a spell on everyday life—no, it breaks the spell *from* everyday life!—and bathes our earthly sojourn, wherever we may be, and whatever may be our lot, with the glory of God.

THE CHURCH

In many ways, we evangelicals are the products of an "emergency church," a church of the frontier that had to make do with what it had without much fanfare or forethought. Our ancestors were interested in getting people saved before they walked twenty miles back to the farm and disappeared for a year or two. Their "gathering together" was difficult and sporadic.

This was not the case even in the New Testament. Early Christianity was an urban affair; it never faced an organizational challenge such as frontier America presented. The gospel spread on the frontier through individuals who in some cases went to a church meeting only a few times a year, read their Bibles at home, and developed a personal life of prayer and devotion.

The sustaining community life that has been the normal mark of Christian faith was much less present in frontier American Christianity. Evangelicalism was a powerful and important adaptation of the faith to this emergency situation, a situation which was not in every way the norm. Our grandparents had little reason to reflect upon the Church. As Christians, they knew that they were a part of a worldwide body of believers, but it was a truth that had little impact on them. Their faith was much more individualistic.

Now, however, we are no longer on the frontier. Most of us live in urban centers where we regularly attend a local church. It is time to come to grips with the question, "What exactly is the Church?" Is the Church what we call the gathering of Christian people, or is the Church the institution founded by God to which people gather who wish to become Christians? What is our obligation to the Church? Who has the authority to begin a local church? What does a legitimate Christian church look like? These are important questions which should be considered as we forge a theology for the emerging American Church.

WORSHIP

The church I pastor contains hundreds of people who have left other assemblies. When they are asked the reason why, the overwhelming majority say that it is because they had no opportunity to worship in their old churches. This generation of Christians does not want a lecture; it wants to worship. We had better start understanding what that means.

Our theology should center around worship. We are not primarily called together to figure God out, or to reflect on esoteric questions. We are called together to adore the name of God.

I remember asking an Eastern priest what theologians he enjoyed reading. He responded that a theologian was anyone who prays! That is literally true. A man or woman who wants to "study God" should begin by loving him, praising him and receiving him at the altar of his or her church. Our seminaries teach us every woolly idea they believe relevant to modern life, but they do not attempt to take us into the presence of the Almighty. One wonders if they know the way.

I have found several writers to be helpful in coming to an understanding of worship. Jack Hayford, a Pentecostal, is a godly man who has a heart for the whole Church. His book, *Worship His Majesty*, is a delightful introduction to heart-felt worship. Alexander Schmemann's *For the Life of the World* should be required reading for anyone who leads us to the Lord's table. Robert Webber's *Worship is a Verb* is a good introduction for evangelicals into embracing the whole Church's experience of worship.

EVIL

If there is anything our theology must regain, it is an understanding of evil. We live in an age of tarot cards, ouija boards, channeling and dial-a-psychic. Dorothy, this is not Kansas anymore! While exhorctism is not a major focus of my ministry, I have had enough experience to realize that there is a demonic world, and that it is alive and well within modern America and the Church.

In a pantheistic society, spiritual force is thought to be amoral. Such a society will seldom discuss evil, just "spiritual phenomena." Yet, we must judge spiritual influences, because the Bible teaches that it can come from either of two different kingdoms. When the Church is influenced by humanism she tends to be skeptical of spiritual experience, either good or evil. But as the Church becomes influenced by pantheism, she is apt to indulge in spiritual experience because it *is* spiritual experience, and to resist judging the origin of the experience. St. John writes, "Dear friends, do not believe every spirit, but test the spirits to see whether they are from God" (1 John 4:1). Not all spiritual phenomena are benevolent.

As our nation becomes more and more pantheistic, we will have to have a better understanding of the demonic and what to do about it. The ancient and biblical rite of exorcism, the casting out of evil spirits, has to be rethought, particularly by Protestants. The ancient churches and Pentecostals have long practiced it. Sometimes one hears of weird goings-on in the name of exorcism. No matter—it is a viable and necessary part of the Church's offense and defense against the powers of darkness.

If you believe Satanic forces to be only metaphorical and psychological, I'll assure you that you have never encountered the real thing. If you remain in ministry in the coming days, you will encounter it, whether you are a Baptist, an Episcopalian or a member of the Salvation Army.

EVANGELISM

We Americans are known the world over for our entrepreneurial character. Sometimes that side of our national per-

sonality is praised, sometimes ridiculed. We "wheel and deal."
We are innovators. We understand capital. We are unbelievably affluent. Anyone who does not believe that has never
lived abroad. There are places in the world with more wealth,
but no place with our popu-
lation is able to spread the
wealth as effectively. One may
offer many criticisms about
our country, but even in our
current economic distress we
remain a land of plenty.

> **OUR NATION HAS
> BEEN CALLED
> INTO BEING SO
> THAT THE
> GOSPEL MAY BE
> PROCLAIMED TO
> ALL PEOPLES OF
> THE EARTH.**

Why is that? We have
been blessed with great natural resources, but that is true
of Russia and India. Why are
we given these gifts and this
national entrepreneurial dis-
position? I believe that if we
look at it in light of our history and our faith, there is only
one answer: *Our nation has been called into being so that the
gospel may be proclaimed to all peoples of the earth.* If this is so,
then all our wealth, all our technology, and all our entrepreneurial ability are given to us as tools to bring the nations to a
saving knowledge of Jesus Christ. The emerging American
Church must be a missionary church.

The driving purpose behind God's covenant with
Abraham is that *"all peoples on earth will be blessed through
you"* (Genesis 12:3). Perhaps this takes you by surprise. World
evangelism may not be your cup of tea. But look at how God
deals with the issue.

Are you an ecumenically-minded person? Jesus says that
the purpose of Christian unity is *"to let the world know that
you sent me and have loved them even as you have loved me"*
(John 17:23). Are you a sacramentalist? Jesus said, "This
bread is my flesh, which I will give for *the life of the world*"
(John 6:51). Are you a charismatic? Do you believe that renewal of the church is the main consideration of the hour?
Listen to the Word of the Lord: *"you will receive power when*

the Holy Spirit comes on you; and you will be my witnesses in Jerusalem, and in all Judea and Samaria, and to the ends of the earth" (Acts 1:8).

Elton Trueblood remarked that "the early Church did not have a missionary arm, it was a missionary movement."[46] The Church has a mandate from God to evangelize the nations, and the Church in no other nation has the wherewithal we have to do the job. The American Church's main contribution is to fund the evangelization of the earth. God has given us the means to do it.

THE CULTURAL MANDATE

One of my great heroes is Loren Cunningham, a man I consider to be one of this century's most important Christian leaders. He represents what I think of as an emerging American Christian. I am honored to call him a friend. He often says that there is not one, but two Great Commissions—one to preach to every creature, and one to disciple the nations. I have heard him say that while evangelicals and Pentecostals are better at the first commission, the matter of preaching to every creature, the so-called "high churches" seem to deal better with the second one. To disciple a nation means to transform the culture of a people in the light of the gospel teaching.

One of C. S. Lewis' most interesting books, *That Hideous Strength*, tells a story that takes place in a small college town in England. In the college there is an elite visionary group whose agenda is to capture the thought life of the city, to rearrange the values by which the community orders its affairs. At the same time, some relatively insignificant people are providentially brought together to fight the elite. The plot becomes complicated when ancient men resurrect to help in the fight against the elite. Lewis uses this rather strange literary device to compare the ancient values of the English nation with those of the new elite.

Lewis shows how each nation has conflicting ideas about what it is and what its aims in the world are. He finishes his story by telling us that every nation, as every individual, has a good image and a bad one. England's gift is to demonstrate the dignity of the human being. At its best, English culture encourages us to a higher plane. The bad side of England is a distortion of this call to dignity. English culture can be arrogant and insensitive to the customs and cultures of others. He briefly mentions other nations, and what their calling in the world seems to be. He shows also how their role is often satanically perverted into a parody of what God intended.

The American Church has ignored the culture for a long time. Our periodic national revivals have been sweeping and powerful, but have not often extended to the whole of our culture. The gospel in our country tends to be segregated to things that are overtly spiritual. This sends the signal to the American unbeliever that the gospel is something unconnected with life.

We need a resurgence of arts that are birthed from a Christian world view. We need Christian insight in the political and economic life of the nation. We need the application of Christian principles to the medical arts of the nation. We are in great need of Christians who will take the cultural mandate seriously, who will disciple this nation for the cause of Christ. That is one of the great tasks awaiting the emerging American Church.

A theology for the emerging Church must address the issues identified in this chapter. It must prepare a conceptual framework for a new generation that will give the broad plan for *what* needs to be done, and *why* it needs to be done. It is time for a theology for people who pray, who are faithful to the faith once delivered to the saints and who have a vision for the reevangelization and Christianization of our country.

CHAPTER 17

NOW WHAT?

We have explored our emerging culture, the state of our existing Christian churches, and what I believe to be the spiritual needs of our times. You may be saying "now what?"

My personal quest, which began with that strange and unexpected vision on a cold West Virginia morning, and which led me through the breadth of American Christendom, has left me with some answers. I have seen the Church in her strengths and her weaknesses. I have been mostly amazed at her strength. The combination of gifts that the various tribes of Christendom offer are more than adequate to see us through whatever we may have to face. But make no mistake, the days ahead demand their combination.

The prayer of the Lord Jesus is, "that all of them may be one, Father, just as you are in me and I am in you . . ."—and here is the heart of his request—"that the world may believe that you have sent me" (John 17:21). He shows us the key to reaching our world in that prayer.

Our country needs the voice of a united people of God, who not only proclaim the truth as it has been taught through the ages, but who live it in their everyday lives. People need a Church that introduces them to the living presence of a risen Lord. They must hear a faith proclaimed that doesn't flee from the world to hide behind stained glass but which reinterprets all of life in the light of its own values. They must have something which endures, which breathes an ancient and timeless air, but which faces modern life without fear.

If we hope to keep this generation of Americans in a church long enough to instruct them in Christian faith, then they must be able to leave our worship services saying, "I have been in the presence of the most high God."

This generation will forgive Christians for almost all our sins, but they will not forgive us for not being serious about the gospel. If we don't believe it, they demand that we abandon it. Jesus himself agrees with this demand, for he says, "because you are lukewarm—neither hot nor cold—I am about to spit you out of my mouth" (Revelation 3:6). We must become a community of flaming truth.

So what will this "on-fire faith" look like? It will look like whatever Christian tradition it shines through. One or another expression of the Church is not more adequate to face the challenge than the others. However, there are common characteristics we may expect to find in any expression of the emerging American Church.

IT WILL AFFIRM THE FAITH OF THE AGES

We cannot be believable if we continue to reinvent our faith for the convenience of each new decade of pagans. If we proclaim truth, then it has already been truth, and will be truth forever. The lowest common denominator among us ought to be "that which at all times and in all places has been believed by the people of God." The two great creeds of the Church and the Holy Scriptures defines it. Liberal Christianity, and sectarian movements on the right and left, sometimes cross the line and no longer represent that common denominator.

Though we do not have the authority to judge an individual's eternal salvation, we do have an obligation to hold our brothers and sisters accountable to the faith once delivered to the saints. Though the culture of an individual church may differ widely from its sister congregation, the emerging Church must be doctrinally legitimate. That is, it must hold to our common faith as it has been believed from the beginning.

> WE DO HAVE AN OBLIGATION TO HOLD OUR BROTHERS AND SISTERS ACCOUNTABLE TO THE FAITH ONCE DELIVERED TO THE SAINTS.

Liberal Christians must return to the faith. The faithful within the mainline denominations must stand firm for the faith. Charismatics and Pentecostals must learn more about the faith. Evangelicals must rejoice in the faith.

We all must teach our people what the faith is all about.

In Christ Church we allow no one into leadership who has not taken our catechism course. In that six months' study we memorize the books of the Bible, introduce our view of Scripture, memorize the Apostles' Creed and learn the Ten Commandments. As we are learning about all of this, we experience it. We take communion on the night we teach that subject. We baptize the Sunday after we teach on baptism. We pray for the Holy Spirit on the night we teach about the Holy Spirit. When we finish the catechism, we confirm those who make it through. We want our leaders to know what their faith is all about.

IT WILL REGAIN AUTHORITY

We must regain the authority to proclaim the gospel to our country. We will do that by cleaning up our lives, by becoming accountable, by rejecting the celebrity model of ministry and by doing "your best to present yourself to God as one approved, a workman who does not need to be ashamed and who correctly handles the word of truth" (2 Timothy 2:15).

We will not be afraid to speak if we have the lives to back up what we say. If we preach against abortion, we must take care of single mothers and unwanted children. If we stand against homosexuality, we must still give compassionate care to the victims of AIDS. We must walk the walk and not just talk the talk.

We must regain authority for our leaders. They must become shepherds, well known for kindness, honesty and integrity. The American people don't believe preachers are on the level. Sometimes they aren't. We must hold ourselves to the kind of life which wins respect for our office.

IT WILL REGAIN MYSTERY

The success of the New Age movement is proof that modern people are not asking for a religion with answers to every question. They are looking for an encounter with that which lies beyond nature.

Christian faith can answer this need because it embraces a universe that is larger than our five senses. It claims to prepare us for our eternal state, where our powers of comprehension will be infinitely greater than they are at present. For now, Christianity teaches us to live patiently with paradox and mystery. It teaches us that when our understanding reaches its limits, we can to trust in the revelation given to us. This causes us to reach, and it is a stimulus rather than an impediment to intellectual growth.

We worship. There is a time to cease rationalizing, to simply bow down before the awesome presence of the eternal God. This generation of Americans wants to worship. Too many times our churches have only preliminaries. It's time to humble ourselves and to make God, rather than ourselves and our programs, the center of our worship.

We must regain piety in the good sense—a humble and wholesome attitude toward sacred things.

We must recover the sacraments, not just the perfunctory observance of them, but we need to learn to pass through them into the court of heaven. They should be windows in the wall of our material world through which we glimpse the glories of the world to come.

Evangelicals need to stop teaching long enough to worship God in mystery and awe. Pentecostals need to calm down sometimes and confront the awesome God in respectful silence. Sometimes we make too much noise; it covers up the convicting voice of the Holy Spirit. Liturgical Christians need to recover the power that should move through the form. They need to reconsider what the rite is all about.

IT WILL CELEBRATE

The emerging American Church will be a movement of joyful people. After we have worshiped and meditated on God, there should be a time to rejoice, to celebrate. We should be able to clap our hands, to shout in a loud voice if we wish and to sing and dance. God made us emotional creatures. The Lord delights in our delight of him. So God's people should celebrate, before the rocks cry out!

Evangelicals and liturgical Christians need to stop quenching the joy of God's people. When Christians want to raise their hands, they should do so without feeling ashamed. If we have anything to rejoice about, then there should be times of rejoicing.

IT WILL EMBRACE ALL OF LIFE

A Christian's vocation, whatever it may be, should fall under the Lordship of Christ. What does a God-centered sociology look like, or a Christ-centered medical practice? Does our Christian faith influence the way we conduct business or live out our marriages? It must. It is time for the churches in America to address life, to stop making excuses for our intellectual, artistic and spiritual stupor. Our faith should swallow up the rest of our world and reinterpret it, not be a small area on the edge of life.

Pentecostals and evangelicals must stop quarantining spirituality to such a narrow slice of life. We need our faith applied to the whole spectrum of human existence. In this, the old mainline Protestants and the liturgical Christians have much to teach the rest of us.

IT WILL EMBRACE THE WHOLE CHURCH

There will always be differences among Christians. Some will want quiet services and some will want loud ones. Some will emphasize this doctrine, some will emphasize another. The emerging American Church, however, will borrow from the tribes of Christendom whatever it needs for this hour. We will learn that the treasures of the Church belong to us all. Wesley doesn't belong to the Methodists, and Graham doesn't belong to the Baptists. Both belong to all of us. So while variety will continue in the body of Christ, churches will be borrowing elements from outside their own traditions, making for some rather interesting cultural blends.

It will be all right for Lutherans to speak with tongues. It will be all right for a Pentecostal to make the sign of the cross. It will be perfectly in order for a Baptist to observe Lent. Charismatics will kneel if they wish for the Eucharist. The treasures belong to us all.

IT WILL EVANGELIZE AND DUPLICATE ITSELF

In this age we may well complete the Great Commission. The remarkable strides made in missionary strategy, the fall of restrictive governments and the technological advances of our times leave us without excuse. We must get on with the job of winning the world to Christ. It can be argued that this is the reason why our country was raised up—to spread the gospel to every creature. It is time all American churches wake up to the cause of world evangelism.

Ralph Winter and his Center for World Missions, Loren Cunningham and his Youth With A Mission, David Barrett and his statistics and analysis, are available to all Christians of all stripes. Agencies like these can network us together as we get serious about fulfilling the Lord's last orders to his Church.

With the help of people like these, every congregation in this country, no matter how small, can duplicate itself anywhere in the world! It just takes study, prayer and commitment. We need church planting in our inner cities in the worst way. Only the vigorous planting of churches will allow us to reach into the hell now engulfing them.

The possibility of the emerging American Church staggers the imagination. It holds the potential of finishing the work of the Church on the earth and of pushing back hell's rising tide. The writer of the popular song was wrong: the Father, Son and Holy Ghost did *not* take the last train for the coast. The current apostasy of our times is reversible.

The Lord of Glory stands at the door of our country and knocks. If any church will let him in, he will take up his residence there. We can humble ourselves and pray until he hears from heaven and heals our land. If we will, then he will. That is the hope for the emerging American Church.

NOTES

[1]"Orthodoxy," *The Collected Works of G. K. Chesterton* (San Francisco: Ignatius Press, 1986).

[2]See *Lila: An Inquiry into Morals* (New York: Bantam Books, 1991).

[3]Hall of Names, Scott Family, Blue Mist, Old Cleeve Minehead, Somerset UK TA246HN

[4]Amaury de Reincourt, "The Eye Of Shiva," *Eastern Mysticism and Science,* (New York: William Morrow and Company, Inc., 1981).

[5]*Encyclopedia of Philosophy*, 3:433.

[6]Francis Bacon (1561-1626), *Essays, Of Truth.*

[7]Elton Trueblood, *General Philosophy* (Grand Rapids: Baker Book House, 1963).

[8]See Durant's introduction to the American philosophers in his book *The Story of Philosophy*, (New York: Simon & Schuster, 1961).

[9]C. S. Lewis, "Equality, Present Concerns," *Essays by C. S. Lewis,* 1943.

[10]C. S. Lewis, "On the Transmission of Christianity," *God in the Dock,* 1946.

[11]C. S. Lewis, "Screwtape Proposes a Toast," *The Screwtape Letters,* 1941.

[12]Anka, Francoise, Revaux, Thibault. Publisher: Spanka Music Corp., Don C. Publications BMI, Inc.

[13]Anthony Harrigan, *National Review,* January 11, 1984.

[14]C. S. Lewis, *The Weight of Glory,* 28-29.

[15]Trueblood, *General Philosophy.*

[16]G. K. Chesterton, *The Ethics of Elfland.*

[17]Will Durant, *Story of Philosophy,* (New York: Simon & Schuster, 1961).

[18]F. F. Bruce.

[19]Frank Lloyd Wright, *Writings and Buildings,* Kaufmann and Raeburn.

[20]*Writings and Buildings.*

[21]Joe McGinnis, *The Selling of the President* (Harmondsworth: Penquin Books, 1970).

[22]Elton Trueblood, *The Incendiary Fellowship.*

[23]Bishop John Spong, *Rescuing the Bible from Fundamentalists* (New York: Harper & Row, 1992).

[24]C. S. Lewis, *Modern Theology and Biblical Criticism: Christian Reflections.*

[25]Appalachian folk hymn.

[26]For statistics on Pentecostalism, see David Barrett's *Encyclopedia of World Christianity.*

[27]For a full treatment of Kenyon's contribution to the faith movement, see *A Different Gospel* by D. R. McConnell,

(Peabody, Ma.: Hendrickson Publishers, 1988).

[28]Donna Steichen, *Ungodly Rage: The Hidden Face of Catholic Feminism* (San Francisco: Ignatius Press).

[29]Barrett, *World Christian Encyclopedia.*

[30]*Touchstone Magazine* is available from: The Fellowship of St. James, 330 W. Cullom Ave., Chicago, IL 60618-1218.

[31]*First Things* is available from The Institute on Religion and Public Life, 156 Fifth Avenue, Suite 400, New York, NY 10010.

[32]Preface to *Christian Reflections.*

[33]C. S. Lewis, *Preface to Paradise Lost.*

[34]Thomas Howard, *C. S. Lewis, Man of Letters*, 92.

[35]Roger Grainger, *The Language of Rite* (London: Darton, Longman and Todd Publishers), 37.

[36]Grainger, 103.

[37]Grainger, 98.

[38]Grainger, 107.

[39]Grainger, 109.

[40]Quoted in *The Story of Philosophy* by Will Durant (New York: Simon and Schuster, 1961).

[41]Sufism is an Islamic mystical movement.

[42]C. S. Lewis, "Chiefly on Prayer," *Letters to Malcom,* 65.

[43]The writings of these three authors are available from St. Vlaimir's Press, Crestwood, New York, 10707.

[44]C. S. Lewis, *A Preface To Paradise Lost* (Oxford University Press), 17.

[45]See *Man's Search For Meaning,* Viktor Frankl.

[46]Elton Trueblood, *The Incenery Fellowship,* 112

7